ROME AND THE ARABS

Bust of Emperor Philip
Vatican City, Vatican Museum

ROME AND THE ARABS

A PROLEGOMENON
TO THE STUDY OF
BYZANTIUM AND THE ARABS

IRFAN SHAHÎD

Georgetown University

DUMBARTON OAKS
RESEARCH LIBRARY AND COLLECTION

Washington, D.C.

bur
DS
62.25
.S52
1984
copy1

Library of Congress Cataloging in Publication Data

Shahîd, Irfan, 1926–
Rome and the Arabs.

Includes index.
1. Arabs—History—To 622.   2. Rome—History—Empire,
30 B.C.–476 A.D.   3. Arabs—Rome.   4. Near East—
History—To 622.   I. Title.
DS62.25.S52   1984   937'.004927   83-8930
ISBN 0-88402-115-7

TO

ADRIAN NICHOLAS SHERWIN-WHITE

Contents

Preface

This book treats the Arab presence in the Roman-controlled Orient in the four centuries or so which elapsed from the Settlement of Pompey in 63 B.C. to the reign of Diocletian, A.D. 284–305, and its emphasis is on the Arab-Roman relationship. It is written as a prolegomenon to this relationship in the Byzantine period of three centuries from the accession of Constantine to that of Heraclius. It is hoped that the elucidation of both these periods, the Roman and the Byzantine, will serve as a background for answering the largest question in Arab-Roman relations, namely, why the Arabs were able in the seventh century to bring about the annihilation of the Roman imperial army at the decisive battle of the Yarmūk (Hieromax) on 20 August, A.D. 636, a much more fateful day, as it turned out, than 28 August, A.D. 378, when the Goths annihilated the Roman army at Adrianople.

The sober approach to answering this question is to follow the fortunes of this ethnic group, the Arabs, in the course of the seven centuries (exactly seven centuries from 64/63 B.C. to A.D. 636) of their relations with the Romans. The study of the past may not be helpful for predicting the future, but it is helpful for the study of another past, posterior to it and related to it. Pompey was able to disperse and control the Arabs in the first century B.C., and Aurelian was able first to beat them and then to crush them completely four centuries later. When these two Roman successes in the distant past are brought within the long perspective of seven centuries the climax of which was the resounding Roman failure in the seventh, surely the latter can be illuminated by the two previous successes, the study of which reveals the fragility of the political structure which the Arabs had erected in the Roman period and the consequent vulnerability of their position. This, then, is the first in a series of studies on Arab-Roman relations in these seven centuries, concentrating on a range of problems relevant towards solving the major problem of these relations and their climax, namely, the Arab Conquests in the seventh century.[1]

The Arabs who figure in these pages are those of what is termed in this book *the Orient,* the region which is coterminous with the later Byzantine administrative division called the Diocese of Oriens, which comprised Syria in the largest sense from the Taurus to Sinai, Roman Mesopotamia, and Egypt, east of the Delta. This is the region in which the Arabs of the Roman Empire were to be found, and it is also what might be termed the Semitic Orient since not only the Arabs but the Aramaeans and the Jews too lived within its confines. It has been necessary to operate with this term since Syria, even in the largest sense, excluded Egypt and Mesopotamia, in which the Arabs were also to be found. Thus recourse was had to the Byzantine administrative division which is so convenient in that it happens to be the area where the Semitic peoples of the empire, including the Arabs, were to be found. The Orient is a more valid and meaningful geographical unit of historical study than the various provinces with their artificial boundaries. Thus the ethnic history attempted in this book is also a regional history, an ethno-regional history of the Arabs in the Roman-controlled Orient, the very same one in which the Muslim Arabs battled the Romans, which they were able to wrest from Byzantium in the seventh century, and where the Semitic complexion of the region was a factor both in its conquest and also in its retention after the military phase of the conquest was over, unlike the Anatolian region north of the Taurus which was never conquered or retained and which had no Arab or Semitic complexion. It is the ethnic history of a people in one specific region, in which the strictly Arab zone has been identified and separated from the general Semitic one. Finally, the two termini of the period chosen for the chronological framework of this book, from the Settlement of Pompey to the reign of Diocletian, make it a genuine historical period in the history of Arab-Roman relations and preludes the

[1]On these three periods and the trilogy of works related to them, see the present writer in *Byzantium and the Arabs in the Fourth Century* (abbreviated as *BAFOC*), Pref., sec. 1; for the third period and the third part of this trilogy, which treats the Arab Conquests in the seventh century, see *ibid.*, Intro., II. 3. On *BAFOC*, see *infra*, pp. xii–xiii.

Byzantine one of three centuries that followed, during which the
nature of this Arab-Roman relationship experienced a drastic quali-
tative change. Thus it is a sharply focused history, not of the Arabs
in their entirety, but of one group of Arabs, the Roman Arabs,
who lived not in the entire Arab area but in only one area, the
Roman Orient, and limited to a genuine historical era, the first
four centuries of the Roman period from Pompey to Diocletian.

It is only a survey of the Arab presence in the Roman-controlled Orient and of Arab-Roman relations, and might be described as an interpretative essay. These relations have been treated
in standard histories, but sporadically and intermittently, and this
has tended to obscure the strand of continuity in these relations and
the major lines of its development. It is, therefore, hoped that this
diachronous treatment, brief and quick as it is, will provide the
student of this period with a continuous narrative of the history of
this ethnic group which played an important role in the history of
the Roman Orient in these four centuries, thus making more intelligible what has been obscured by misleading geographic and
gentilic terms.

In view of the fact that *Rome and the Arabs*[2] is an interpretative
essay, no attempt has been made to provide an exhaustive bibliography or a chapter on the sources. The bibliography consequently
remains skeletal, but it is fairly comprehensive for the five chapters
of the topical studies. The sources are sparse and uneven and their
character and limitations will become evident to the reader as he
peruses the various chapters one after the other. Responsively to
the bipartite division of the nine studies which constitute this
book, no intensive study of the sources or their authors has been
undertaken for Part I because it consists of interpretative surveys
based on data already established by others who have examined
these sources.[3] But the sources for Part II, the topical studies, as
well as their authors, have been subjected to intensive investigation.
They are mainly literary, but epigraphy has not been neglected.[4]

---

[2]Sometimes abbreviated as *RA*.

[3]See *infra*, p. 43 note 1.

[4]In *BAFOC*, it plays a much more important role: the longest section in the
book (chap. 1, sec. I) analyzes the Arabic Namāra inscription, and chapter 6 is
devoted exclusively to two Greek inscriptions.

However, only inscriptions that are significant and relevant to the larger concerns and themes of this book have been taken into account.[5]

The Introduction explains in detail how *Rome and the Arabs* is constituted and structured. Furthermore, it presents the range of problems that this book grapples with in the treatment of Arab-Roman relations in this period of four centuries. It is hoped that the identification of these problems will lead to an increased interest in them and in the people that created them for those whose main concern is this Roman period, and that this interest will lead to a more detailed discussion of these problems than has been possible in a work that is only a prolegomenon to the study of the Byzantine period.

Because of the very structure of the book, some sentences or paragraphs may sound repetitive. But the repetitiveness is only apparent; certain data are sometimes used in various contexts to illuminate different aspects of the Arab-Roman relationship. The abundant use of Arabic and Roman numerals as well as the letters of the alphabet for paragraphing is intended as a visual aid to the reader for a better comprehension of the sometimes complex and involved argumentation, especially in the chapters of Parts I and II.

As has been mentioned earlier, *Rome and the Arabs* is an introduction to the detailed study of Arab-Roman relations in the three centuries of the Byzantine period. These have been intensively researched by the present writer in the course of the last ten years or so, and the fruits of these researches will appear in three separate volumes. Since reference is made in this book to two of them, the following abbreviations have been used: *BAFOC* for *Byzantium and the Arabs in the Fourth Century*; and *BAFIC* for *Byzantium and the Arabs in the Fifth Century*. The manuscript of the first of these volumes has been completed, and goes to press at approximately the same time as does this on *Rome and the Arabs*. It is

---

[5]Such as the Latin and Greek inscriptions found respectively at Dūmat al-Jandal and al-Ḥijr (Madā'in Ṣāliḥ), important to the vexed question of the boundaries of the Provincia Arabia; see *infra*, p. 20 note 5. And such also is the Ruwwāfa Bilinguis for the discussion of the term *Saraceni*, to which an appendix has been devoted; see *infra*, pp. 138–41. For those who depend on epigraphy in a large way because it is relevant to their specialized work and the restricted area in the Orient with which they deal, see *infra*, p. 63 note 42.

hoped that it will not be long before the two other volumes will be ready for publication.

The manuscript has benefited most from the comments of Mr. Sherwin-White who has given so much of his time and energy to reading it. It is, therefore, only natural that *Rome and the Arabs* should be dedicated to the well-known Roman historian from whose tutorials at the College of St. John the Baptist I have derived much of my knowledge of Roman history.

DECEMBER 1981   WASHINGTON, D.C.

Acknowledgments

The nine chapters of Parts I and II of this book, with the exception of Chapters V and IX, were ready in 1978 and the winter of 1979 and were then read by Professor G. W. Bowersock. Chapters V and IX were written in 1976 and in 1980 respectively, and both were also read by Professor Bowersock. I should like to thank him for reading these chapters and for supplying me with bibliographical items on Roman military history, especially his own contributions to *Limesforschung*. Chapters VI and VII were read by Professor T. D. Barnes, and I am grateful to him for his comments. His letter of 27 March 1979 led me to add the appendix to Chapter VI on Philip the Arab. Professor Franz Rosenthal was good enough to read Chapter IX in the winter of 1980, and I should like to thank him for his comments. The last to read the manuscript were my tutors at Oxford, Messrs. C. H. Roberts and A. N. Sherwin-White. Very warm thanks are due to them for their comments which reached me in the summer and autumn of 1980. Because of the importance of Mr. Sherwin-White's detailed comments on the first three chapters, I have devoted to them a special epilogue (pp. 163–68). The comments of the anonymous readers have been helpful, especially in reminding me that a book such as this is likely to raise many questions in the minds of Roman historians, and for this I am deeply grateful. Their comments have persuaded me of the desirability of elaborating on what I had briefly said in the Preface concerning what the book is and what it is not, and to this purpose I have devoted section II of the Introduction. I have discussed various aspects of the manuscript with my colleague, Professor John Callahan, and I should like to thank him very warmly for his many comments. Professor Albert Jamme, W. F., drew the sketch maps which appear at the end of the book, and I wish to express my gratitude to him for doing this.

A heavy debt is owed to Dumbarton Oaks, where my Associate Fellowship has enabled me to conduct my researches in ideal surroundings. For this I am grateful to its Director, Professor Giles Constable, as I also am to Professor Peter Topping for advice on various matters pertaining to the improvement and publication of this book. The editorial and library staff has greatly facilitated my work, and I should like to thank them for their assistance and courtesy.

A debt of a different kind is owed to the couple who felt warmly towards my researches and gave generously to their publication. I should therefore like to end these acknowledgments by expressing to Ludwig and Mir Tamari my deep gratitude for their sentiment and contribution.

Abbreviations

AB: *Analecta Bollandiana*

BAFIC: I. Shahîd, *Byzantium and the Arabs in the Fifth Century*

BAFOC: I. Shahîd, *Byzantium and the Arabs in the Fourth Century*

BHG: *Bibliotheca Hagiographica Graeca*

BHL: *Bibliotheca Hagiographica Latina*

Bonn: Corpus Scriptorum Historiae Byzantinae

BZ: *Byzantinische Zeitschrift*

CAH: *Cambridge Ancient History*

Cities: A. H. M. Jones, *Cities of the Eastern Roman Provinces*

CHI: *Cambridge History of Islam*

CSEL: *Corpus Scriptorum Ecclesiasticorum Latinorum*

DHGE: *Dictionnaire d'Histoire et de Géographie Ecclésiastique*

DOP: *Dumbarton Oaks Papers*

EI: *Encyclopaedia of Islam*

GCS: *Die griechischen christlichen Schriftsteller der ersten {drei} Jahrhunderte*

HA: *Historia Augusta*

HE: Eusebius, *Historia Ecclesiastica*

HN: Zosimus, *Historia Nova*

JAOS: *Journal of the American Oriental Society*

JRS: *Journal of Roman Studies*

JSS: *Journal of Semitic Studies*

LRE: A. H. M. Jones, *The Later Roman Empire*

MGH: *Monumenta Germaniae Historica*

ND: *Notitia Dignitatum*

OTS: D. F. Graf and M. O'Connor, "The Origin of the Term Saracen and the Rawwāfa Inscriptions"

PG: *Patrologia Graeca*

PL: *Patrologia Latina*

RA: *Rome and the Arabs*

RAC: *Reallexikon für Antike und Christentum*

RE: *Paulys Realencyclopädie der classischen Altertumswissenschaft*

RM: R. Grosse, *Römische Militärgeschichte*

SC: *Sources Chrétiennes*

SDAF: D. F. Graf, "The Saracens and the Defense of the Arabian Frontier"

TU: *Texte und Untersuchungen*

ZDMG: *Zeitschrift der Deutschen Morgenländischen Gesellschaft*

Introduction

T his book can be described as a triptych the first part of which consists of four chapters of interpretative surveys, the second of five chapters of topical studies, and the third of six divisions of synthesis and exposition. The complex nature of the book, consisting as it does of three parts that reflect three different historical operations, makes it necessary to explain and discuss this tripartite structure for the more profitable perusal of this book and also for introducing the problems whose synoptic presentation should conduce to a better comprehension of *Rome and the Arabs*.[1]

I

The nine chapters of the first and second parts turn around three major themes: (1) military and political relations, (2) cultural contacts, and (3) what might be termed the image of the Arabs in the mirror of Graeco-Roman historiography. These three themes are most relevant to the ultimate and important question of the Arab Conquests.[2] The preponderance given to political and military problems in works on this period has tended to obscure the importance of cultural relations; hence the attention paid to these in five of the nine chapters of Parts I and II. As will be seen when the volume on the seventh century comes out, cultural relations are extremely important for understanding the problem of the Arab Conquests, which belong as much to the history of ideas as to the history of war; for the moving spirit behind them was a religion, Islam, an Abrahamic religion which appeared in the midst of a Judaeo-Christian environment.[3]

In addition to these remarks of a general nature, the following

---

[1]For the problems and major themes of Arab-Byzantine relations in the three centuries that follow, see *BAFOC*, Intro., II.

[2]Further on this, see *infra*, p. xxix.

[3]On the complex problem of the image and the "four mirrors," see *BAFOC*, chap. 7, sec. V. A preliminary statement on its relevance to the discussion of the

observations may be made on each of the chapters of Parts I and II and on Part III, the Synthesis.

A

1. The first chapter in Part I is the basic one. It reveals the extent of the diffusion of the Arabs in the Orient when Pompey appeared in 64 B.C. and the fact that what Pompey had on his hands in the region from the Taurus to Sinai was to a large extent an Arab problem.[4] Thus the Settlement of Pompey becomes the terminus a quo in the history of Arab-Roman relations, and the disclosure of its Arab profile lengthens the perspective of Arab-Roman relations by some four centuries. This long perspective enables the confrontation between the Romans and the Arabs in the third century A.D. to be better understood as it does also the much more important one in the seventh.[5]

2. The second chapter treats diachronously the history of Arab-Roman relations in the four centuries or so from the first century B.C. to the third century A.D. It is a natural sequel to the first chapter which identifies the Arab groups in the Orient and the extent of the Arab diffusion in the region. It is the story of how Rome dealt with her Arabs in the course of the four centuries that elapsed after the Settlement of Pompey had involved her with the Semitic group—the second it had to deal with after the Carthaginians three centuries before.[6] It is thus concerned with political

---

battles of early Islam against Byzantium was made by the present writer in a paper entitled "The Sons of Ishmael: the Self-Image," read at a symposium, "Byzantium and Islam," which was held at Hellenic College, Brookline, Mass., 11 April 1981.

[4]The discussion in this chapter and the following two should not give the impression, as in fact it has to one reader, that "the Romans confronted an ethnically and culturally cohesive Arab nation." Exactly the opposite is true of the Arabs of Rome, who were not a nation in this period but consisted of various groups, disunited and often at war with one another. Hence the word *nation* is never used of Arabs in this book, and instead the term *presence* is employed.

[5]Parenthetically, it makes of the Arab-Roman relationship from its inception in 64 B.C. to the crucial terminus in A.D. 636 (the date of the battle of Yarmūk) a period of exactly seven centuries. The Settlement took place partly in 64 B.C. and partly in 63 B.C.; see Epilogue, *infra*, p. 165.

[6]In an interpretative chapter such as this, the sequence of Arab-Roman relations is naturally not presented as a continuum. After the Settlement of Pompey, what matters are the three major annexations—Nabataea, Osroene, and Palmyrena. What took place between the Settlement of Pompey and the reign of

and military problems and with the gradual annexation of the
Arab client-kingdoms. Although Palmyra with its Odenathus and
Zenobia is more exciting than Petra and its Nabataean kings, and
although the Palmyrene episode was a major upheaval in the history
of Rome in the third century, it is the annexation of Nabataea and
its conversion into the Provincia Arabia in A.D. 106 that is more
important to study for the rise of Islam and the Arab Conquests,
since for some five hundred years the Provincia becomes an important fact and factor in the history of Ḥijāz—the Cradle of Islam.
Thus more research on the Provincia should be welcome to both
the Arabist and the Islamicist.[7]

3. The third chapter deals with the Arab factor in Roman
history in the century of the imperial crisis. Had it not been for
the epithet "the Arab" that describes Emperor Philip, few would
have been aware of his Arab origin, and he is not as important as
the half-Arab Severi earlier in the century or the Palmyrenes later in
the same century, whose Arab ethnic affiliations are not explicitly
stated and have consequently been obscured. This third chapter
thus reveals the strength of the Arab presence in the third century
A.D. as the first chapter reveals it in the first century B.C., and,
what is more, it draws attention to its being not merely an element
but a factor in the making of Roman history. This was the climax
of Arab-Roman relations in the Roman period and, perhaps, this
very fact holds the key to understanding the anti-Arab sentiment
in the works of Graeco-Roman historians who wrote on this third
century, as will be explained in the chapter on Zosimus who represents the climax of vituperation and racial prejudice.

4. The fourth chapter deals with cultural contacts and contributions beginning with the Idumaean Herod. The main theme of
the chapter is the contribution of the Arabs, especially that of the
Herodians and the Nabataeans, to the urbanization of the Orient
and, through urbanization, to its higher culture. Their intense

---

Trajan is relatively unimportant compared to these three annexations, and, consequently, what the Julio-Claudians and the Flavians did in the first century A.D. is
only referred to in the most cursory fashion; see *infra*, pp. 18–19.

[7]Hence the importance of the detailed work that is being done on the
Provincia by a number of scholars, for whom, see *infra*, p. 63 note 42. On the
discussion of the *Notitia Dignitatum* in sec. III of Chap. II, see the remarks on
Chap. V, further on in this Introduction.

involvement in the religious life of the region, especially in paganism and Christianity, is pointed out. The Severan emperors and empresses were involved in the former, while the Emperor Philip and Abgar, king of Edessa, were involved in the latter and, indeed, were the first rulers in history to adopt Christianity. Attention is drawn to the role of the Arabs in the development of Edessa as the great Christian center of the Semitic Orient and in the development of an urban center which is lesser known to the Roman historian, namely, Ḥīra, which belonged to the Sasanid sphere of influence but which nevertheless played an important role in the history of the Roman Orient.

The Arab historical personages of this period are often masked by their Graeco-Roman names, and their assumption of these names has concealed their participation in and contribution to what has aptly been termed the "harvest of Hellenism."[8] Porphyry, whose Semitic name was "Malik" before he assumed his Greek name, could possibly have been an Arab. But such a name as Iamblichus, that of the Neo-Platonist and of his namesake, the writer of the novel *Babyloniaca* or *Rhodanis and Sinonis*, is certainly Arabic, and both the philosopher and the novelist were Arabs. In this period, Arabic names could have been assumed only by Arabs, unlike the Islamic period when, with the prestige of Arabic names, non-Arabs assumed such Arabic- (and Islamic-) sounding names that it is impossible to argue from the assumption of an Arabic name to the Arab nationality or origin of its holder. Intensive research could produce more names of Romans of Arab origin who contributed to the Graeco-Roman culture in this Semitic Orient.[9]

---

[8]See F. E. Peters, *The Harvest of Hellenism* (New York, 1971).

[9]If Porphyry turns out to be an Arab, then the Arabs would have contributed two Neo-Platonists in this Roman period and would have been involved in that philosophy long before their well-known involvement in it in the Islamic period, for which, see M. Fakhry, *A History of Islamic Philosophy* (New York, 1970), pp. 32–44, 125–83.

Prof. G. W. Bowersock has just turned up three third-century Arab sophists from Petra who had been masked by their Greek names—Heliodorus, Callinicus, and Genethlius. The first, according to Philostratus, made a strong impression on Caracalla. The second wrote a treatise on rhetoric and presented it to Virius Lupus, the governor of Arabia, and later presented Queen Zenobia with a history of the city of Alexandria; he was distinguished enough to practice rhetoric in Athens itself. The third also practiced rhetoric in Athens and was the rival of his compatriot. See G. W. Bowersock, *Roman Arabia* (Cambridge, Mass., 1983), pp. 135–36.

These first four chapters are thus interpretative,[10] based on the work of historians who have researched this period of four centuries and who have presented it from the Roman viewpoint. The present writer has traversed very quickly the same ground but presented the history of this period from a different point of view, that of the Arabs of the Orient, and in so doing has attempted an ethnoregional historical sketch, but still within the framework of Roman history.[11]

B

1. The first chapter in Part II analyzes that important document, the *Notitia Dignitatum*, already discussed in Chapter II of Part I, but in a different context and in a preliminary fashion, preluding the more detailed treatment in this chapter, which is entirely devoted to it. The attention of the reader may be drawn to the bibliography on the *ND* which appears in Chapter II and which supplements the much fuller bibliography in this chapter. It is an early fifth-century document and its inclusion in this book is explained in the introductory paragraph of this chapter, in which its discussion is a contribution to the study of ethnic units in the Roman army.[12]

2. The second chapter is an intensive study of the Christianity of Philip the Arab, which the present writer has argued is certain and must not be left in the realm of the possible or even the probable. The claim put forward for Constantine as the first Christian Roman emperor is thus contested in this chapter in which also some questions of Eusebian scholarship are raised.

Philip was the only Arab Roman emperor and the first Chris-

---

[10]Hence little attention has been paid to the enumeration of facts about such major Arab historical figures as Herod, Zenobia, and Odenathus since these have been treated extensively and a knowledge of these facts on the part of the reader has been assumed by the present writer. The chapters remain strictly interpretative, not narrative.

[11]Much remains to be done on the Arabs as a factor in Roman history in the third century. For the Palmyrene and Edessan Arabs, archeology is providing challenging prospects for a better understanding of their roles. On what has been said, with equal truth, about the Provincia Arabia, see *supra*, note 7 and *infra*, p. 63 note 42.

[12]After so much has been written on the *ND* since the time of E. Böcking and O. Seeck in the nineteenth century, it is hoped that a new edition of this document will be prepared with a full commentary and with maps for the many posts and stations of the military units listed in it.

tian Roman emperor. Both facts give him a place in a book entitled
Rome and the Arabs, the three major themes of which are military,
political, and cultural. Before their appearance on the stage of
world history as Muslims in the seventh century, the Arabs had
walked the pagan and then the Christian way, and this book treats
these two phases in their religious history. When one of them, a
Christian, becomes the head of the Roman state, the fact and the
attendant circumstances cannot be left out in the discussion of the
second phase of the Arab spiritual journey, namely, Christianity.[13]
And likewise, when an Arab vassal of the Romans converts to
Christianity around A.D. 200 and enables his capital, Edessa, to
develop as the great Christian center of the Semitic Orient, he,
too, cannot be left out of a book entitled *Rome and the Arabs*; hence
the special appendix devoted to Abgar VIII in the following chapter,
"Eusebius and the Arabs."[14]

3. The third chapter opens a series of three dealing with one
theme, namely, the image of the Arabs in the mirror of secular and
ecclesiastical Roman historiography. These three are related to the
preceding chapter in this part and to the fourth chapter in Part I.
Thus the five form one group treating cultural matters.

The inclusion of this chapter, "Eusebius and the Arabs," calls
for an explanation. Although he was a contemporary of Constantine, Eusebius did write towards the end of this Roman period,
but what is more important is the fact that the Arabs who appear
in the pages of his *Ecclesiastical History* all belong to this very
Roman period with which this book deals. Their ecclesiastical
image is important in view of the fact that the Arabs of the seventh
century who carried out the Conquests were professors of a new
faith, but one that was related to the Judaeo-Christian tradition.
Tracing the history of Christianity among the Arabs is thus relevant
to answering the question of why in the seventh century the Arab
conquerors appear not as the Germans in the West (i.e., Christianized barbarians), but as Muslim Arabs, a fact which raises the
important question of whether the Christian mission to the Arabs
in pre-Islamic times may be considered to have failed.

4. The fourth chapter deals with the image of the Arabs in
secular Roman historiography as it is reflected in the *Historia Nova*

---

[13]See the last sentence in the observations on Chap. VII, "Eusebius and the
Arabs," *infra*, lines 30–35.

[14]See *infra*, pp. 109–12.

of Zosimus, whose *floruit* may be assigned to ca. A.D. 500. The case for the inclusion of Zosimus rests on the fact that he is probably the best representative of this secular Roman tradition and its perception of the Arabs; even more important, the Arabs that figure in his *HN* are mostly those of this Roman period, especially the third century, with chapters on the Emperor Philip and the Palmyrene Arabs. Furthermore, his sources for these Roman Arabs go back to the Roman period, most probably to Dexippus in the third century. Finally, he is not merely an ethnologist, but an analyst of Roman decline. Hence the image of the Arabs in his *HN* is doubly important both as an image and as an illustration of Zosimus's views on that decline. In addition to the Arabs of the third century, those of the fourth, of Queen Mavia, appear in the *HN*. A discussion of them has been included, partly because they, too, illustrate Zosimus's theory of Roman decline and partly because this book preludes *Byzantium and the Arabs in the Fourth Century*.[15]

5. The fifth and last chapter of Part II is the third which deals with the problem of the image of the Arabs. It is a detailed discussion of the most common and historically most important appellation that has been applied to the Arabs in ancient and medieval times, both in Latin and in Greek Christendom, namely, *Saracens*. The discussion of its etymology is important because of its relation to the cultural overtones that the term carries. The most recently suggested etymology is also discussed; in the opinion of the present writer, it rests on a mistranslation of a term in the Thamudic inscription found in northern Ḥijāz. It was this term *Saraceni* that prevailed towards the end of the Roman period and projected the image of the Arabs as nomads, an image that must have carried conviction by the coincidence of the Roman dismantlement, in the third century, of the Arab military establishment, which rested on such urban centers as Edessa and Palmyra.

The study of the image of the Arabs in Roman times has received little attention from ancient historians, and it is hoped that these three chapters will fill this gap and do justice to this theme.[16]

---

[15]In which there is a substantial chapter on Queen Mavia, for which, see *BAFOC*, chap. 4.

[16]These three chapters should be supplemented with relevant material in a long chapter (7) on Ammianus Marcellinus in *BAFOC*.

C

In a real sense, the Synthesis, the third part of this triptych, is the climax of the book and it is indispensable for its comprehension. The preceding two parts, contrasting so sharply with each other as general interpretative accounts and special intensive studies, range far and wide over the vast panorama of Roman history in the course of four centuries. Consequently, some readers may find it difficult to follow the thread of narrative, interrupted as it is by appendices and the highly specialized discussions of Part II. The Synthesis, on the other hand, provides the reader with a sequent narrative revolving around the major themes of Arab-Roman relations. It clamps together the summaries, the conclusions, and the implications that may be drawn from each of the chapters that precede it. The Synthesis thus represents the present writer's final vision or perception of the various dimensions of the Arab presence in the Roman-controlled Orient.[17]

As the Synthesis is based on the nine chapters of the two preceding parts, support for each statement in it will be found in these nine chapters, as will also be found the necessary documentation. Hence all footnotes have been banished from it. This will ensure that the flow of the presentation will not be interrupted and the attention of the reader will not be distracted. The Synthesis is composed of six sections, and thus its component parts do not exactly correspond to the nine chapters on which it is based; some sections draw on materials from various chapters. The following observations, therefore, will be helpful as a guide:

1. Sections I–III correspond to Chapters I–III of Part I respectively.

---

[17]The reader should not be surprised that King Abgar, noticed in a short appendix (pp. 109–12), is given more space in the Synthesis (pp. 155–56) than Emperor Philip, who is given only half a paragraph (p. 155), although he had been discussed at so much length in Chapter VI (pp. 65–93). The analytic part of the book, Part II, is a workshop of sorts where the length of the chapter is dictated not only by the importance of the topic but also by its status in the literature. In the Synthesis, however, only the historical significance of each theme determines the space allotted to it. The Synthesis in its entirety is so proportioned as to reflect the relative importance of the major themes to each of which space is allocated accordingly. The last section (VI) on Diocletian (pp. 159–61) reflects this most accurately.

2. Section IV draws on Chapter IV of Part I and Chapters VI and VII of Part II.

3. Section V draws on Chapters VII–IX of Part II.

4. Section VI, which closes the Synthesis, draws on material from Chapter II of Part I and Chapter V of Part II.

II

In the preceding section the structure of this book and the manner in which its three parts are related to one another have been explained. It remains to make some remarks on the book as a whole or, rather, to amplify what was briefly said in the Preface concerning its scope and nature, its character as a prolegomenon, and its relation to the other parts of the trilogy. This amplification seems necessary in view of the thoughts which actually crossed the minds of some readers[18] of this book when it was still in manuscript form, in spite of what was said in the Preface. It was perfectly natural for Roman historians to raise such questions and the only way to answer them adequately is to restate in clear terms and in an amplified form what *Rome and the Arabs* is and what it is not.

A

This book could have appeared as the first part of a larger work entitled "Byzantium and the Arabs before the Rise of Islam," supplying the Roman background of these relations, but prolonged reflection convinced me that this would have obscured the importance of the theme "Rome and the Arabs," an importance that warrants its being presented as a separate work. Familiarity with the Roman period is fundamental to the understanding of much that was to happen later in the Byzantine; and its two Arab-Roman confrontations are major ones that are more significant, at least militarily, than those of the Byzantine period of three centuries or so that followed—excepting the reign of Heraclius, which witnessed the Arab Conquests.

Indeed, certain portions of this book had formed part of *BAFOC* before they were separated from the latter. The separation has redounded to the advantage of both volumes. It has made even clearer in the mind of the present writer certain problems which

---

[18]See *supra*, Acknowledgments, p. xv.

otherwise might have remained obscure or altogether unidentified. The separation has given the book its own identity, slim and introductory though it is. The problems of the three periods, the Roman of four centuries, the Byzantine of three centuries, and the Islamic beginning with the seventh century, have become clearer in the mind of the author, as the identity of each of these genuine historical eras in the history of Arab-Roman relations has emerged and as the strands of continuity that run through these three periods have, consequently, become discernible.

In spite of the strong identity that the book has, derivative from the identity of the period that it treats, it remains in execution a prolegomenon to the history of Arab-Byzantine relations in the three centuries which elapsed from the reign of Constantine to that of Heraclius. It is especially related as a prolegomenon to one of the three volumes that treat this Byzantine period, namely, the first, *BAFOC*, from which it was separated. The two books should therefore be read together since they are so closely related.

This close relationship is evident everywhere in *RA*, most clearly in Part II, where the titles of the first four chapters are revelatory of this relationship: "*Notitia Dignitatum*"; "The First Christian Roman Emperor: Philip or Constantine?"; "Eusebius and the Arabs"; and "Zosimus and the Arabs." The fifth chapter, which partly treats the image of the Arabs, has close relations with the same theme in *BAFOC* and with the chapter in it on Ammianus Marcellinus. *RA* supplies the substrate for the image in *BAFOC*.

The Synthesis is the closest point of articulation between *RA* and *BAFOC* and was written as the gateway to the latter. It telescopes the history of four centuries and prepares for the more profitable reading of the history of the century or so treated in *BAFOC*. The reader is, therefore, urged to peruse it carefully before embarking upon *BAFOC*. How closely the two works are articulated is best reflected in section VI of the Synthesis, on Diocletian, who ended one era in the Arab-Roman relationship and opened another, that of the *phylarchi* and the *foederati* of the Byzantine period.

B

The preceding section has explained what *Rome and the Arabs* is; it remains to explain what it is *not*.

Only the author knows his work intimately, and this author is more aware than anyone else how more comprehensive and like-

wise exhaustive the treatment in this book could have been. But
Rome and the Arabs is strictly introductory and interpretative. It is
written from the point of view of an Arabist and Byzantino-arabist
as a prolegomenon to a work entitled *Byzantium and the Arabs* and
is addressed primarily to Arabists and Byzantinists. Only second-
arily is it a contribution to Roman history and addressed to Ro-
manists. These naturally will not find it a comprehensive, let alone
exhaustive, study of the Arab presence in the Roman-controlled
Orient and of Arab-Roman relations in this period, although the
treatment in the second part, consisting of topical studies, is rea-
sonably exhaustive. They will find that it emphasizes the military,
political, and cultural aspects of Arab-Roman relations, not the social and economic. *Inter alia*, this emphasis is derivative from the
fact that *RA* is a prolegomenon to the series of volumes, *Byzantium
and the Arabs*, that deals with the succession of three groups of
foederati in the course of these three centuries, the shield of Byzantium against the Arabian Peninsula, whence in the seventh
century the Arabs issued as Muslims. As the climax of these researches is the Muslim Conquest in the seventh century, the emphasis on military and political history is understandable. The field
is open to those who are interested in the social and economic
history of this Roman period, and I look forward to the appearance
of such a complementary treatment. [19]

Repeated reference to the Muslim Conquests in the seventh
century could raise the expectations of the reader of this book to
look for an explanation of the Arab victory in the seventh century.
But *RA* is only the first of a series of volumes which deal with
Arab-Roman and Arab-Byzantine relations in the pre-Islamic period. In addition to illuminating the history of these relations in
this period, I wanted this series of books to serve as a *background*
for solving the problem of the Islamic Conquests. *Rome and the
Arabs* deals with the most remote part of this background and is
not meant to solve the problem of the Conquests. That problem
belongs to the volume on the seventh century. But the present
volume offers some relevant data, and crucial data will be offered
in the volume on the sixth century, closest to the seventh and the
period of the Conquests.

---

[19]On the paucity of the sources on the social and economic history of Arab-
Byzantine relations in the fourth century, see *BAFOC*, Intro., note 19.

Nevertheless, and in spite of its being restricted in scope and introductory in nature, *Rome and the Arabs* is the first book that treats the Arab presence in the Roman-controlled Orient in this genuine historical period from Pompey to Diocletian. In writing it, I have isolated the significant and relevant data, interpreted them, discovered the historical context to which each cluster of data belongs, and finally set the Arab component within the continuous stream of Roman history. This is the extent of my involvement in this period. To have written its history comprehensively and exhaustively would have changed the nature and extent of my involvement. But teamwork is important in this case, as is interdisciplinary dialogue with colleagues who work in allied fields and branches of ancient and medieval studies. The present writer has still to publish the remaining part of his researches of many years on the trilogy of Arab-Roman-Byzantine relations. Thus the principle of the division of labor suggests that a comprehensive and exhaustive history of these four centuries of Arab-Roman relations be undertaken by another scholar.

This is how the appearance of *Rome and the Arabs* as a separate book rather than as an introductory part of *BAFOC* may be said to justify itself. I hope that it will arouse the interest of Roman historians in this neglected branch of Roman studies and that its very restrictions, those imposed by the present writer on scope and treatment, will attract the attention of a Roman historian whose gaze, unlike that of the present writer, is not riveted on the Byzantine period, but on the Roman, and who is primarily interested in it per se and not only as a prolegomenon to another period. Such a scholar will be able to do full justice to this theme by treating it comprehensively and exhaustively and will thus produce a book that has a more independent existence than the present one. If *RA* does this, it will have performed another function, a heuristic one, by inspiring the composition of a bigger and better book.

I cannot think of a scholar more qualified for this alluring task than the one who does belong to the establishment of Roman historians and is indeed a distinguished member of it, the one who has gone out of his way to equip himself with knowledge of Arabic, Aramaic, and Hebrew for a better comprehension of the Roman-controlled Semitic Orient—Glen Bowersock.

Postscript: The hopes and expectations expressed in the last paragraph of this Introduction have been partially fulfilled. Professor Bowersock published *Roman Arabia* in the summer of 1983, and I hope he will now turn his attention to the other "Arabias" in the limitrophe and the more comprehensive theme, "Rome and the Arabs." *Roman Arabia* appeared after the proofs of *RA* and *BAFOC* had been corrected; for this reason I was unable to profit from the wealth of new material and the refined scholarship of this book except for making an addition to footnote 9 of this Introduction.

PART ONE
INTERPRETATIVE SURVEYS

I

The Arab Presence in the Orient
in the
First Century B.C.

I

The extent of Arab diffusion in the Orient in the first century B.C., more precisely around 63 B.C., the year of Pompey's Settlement, should be apparent from the following enumeration of Arab groups in that region, running from the north to the south:[1]

    1. The Osroeni[2] were in possession of Edessa, which they had

---

[1]Strabo is the principal Greek historian who attests in bk. XVI of his *Geography* the Arab presence in the Orient in the first century B.C. in an explicit and detailed manner; see *Geography,* XVI.i.26–28; ii.1, 16, 18; iii.1. Modern works that specifically treat the theme of the Arab presence in the Orient are perhaps best illustrated by R. Dussaud's *La pénétration des Arabes en Syrie avant l'Islam* (Paris, 1955); for the Arab penetration of the entire Fertile Crescent, see E. Merkel, "Erste Festzetzungen im fruchtbaren Halbmond," in F. Altheim and R. Stiehl, eds., *Die Araber in der alten Welt* (Berlin, 1964), vol. 1, pp. 139–80, 268–372; and Carlos Chad, *Les dynastes d'Émèse* (Beirut, 1972), pp. 18–24. More convenient to use because it is written from the point of view of a Roman historian is A. H. M. Jones, *Cities of the Eastern Roman Provinces,* 2nd rev. ed. (Oxford, 1971), which will consequently be referred to repeatedly and will henceforth be cited as *Cities.* Th. Mommsen's old work, *The Provinces of the Roman Empire,* trans. W. P. Dickson (New York, 1887), vol. 2, has not outlived its usefulness for the study of the Arab presence in the eastern provinces.

    This chapter does not aim at an exhaustive listing of all references in the sources to the Arabs in the Orient; rather it seeks only to indicate the Arab presence by gathering together what has been scattered in the sources and in modern works in order to reflect the extensiveness and intensiveness of that presence in the Orient as a whole, and not only in Mesopotamia or in Syria or in Egypt, but in all these three areas of which the Orient consisted before Egypt was separated from it ca. A.D. 380. Hence also the restricted but select bibliographical items for these introductory chapters on the Roman period, even for such large and important Arab groups as the Nabataeans and the Palmyrenes.

    [2]Better known as Abgarids, the name of the dynasty that ruled Edessa, most of whose members were named Abgar.

occupied and ruled since the second century B.C. and which they continued to rule till the middle of the third century A.D. Of all the Arab groups who succeeded in establishing a presence in the Trans-Euphratesian region of Mesopotamia, the Osroeni of Edessa were the most important.[3]

2. To the south of the Taurus range and in the region of Antioch, there was another Arab group, under the rule of one ʿAzīz by name, who played an important role in the affairs of the last two Seleucids, Antiochus XIII and the claimant, Philip.[4]

3. To the east of this Arab group, there ruled in Chalcidice various Arab princes such as Alchaedamnus of the Rhambaei, Gambarus, and Themella.[5]

4. Farther to the east, there were the Arabs of Palmyra,[6] who were to become a dominant factor in the history of Arab-Roman relations in the third century A.D.

5. In the valley of the Orontes, in Emesa and Arethusa, there ruled another group of Arabs under Sempsigeramus, a dynast who collaborated with his neighbor to the north, ʿAzīz, in interfering in the affairs of the last two Seleucids.[7]

In addition to the above-mentioned five groups, four of whom were in possession of a large portion of what had been Seleucid Syria,[8] there were the following Arab groups, who were in possession of much of what had been Ptolemaic Syria:

---

[3]On the strong Arab element along the Euphrates and in the Trans-Euphratesian region, Strabo is very informative; see *Geography*, XVI.i.27–28; ii.1; iii.1; also Pliny, *Natural History*, V.xxi.87. For more on the Arab penetration of the whole Mesopotamian region in pre-Islamic times, see *infra*, pp. 7–8 and p. 61 note 39.

[4]On ʿAzīz, see G. Downey, "The Occupation of Syria by the Romans," *Transactions and Proceedings of the American Philological Association*, 82 (1951), pp. 150–51.

[5]*Cities*, p. 256; Gambarus and Themella are not mentioned till Caesar's time; see *ibid.*, p. 455 note 41.

[6]They receive their first mention in the sources in Antony's time; see *ibid.* On their later prosperity, see *ibid.*, pp. 265–66; for more on the Palmyrenes, see *infra*, pp. 22–24.

[7]A rare instance of collaboration among the Arab dynasts of the region at this time; on the agreement between these two Arab dynasts to divide between themselves the débris of the kingdom of the Seleucids, see A. Bellinger, "The End of the Seleucids," *Transactions of the Connecticut Academy of Arts and Sciences* (New Haven), 38 (June 1949), p. 83.

[8]For more detailed documentation of the Arab presence in Seleucid Syria, see *Cities*, p. 455 note 41.

6. The Ituraeans, an old Arab people known to the classical sources since the days of Alexander the Great, inhabited and ruled both Lebanon and Anti-Lebanon; from the latter they expanded into and conquered Batanaea, Trachonitis, and Auranitis.[9]

7. To the south were the Nabataeans of Petra, in possession of extensive territory that included Trans-Jordan and the Sinai Peninsula, and in the first century B.C. they were in occupation of Damascus itself. They were the most important Arab group in the area and possibly the oldest.[10]

8. The Idumaeans inhabited southern Palestine to the west of the Dead Sea, whither they had been pushed westward by the Nabataeans in the fourth century B.C. However, it was not until the fall of the Hasmonaeans in the second half of the century that the Idumaeans under Herod the Great became with Rome's support politically dominant for more than a century both in Palestine and in southern Syria.[11]

9. Finally, there were Arabs living in Egypt even in pre-Christian times between the Nile and the Red Sea, in the Ptolemaic nome called Arabia, in Arsinoites (Fayyūm) across the Nile, and in the Thebaid.[12]

---

[9]The Ituraeans had two capitals, a religious one (Heliopolis) and a secular one (Chalcis-sub-Libano), and their rulers wielded both religious and secular authority. According to Stephanus of Byzantium, Chalcis was founded by Monicus the Arab, perhaps the same as Mennaeus, the father of Ptolemy, who ruled the Ituraean principality in the first century B.C. On the Ituraeans, see *Cities*, p. 254 and p. 454 note 37; also, Jones's article "The Urbanization of the Ituraean Principality," *JRS*, 21 (1931), pp. 265–75.

[10]*Cities*, p. 255, and p. 454 note 38. Of all these Arab groups in the Orient, the Nabataeans share only with the Ituraeans an Ishmaelite origin; their eponyms, Nabaioth and Yetur, are mentioned in Gen. 25:13, 15, as two of the twelve sons of Ishmael.

[11]See M. Avi-Yonah, *The Holy Land: A Historical Geography* (Grand Rapids, Michigan, 1966), pp. 86–107. The Idumaeans owed their political dominance and the extension of their territories to the Romans as did the Palmyrenes, who especially prospered after the Roman annexation of the kingdom of the Nabataeans, their neighbors to the south; on the prosperity of Palmyra, see *Cities*, pp. 265–66. For details of Pompey's Settlement in Seleucid and Ptolemaic Syria, see *ibid.*, pp. 256–60.

[12]For more on the Arabs in Egypt, see *infra*, Chap. V, note 32, and also *infra*, p. 7 notes 18–20. On the Arabian nome, see *Cities*, pp. 298–99, and p. 470 note 2.

II

All the groups listed in the preceding section—Osroeni, Palmyrenes, Ituraeans, etc.—were Arab. And yet this pervasive Arab presence in the Orient has been accidentally obscured by terminology, both gentilic and geographic.

A

Although the classical historians[13] who wrote on the history and geography of this region were aware of the ethnic affiliation of these groups, yet they did not normally refer to them by the generic term *Arab*, but by specific designations.[14] In so doing, these authors reflected the fact that each of these Arab groups had developed its own identity during a long period of historical development, but they also unwittingly obscured the other and larger fact that all these groups belonged to the same ethnic stock and were Arab.[15] This has made the student of the Roman East in this period oblivious of the pervasive Arab presence in the Orient in the first century B.C., a matter of considerable importance for understanding the history of this region in both the Roman and Byzantine periods.[16] Historians in modern times have used various terms to designate the Arabs of the Orient in the Roman period, such as *Semitic*, *Aramaean*, and *Syrian*. Something could be said for the application of these terms in view of the fact that the Arabs were Semites, that they were in some respects Aramaicized, and did in fact live in Syria, but these designations conceal the ethnic and cultural identity of these Arab groups. The term *Semitic* is too wide,

---

[13]Especially Strabo; see *supra*, notes 1, 3.

[14]Unlike the Greek and Latin historians of the three centuries of the Byzantine period; these never refer to the Arab *foederati* by their tribal affiliations but only by the generic term *Saracens*. Nonnosus is an exception who refers to the Kindites, but these were living *extra limitem* in the Arabian Peninsula; for Nonnosus and Kinda, see the present writer in "Byzantium and Kinda," *BZ*, 53 (1960), pp. 57–73.

[15]In this respect they were like the Germanic tribes enumerated and discussed by Tacitus, but while the reader would have been aware that the long list of tribes enumerated by that author—Batavi, Chatti, etc.—were Germanic, if only because of the title of Tacitus's work, the *Germania*, let alone its introductory chapters, the student of the first-century Orient would not have concluded or easily concluded that the tribes listed earlier in this chapter were all Arab.

[16]On these problems, see *infra*, p. 16 notes 50–51.

Aramaean is too restricted to subsume Arab under it, and *Syria* is a geographical expression. [17]

B

The diffusion of the Arabs in the Orient was reflected by the fact, not often realized, that there was not only one Arabia in it— the ex-Nabataean kingdom converted into a province in A.D. 106— but also two other Arabias, one in Mesopotamia and another in Egypt.

1. The Arabs had established themselves in Egypt in very early times,[18] and the fact is reflected onomastically by the application of the term *Arabia* in Ptolemaic times to the nome in the Eastern Delta whose capital was Phacusa and by the institution of the office of arabarch.[19] It is the same Arabia that Egeria traversed in her travels centuries later.[20]

2. Much more important than "Arabia in Egypt," culturally and otherwise, is "Arabia in Mesopotamia," where the Arabs had established a deep and pervasive presence from very early times, reflected as early as the time of Xenophon in the application of the term *Arabia* to one of the districts of the Mesopotamian region and perpetuated in later Roman and Byzantine times both in Syriac and in Latin as Bēth-ʿArabāyē and Arabia for the regions east and west of the Khābūr respectively.[21] However, after the dismantling

---

[17]The tendency to treat the various ethnic groups of which Syria consisted as Syrians is apparent in such a work as Philip K. Hitti's *History of Syria* (London, 1951), although the author does have a chapter (29) entitled "Pre-Islamic Syro-Arab States"; the chapter, however, informative as it is for the general reader, contains some misconceptions, as in its opening paragraph on p. 375. Fergus Millar conceives of Syria as divided between only two cultures, Greek and Aramaic; this division may be said to be valid generally but it obscures the Arab element and zone in Syria by subsuming it under the Aramaic, even in the limitrophe where the Arab element was strong, as in Palmyra; see Fergus Millar, "Paul of Samosata, Zenobia and Aurelian: the Church, Local Culture and Political Allegiance in Third-Century Syria," *JRS*, 61 (1971), pp. 1–17. On what might be termed the Arab zone in the Orient, see *infra*, pp. 14-16.

[18]On this, see *infra*, Chap. V, note 31.

[19]See R. Stiehl, "Araber in Ägypten," *Lexicon der Ägyptologie*, 1, 3, p. 360.

[20]On Egeria's travels in "Arabia in Egypt" in the fourth century, see *BAFOC*, chap. 8, sec. III.

[21]In addition to what has been said above on the Arab presence in Mesopotamia, represented by the Osroeni of Edessa, west of the Khābūr, it might be mentioned that the Arabs succeeded in establishing themselves not only in the steppes of

of the Arab establishment in Mesopotamia in the third century
by both the Persians and the Romans, who terminated the independence of Ḥatra and Edessa respectively, the Arab presence in
Mesopotamia was obscured by the new administrative designation
given to the region. In Byzantine times, Roman Mesopotamia west
of the Khābūr was divided into three provinces—Mesopotamia,
Osroene, and Euphratensis; none of the three designations suggested an Arab presence, and only well-informed students of provincial history and the historical geography of the Orient might
remember that Osroene was derived from the name of the Arab
tribe, Osroeni.

Thus the provincial onomasticon devised for the Orient concealed the extent and depth of the Arab presence in that region.
Although it had reflected it partially through the three Arabias,
yet the Ptolemaic nome was relatively unimportant, while Arabia
in Mesopotamia lapsed officially as an administrative name. Only
ex-Nabataea, the Trajanic Provincia Arabia, reflected onomastically
the Arab character of the province. But, as has been shown in the
preceding section, the Arab presence in the Orient in the first
century was pervasive; and it persisted throughout Roman and
Byzantine times, however obscured it was by the designations
given to the newly created provinces, especially the limitrophe
ones, and by the Graeco-Roman names that its acculturated Arabs
assumed.

III

When the Romans appeared in the East in the first century
B.C., the Arabs in the Orient had had almost three centuries of
relations with the Seleucids and the Ptolemies and an even longer
relationship with the Semitic peoples of the region, especially the
Aramaeans and the Jews, by all of whom they had been influenced.
The new masters of the Orient subjected the Arabs to new influences which emanated from such areas as the imperial administra-

---

the region but also in many of its urban centers where Arab dynasties ruled to
the east of the Khābūr: there was Ḥatra, the great Arab fortress balancing Edessa
to the west of the Khābūr, and Singara, the capital of the Arab tribe called
the Praetavi. For these and other Arab dynasts and cities in Mesopotamia, see
Cities, pp. 216, 220; see also *infra*, Chap. V, note 31; for Arabia east of the
Khābūr in Xenophon, see *Anabasis*, I.5.1.

tion and the army. With the extension of *civitas* to all the *peregrini* in A.D. 212, the "Romanization" of the Arabs may be said to have reached its highest point.[22]

In spite of all these influences to which the Arabs in the Orient were subjected throughout these many centuries, they did not entirely lose their identity as Arabs, in either the Hellenistic or the Roman period.

1. Influenced as the Nabataeans were by the Hellenistic culture of their Macedonian neighbors, Ptolemies and Seleucids, and philhellenes as some of their kings were, they remained Arab in ethos and mores and above all in their use of the Arabic language.[23] Like the rest of the peoples of the Semitic Near East, they used Aramaic as the language of their inscriptions and international relations, but Arabic remained the language of everyday life in Nabataea.[24] What Fr. Cumont wrote of them in 1936 remains true today: ". . . Greek civilization was only skin deep, and under the native princes they kept their own alphabet, their own religion and traditional laws, and remained faithful to their ancestral customs as to their Semitic rites."[25]

The degree to which the various Arab groups kept their identity no doubt varied; yet a residue of that identity must have persisted, however faint it may have become, as in the case of the Idumaeans, who were finally absorbed into the Jewish nation.[26]

[22]For some aspects of Latinization, see Fr. Cumont in *CAH*, 11, pp. 624–25.

[23]See Hitti, *History of Syria*, pp. 288, 383–84. On the use of Arabic in the celebration of the pagan liturgy of Petra in the 4th cent. A.D., see "St. Jerome and the Arabs" in *BAFOC*, chap. 8, sec. II.

[24]The Jews did not lose their identity when they adopted Aramaic as their spoken language and the Nabataean Arabs did not either, especially as, unlike the Jews, they used Aramaic only epigraphically and in their relations with the outside world for commercial and diplomatic transactions.

[25]*CAH*, 11, p. 616.

[26]Avi-Yonah, *The Holy Land*, p. 65. Yet, in spite of some significant gestures to the Jews, including the enlargement of the Temple, the Jews disliked Herod, the Idumaean, and did not consider him one of them. This antipathy could only have alienated him and diluted his sense of Jewish belonging.

Evidently Ptolemy discussed the difference between the Jews and the Idumaeans; see M. Stern, *Greek and Latin Authors on Jews and Judaism* (Jerusalem, 1976), vol. I, p. 356. This book may be consulted on such Greek writers on the Jews as Molon and Polyhistor, mentioned in the chapter "Eusebius and the Arabs," *infra*, p. 100, in addition to E. Schürer's *A History of the Jewish People in the Time of Jesus Christ*, cited *infra*, p. 100 note 40.

2. What has been said of the Nabataeans is roughly true of
the Palmyrenes in the Roman period,[27] during which different Arab
groups in the Orient were influenced and affected by Romanization in different ways and in varying degrees. The Arabs of the
Orontes—those in Emesa, for instance—were probably more affected than the Palmyrenes, but the chances that they kept much or
something of their Arab identity are good.[28] This is reflected in the
survival of Arabic personal names among them, such as Soaemias
and Elagabalus, and, what is more important, in their continuing
devotion to their old religious rites, of which the princes of Emesa
were also priests. When an identity is related to a religious cult,
that identity remains alive because of its very relatedness to such a
tenacious and conservative institution.

Thus despite their long association with the Greeks and the
Romans and the extension of *civitas* to them as to other provincials
in A.D. 212, most of the Arabs of the Orient only acculturated.
Some of them were probably assimilated, such as the Idumaeans
and the Ituraeans, but Graeco-Roman culture remained a superficial
veneer in the life of many of the Arabs of that region. No doubt
the elite among them, individuals who attained prominence in
Roman provincial history, such as the Herodians, may be said to
have been more thoroughly influenced by Graeco-Roman culture,
but it is doubtful whether the bulk of the Idumaeans who lived in
the countryside were influenced to the same degree as their rulers.
Even these, in spite of the Graeco-Roman names they adopted and
their thoroughly Hellenizing and Romanizing policy, most probably remained strangers and foreigners even to the Semitic people
they were closely related to and whose religion they adopted—the
Jews.[29] Thus the Arabs of the Orient may be said to have acculturated, but they did not integrate or fully integrate. It is clearest
in the case of the Nabataeans, who kept their traditional laws,
ancestral customs, Semitic rites, and the Arabic language.

[27]And of the Nabataeans in the Roman period also; on both these Arab peoples,
see *infra*, pp. 14–15; on the persistence of "the old tribal organization of the
Semites" in Palmyra, see *CAH*, 11, p. 624.

[28]See Chad, *Les dynastes d'Émèse*, pp. 13, 29, 82.

[29]See *supra*, note 26. The same was probably true of such figures as Marcus
Julius Philippus, Roman citizen and Roman emperor A.D. 244–49, and yet for
Roman historians he remained Philip the Arab.

The following reasons may be suggested for the retention of their identity by the Arabs of the Orient:

(*a*) They had been in the Orient before the Romans appeared on the scene of Near Eastern history; thus they were not newcomers but old settlers who had been used to absorbing the shock of new conquests, military and cultural,[30] and who, moreover, were in a position of political supremacy as dynasts in the various urban centers when the Romans appeared.

(*b*) The policy of the Romans helped the Arabs maintain their identity since in many cases they left them in control of whatever regions they were masters of politically; thus the experiment of the clientship which endured remarkably long enabled the Arabs to continue growing within the confines of an Arab political and social structure that had been erected before the Romans arrived. Such was the case of the Nabataeans.[31]

(*c*) Important as the two preceding reasons are or may be, there is no doubt that more important than either for the uniqueness of the Arab presence in the Orient and the continuance of the Arab identity is the proximity of the Orient, indeed its adjacency, to that vast ethnic and cultural reservoir of Arab presence—the Arabian Peninsula itself. Unlike the Aramaeans and the Hebrews of the Orient, who had lost contact with the Semitic homeland, the Arabs did not, and the Arab element in the Orient and the Fertile Crescent was constantly replenished by waves of penetrators and immigrants, both seasonal and unseasonal, from Arabia.[32] It was this constant flow from the Peninsula that was the most important element in reinforcing the Arab presence in the Orient demographically and keeping it alive culturally.[33]

[30]Such as the Achaemenid and the Macedonian.

[31]It should also be remembered that *civitas* was not extended to them until as late as A.D. 212, and this fact is also relevant to the discussion of why the Arabs under Roman rule did not shed their identity; for a long period the Roman world had not considered them as belonging to it.

[32]Even after the arrival of the Romans and the Settlement of Pompey, especially before the annexation of Nabataea in A.D. 106 and the destruction of Palmyra in A.D. 272; before those two dates, the limitrophe zone adjacent to the Peninsula was still a Nabataean and a Palmyrene sphere of influence, and Rome had not yet taken over the direct military control of the limitrophe and therewith control of immigration into, or penetration of, the imperial territory in the Orient.

[33]Furthermore, the caravans on which the commercial life of both Petra and Palmyra depended were or must have been major culture carriers, at least in the

The reality of this Arab presence in the Orient and the retention by the Arabs of some[34] form of cultural identity justifies, then, speaking of the Arab factor in the history of the Orient in this Roman period. This factor may be said to have strongly asserted itself in the third century in three related clusters of events,[35] and a recognition of this Arab self-assertion contributes to a better understanding of Arab history, of Roman history, and of Arab-Roman relations in that and the subsequent centuries of the Byzantine period.

IV

The Orient was vast in extent, the Arab groups were ubiquitous within its confines, and they had been subjected to so many cultural influences for so long when the Romans appeared in the East in the first century B.C. And yet, as has been argued in the preceding section, the Arabs of the Orient did retain in varying degrees their cultural identity. The question arises as to what determined for the various Arab groups the degrees of this identity.[36]

---

area of the Arabic language. These caravans crossed the Arabian Peninsula and the Nabataeans and Palmyrenes among them would have been forced to speak the language of the Peninsula for purely commercial reasons even if they were unwilling to use it in Nabataea and Palmyrena, which, as has been argued, was not the case.

[34]Unlike the Arab *foederati* of the three centuries of the Byzantine period in the Orient, these retained a very strong sense of their Arab identity, enhanced by the Roman application of the term *Saraceni* to them and by the non-extension of *civitas*. Their Arab identity is reflected in their employment of the Arabic language, not only as their spoken language as the Nabataeans had done, but more significantly in such areas as the recording of the exploits of a dead king in an inscription and of victories scored over the Romans in poetry; for the Namāra inscription commemorating the exploits of Imru' al-Qays and for the victories of Queen Mavia commemorated in poetry, see the chapters (1 and 4) on the reigns of Constantine and Valens in *BAFOC*. It is only when set against the background of the use of Aramaic by the Arabs of the Orient as their written language in the many centuries of the pre-Byzantine period—Hellenistic and Roman—that the great significance of the Namāra inscription and the Mavian poems composed in the 4th cent. in Arabic becomes evident. These compositions signal a shift in cultural orientation effected by the arrival of a fresh group of Arabs who hailed from regions in the eastern half of the Fertile Crescent where the traditions of literary (and possibly written) Arabic prevailed.

[35]Brought about by the Arab empresses of the Severan dynasty and their sons, by the Emperor Philip the Arab, and by Odenathus and Zenobia of Palmyra; see *infra*, pp. 33–42.

[36]On the desirability of disentangling the Arab zone or layer from the general Semitic or the particular Aramaic one in the Orient, see *supra*, pp. 6–7.

The answer to this question may be stated in terms of closeness to, or remoteness from, the Arabian Peninsula: the closer to that Peninsula, the more retentive of their Arab identity these groups were; conversely, the remoter from it and the closer to the Mediterranean, the less retentive they were of that identity. The operation of this general principle may be illustrated by reference to some representative groups.

A

The Idumaeans were probably the Arab group most assimilated to the non-Arab cultures in the Orient. Idumaea, west of the Dead Sea, was not far from the Mediterranean. Having been for centuries subjected to Aramaicization, Judaization, and Hellenization, the Idumaeans were also subjected to Romanization, and after a century or so of clientship to the Romans, the territories of their rulers, the Herodians, now including the Mediterranean littoral in Palestine, were annexed by the Romans and directly ruled by them. The Idumaeans retained little of their Arab identity.[37]

Close to the Idumaeans were the Ituraeans, who had been subjected to the same influences as the former when the Romans appeared, and whose relations with the Romans also ran along analogous lines. As the Idumaeans reached the shores of the Mediterranean, so did the Ituraeans, and like them they were Judaized. They too may be said to have lost much of their Arab identity.[38]

In roughly the same category but less acculturated were the Arabs of the Orontes who ruled in Emesa and Arethusa. They lived

[37]It was suggested to me by the late Dr. M. Ghul that the Idumaeans were the Arabs of the tribe of Judām of later Byzantine and Islamic times; if so, the Idumaeans, in the course of the following centuries, may have reverted to their Arab cultural affiliations; alternatively, not all of them were assimilated in this Roman period and some may not have moved westward but remained in the deserts of southern Palestine, close to Arab influence from the Sinai and Trans-Jordan. On the Idumaeans, see *supra*, note 26.

[38]Especially those who were *not* in occupation of the Anti-Lebanon whence they expanded into Auranitis, Batanaea, and Trachonitis, close to the Arabian Peninsula and to influences therefrom. Ituraeans were in occupation of the Lebanon and an Ituraean dynast ruled in Arca in northern Lebanon, while Byblus was one of their forts; see *Cities*, p. 456 note 45. Those who inhabited the Anti-Lebanon, Auranitis, Batanaea, and Trachonitis must have retained much of their Arab identity in much the same way that part of the Idumaeans did; but even the Ituraeans of the Mediterranean littoral in Arca seem to have retained an Ituraean identity; on Arca Ituraeorum ca. A.D. 230, see Chad, *Les dynastes d'Émèse*, p. 22.

in the Graeco-Roman fashion and assumed Roman names, and yet they do not appear to be as acculturated as the Idumaeans. Arab names appear among them, but what is much more important is their adherence to the old Arab religion of the sun-god of Emesa; this distinguished them from the Idumaeans and the Ituraeans, who were Judaized, and could argue for their retention of more Arab identity than the latter.[39]

B

It is, however, in the limitrophe—in the frontier provinces of the oriental *limes*—that the Arabs retained their strongest cultural identity. Unlike the Arabs of the Mediterranean littoral and the Valley of the Orontes, these were close to the Arabian Peninsula, and this proximity ensured a constant flow of native strains into these frontier provinces and a constant touch with the Arabic language. The two groups of Arabs who best illustrate this are the Nabataeans and the Palmyrenes—the Arabs of Petra and of Palmyra—who inhabited the area of the oriental *limes* from the Euphrates to the Red Sea, facing the Arabian Peninsula; their territories became the future provinces of Arabia, Phoenicia Libanensis, and Syria Salutaris.

1. For almost two centuries after the Settlement of Pompey in 63 B.C., the Nabataean Arabs had remained independent but clients of the Romans. The annexation of Nabataea and its conversion into a province entailed the acquisition by Rome of a vast territory inhabited by Arabs, and this territory included not only Sinai, Trans-Jordan, and Trans-ʿAraba, but also a large part of Ḥijāz in northwestern Arabia. Its Arabs were the oldest organized Arab group in the region politically and commercially, and their territory, Nabataea, formed probably the most thoroughly Arab and Arabized province in the whole of the Orient.[40] Even in the fourth century, ecclesiastical history testifies to the use of the Arabic vernacular in

---

[39]On the Arabs of Emesa, see *supra*, p. 4, and on the relevance of their religion to their Arab identity, see *supra*, pp. 10–11. Chad's book *Les dynastes d'Émèse* is a mine of information on Arab Emesa and its Arab princes in the Roman period.

[40]Less exposed to the outside world than the Arabs of Palmyra, where Iranian influences from across the Euphrates are striking.

the province for the celebration of the pagan Arab liturgy.[41] The Arab character of Nabataea was reflected onomastically after the annexation in A.D. 106; the new province was called Arabia, and the name thus reminded the student of the provincial history of the Orient of the Arab character of what had previously been Nabataea.[42]

2. The northern half of the Arabian limitrophe was developed rapidly,[43] after the fall of Petra and the annexation of Nabataea in 106, by the Arabs of Palmyra for almost two centuries. Although subjected to foreign influences more profoundly than the Nabataeans, the Palmyrenes remained Arab in ethos and mores and in religious practice.[44] When the Romans destroyed Palmyra in 272 and ruled the area directly, Palmyrena was an Arabized region, the Arab character of which was concealed by the names given in the future to the territory which formed part of Phoenicia Libanensis and Syria Salutaris. Thus unlike Nabataea, which was renamed Arabia, Palmyrena's new name was not reflective of its Arab character, and the non-Arabic and classical terms *Palmyra* and *Palmyrene*,[45] which were applied to the city and the people, further dissociated this group from its Arab origin.[46]

3. Mesopotamia should be included in this enumeration of the frontier provinces which constituted the Arab zone in the Orient. In spite of its separation from the Arabian Peninsula, the Arab element in it in pre-Islamic times was very strong both in

[41]*Supra*, p. 9 and note 23; and for Justinian in the sixth century, the Provincia Arabia was "the country of the Arabs," τὴν ᾿Αράβων χώραν; see the prooimion to the novella (102) on Arabia.

[42]For the Nabataeans, see J. Starcky, "Pétra et la Nabatène," *Dictionnaire de la Bible, Supplément*, 7 (1966), cols. 886–1017.

[43]Palmyrena had been prosperous before A.D. 106, but its prosperity accelerated after that date. On the controversial date of the Roman annexation of Palmyra, see Chad, *Les dynastes d'Émèse*, pp. 105–8.

[44]Their princes kept their Arab names such as Ḥayrān and Uḏayna side by side with the *gentilicium* Septimius; it is noteworthy that the Palmyrenes lived in the consciousness of the Arab historians as Arabs who spoke Arabic; for further discussion of the Palmyrenes in the third century, see *infra*, pp. 38–41.

[45]Aurelian's *cognomen* after the conquest of Palmyra was not *Arabicus* but *Palmyrenicus*. *Arabicus* reflected his victory over a group of Arabs in the region other than the Palmyrenes, but who may have been allied to them; on these two *cognomina*, see sec. III, "Constantinus Arabicus Maximus," in chap. 1 on Constantine in *BAFOC*. On the collocation "Palmyrene Arabs" attested epigraphically, see H. Seyrig, "L'Agora de Palmyre," *Antiquités Syriennes*, 3 (1946), p. 175.

[46]On Palmyra, see J. Starcky, *Palmyre* (Paris, 1952); also his article "Palmyre" in *Dictionnaire de la Bible, Supplément*, 6 (1960), cols. 1078–1103.

the steppes and in the urban centers ruled by Arab dynasts.[47] Thus when the Romans finally terminated the autonomous rule of the Arab Abgarids in Edessa, A.D. 244, they acquired and directly ruled a territory that had been under the rule of Arab dynasts for centuries and where the Arab element was dominant on both sides of the Khābūr, but the names of the future administrative units given to the newly acquired territory, such as Osroene,[48] Mesopotamia, and Euphratesia, did not reflect the strong Arab presence in that region, just as Phoenicia Libanensis and Syria Salutaris did not reflect the same presence in the region that had been Palmyrena.[49]

The Arab zone in the Orient in both Roman and Byzantine times is then the long limitrophe of frontier provinces which before direct Roman rule was applied had been the Arab kingdoms of the Abgarids in Edessa, of the Palmyrenes in Tadmur, and of the Nabataeans in Petra. The identification of this distinctively Arab zone makes it necessary to understand the cultural map of the Orient not in bipartite terms of only Greek and Syriac or Graeco-Roman and Aramaean, but in tripartite terms which include Arab and Arabic as well, dominant in the frontier provinces. The recognition of this fact will disclose for the student of Roman and Byzantine provincial history that under the superficial glaze of Graeco-Roman culture these frontier provinces remained Arab—a fact of considerable importance to the study of the institution of the *phylarchia*[50] in Byzantine times and of the Arab Conquests in the seventh century.[51]

[47]See *supra*, pp. 7–8.
[48]*Ibid.*
[49]For Osroene, see A. von Gutschmid, "Untersuchungen über die Geschichte des Königreichs Osroene," *Mémoires de l'Académie Impériale de St. Pétersbourg*, 35, 1 (1887).
[50]The success of the concept of the *phylarchia* in its new form throughout the three centuries of the Byzantine period must be attributed in part to the fact that these Arab *foederati*, quartered in the limitrophe, were related to its inhabitants, who never forgot or lost their Arab identity. Contrast with the German *foederati* of the Byzantine period, who were quartered in territories not inhabited by a population that was related to them ethnically or otherwise.
[51]A recognition of the pervasive Arab presence in the Orient illuminates other problems, such as the ethnic background of many of the units of the *Notitia Dignitatum* stationed in the Orient (see *infra*, pp. 51–63) and the *ajnād* (the Muslim military themes in Syria) in Umayyad times.

II

Arab-Roman Relations
from the Settlement of Pompey
to the Reign of Diocletian

The Arabs were not Rome's main problem when Pompey took over the eastern command; Mithridates of Pontus in Asia Minor was, and, to a lesser degree, the Parthians across the Euphrates and the remnants of the Seleucids in Syria. However, the Arabs were in control of a large part of the Orient in the first century B.C., and four centuries later, in the third century A.D., they became a serious problem for Rome. The Palmyrenes flung down the gauntlet and succeeded in occupying almost the whole of the eastern half of the empire. They were crushed by Aurelian, and Diocletian was able to hand over to his successors in the fourth century a fairly stable front with Arabia, thus laying the foundation for the new Arab-Byzantine relationship. The preceding four centuries of Arab-Roman relations are thus the background against which may be set the Arab-Byzantine relationship in the fourth. It is therefore necessary to analyze briefly these four centuries of the Roman period[1] both for their own sake and as an introduction to a better understanding of the Arab-Byzantine relationship in the fourth and the following two centuries.

I

These four centuries of Arab-Roman relations are roughly divisible into two periods:

[1]For the historical background of the Arab problem in these four centuries and for the data on which the analyses and the conclusions of this chapter depend, the reader is referred to the relevant parts of the volumes of the CAH: 9, pp. 381–83, 390–96; 10, pp. 247–54, 256–57, 274–75, 279–83, 750–53; 11, pp. 613–27, 630–34, 859–60; 12, pp. 126–37, 174–80, 301–5, 335–37, 396–99.

A

In the first two centuries of this period, Rome dealt primarily not with the Arabs of the Peninsula but with those of the Orient:

1. The tone of Arab-Roman relations in this period was set by the Settlement of Pompey in 64 B.C. After securing the submission of the various Arab dynasts in the Orient, Pompey left the administration in the hands of many of these local dynasts, especially when annexation or direct rule was not called for by strategic or other reasons. Thus in the newly created province of Syria, such Arab dynasts as Sempsigeramus of Emesa and Ptolemy of Chalcis were left in power but as dependents and clients of Rome, as was also Abgar of Edessa across the Euphrates.

2. The main features of Pompey's Settlement survived well into the reign of Augustus in spite of a few adjustments and some seeming[2] departures such as the Roman expeditions against Arabia Felix, out of which nothing came. The Arab vassal states of Emesa and Ituraea remained in charge of internal security and of the defense of Syria against the raids of the nomads from the Arabian Peninsula.

3. The first century A.D. witnessed the beginning of the policy of absorption, of "winding up the Republic," as a result of which the local Arab dynasts start to disappear. In the first half of the century, however, the Julio-Claudians were still pursuing the policy of establishing protectorates and vassal states and applying that

---

Although not very detailed, these chapters in the *CAH* with their bibliographies are adequate.

[2]On the Sabaeans and the Homeritae of South Arabia as a Semitic group cognate with the Arabs, see the present writer in "Pre-Islamic Arabia," *Cambridge History of Islam*, 1, p. 6. On the expedition of Aelius Gallus in 25–24 B.C. see *CAH*, 10, pp. 247–54, and on the controversial expedition of Gaius Caesar a century later, see *ibid.*, pp. 253–54; more recently on the second, see G. W. Bowersock, "A Report on Arabia Provincia," *JRS*, 61 (1971), p. 227, and T. D. Barnes, "The Victories of Augustus," *JRS*, 64 (1974), pp. 22–23. On the relation of the "Parthian arrow" that killed Gaius Caesar (and with it the Arabian expedition) to the cataclysm of the seventh century, see Mommsen's penetrating remarks which, coming from a non-Arabist, are all the more remarkable: Th. Mommsen, *The Provinces of the Roman Empire*, vol. 2, p. 319. His well-known and oft-quoted phrase describing Islam as "the executioner of Hellenism" occurs in that context and in that paragraph; the colorful phrase is only a half-truth the distortion of which may be corrected by appeal to the dictum "without Alexander, no Islamic civilization." On this, see the present writer in "Muhammad and Alexander," *The Third Andrew W. Mellon Lecture* (Washington, D.C., 1979).

policy to such Arab groups as the Herodians, but towards the end
of the century many Arab vassal states had been incorporated under
the Flavians, e.g., Ituraea ca. A.D. 93. Such incorporations, however, were non-significant compared to what was to start happening
in the second century, since Rome continued to deal with the
Arabs of the Orient, while those of the Peninsula were dealt with
indirectly and mainly through such autonomous Arabs as had not
been formally absorbed, e.g., the Nabataeans.

B

In the second century, a new phase of Arab-Roman relations
opened: the policy of absorption, applied at first to relatively small
dependencies and protectorates such as those of the Ituraeans, the
Idumaeans, and the Emesans, gave place to the annexation of larger
units and more important Arab political structures in the Orient
in the second and third centuries. This was the more serious phase
of "winding up the Republic," and it was consummated in three
stages or operations: the first involved the Nabataean Arabs in A.D.
106; the second the Osroenian Arabs of Edessa in A.D. 244; and
the third the Palmyrene Arabs in A.D. 272. The three annexations
raise many problems, but only what is strictly relevant to the context of this chapter will be discussed.

The Nabataeans. The motives behind Trajan's decision to an-
nex Nabataea and the manner of that annexation are controversial,[3]
but more important to the theme of this chapter are other matters,
on which the following observations may be made.

1. The conversion of Nabataea into a *provincia* entailed the
direct incorporation within the *imperium* of a large number of Arabs[4]
who now become provincials and continue to be such for another

[3]The most recent detailed article on this topic and the Provincia Arabia is
D. Graf's "The Saracens and the Defense of the Arabian Frontier," *Bulletin of the
American School of Oriental Research*, 229 (1979), pp. 1–26 (hereafter, *SDAF*). The
author departs from his predecessors who wrote on this topic and makes a case for
the annexation as motivated by a desire to control the desert tribes who disrupted
important trade routes and to restore peace on the eastern frontier; see pp. 6–7
and the conclusions, pp. 19–20. This article has an extensive, up-to-date bibliography, pp. 21–26. See also G. W. Bowersock, "The Annexation and the Initial
Garrison of Arabia," *Zeitschrift für Papyrologie und Epigraphik*, 5 (1970), pp. 37–47;
and M. Speidel, *"Exercitus Arabicus,"* *Latomus*, 33 (1974), pp. 934–39.

[4]A matter of importance to the study both of the ethnic background of the
units of the *Notitia Dignitatum* stationed in the Provincia Arabia and of the Arab
foederati who were stationed in the Provincia in the Byzantine period.

century or so when in A.D. 212 *civitas* was extended to them by an edict issued by the half-Emesene Arab, Caracalla. With its Arabs was also incorporated the extensive Nabataean urban establishment in the Negev, in Trans-Jordan, in Trans-ʿAraba, and possibly in northern Ḥijāz.

2. The annexation of Nabataea also entailed the acquisition by Rome of vast new territories, the precise boundaries of which are difficult to determine but which must have been considerable. That Rome annexed Sinai, the Negev, Trans-ʿAraba, and Trans-Jordan is clear, but what is not clear is the extent of its territorial aggrandizement in Ḥijāz.[5]

3. The creation of the Provincia Arabia brought about important frontier developments and the rise of an elaborate frontier fortification system: the construction of the *Via Nova Traiana* from Ayla to Bostra with a series of forts and fortresses along that road and the construction of another line of forts to the east of that of the *Via Nova* running from Amman to Maʿān. The Roman fortification system of the Arabian frontier presents many problems,[6] but

---

[5]The boundaries of the newly created province of Arabia are a problem, both important and controversial. One view is that the southern boundary of the Provincia extended to Madāʾin Ṣāliḥ (al-Ḥijr) deep in the heart of Ḥijāz; see Starcky, "Pétra et la Nabatène," cols. 898, 921; Bowersock, "A Report on Arabia Provincia," p. 230. Another view is that the southern boundary was "the southern slope of the al-Sherā range"; see Graf, *SDAF*, p. 4, following A. Musil. The epigraphic data that have been found in Dūmat al-Jandal near the southern end of Wādi-al-Sirḥān and in Madāʾin Ṣāliḥ have been variously interpreted to argue for either the former or the latter view. It is easier to accept the former view and to assume that only in later times were the Romans content to maintain a presence or a sphere of influence in Ḥijāz through the Arabs allied to them. For the epigraphic evidence, see G. W. Bowersock, "Syria under Vespasian," *JRS*, 63 (1973), p. 139 note 57, and *idem*, "A Report on Arabia Provincia," p. 230. On the four phases through which, in the view of the present writer, Nabataea went from its conversion into a *provincia* in the reign of Trajan to the incorporation of parts of it into Palestine in the reign of Constantius, see sec. I on the Namāra inscription in chap. 1 of *BAFOC*.

[6]The fortification or defense system of Arabia poses three related problems which have been the subject of a lively discussion: (*a*) as G. W. Bowersock has noted, the term *limes* in *limes Arabicus* must be understood not as a fortified line but as a fortified region or territory; (*b*) Mommsen's concept of a double *limes*, internal and external—inherited by others, such as Brünnow and Domaszewski for Arabia and Poidebard for Chalcidice and the defense system from the Ḥawrān to the Euphrates—is mistaken; for (*a*) and (*b*), see Bowersock, "Limes Arabicus," *Harvard Studies in Classical Philology*, 80 (1976), pp. 219–29; and also Graf, *SDAF*, p. 1; (*c*) the gap in the fortification system of the southern sector of

the large fact which emerges is the transference and application of the *limes* concept[7] to the Arabian frontier with all that that implied: a fixed and clearly recognizable border, at least relative to what had obtained before, and consequently defensive, not offensive, in character.

The Osroenians.   Three centuries after their encounter with Pompey, the Osroenian Arabs were finally absorbed by the Romans. Gordian's campaign against the Persians was successful; his victory near Resaina in A.D. 243 gave the Romans the whole of Mesopotamia, and Edessa, the capital of the Abgarid Arabs of Osroene, this side of the Khābūr, became a Roman colony.[8] Mesopotamia remained Roman, together with Lesser Armenia, according to the terms of the peace that Philip made with the Persians after the death of Gordian.[9]

Thus the Persian campaign of Gordian brought to an end the autonomous rule of an important Arab group in the Trans-Euphratesian region, the Osroenians of Edessa; and the defense of that sector of the frontier which had been partly undertaken by the Arabs of Osroene was now directly assumed by the Romans. Deeper penetrations in the Trans-Euphratesian region were effected by Diocletian towards the end of the century in a campaign that gave the Romans territories across the Tigris.

This annexation, less important for Arab-Roman relations than that of Nabataea, entailed the acquisition by the empire of a large number of Arabs and their territory and brought about important frontier development. But unlike the annexation of Nabataea, this one did not extend the Roman frontier with the Arabian Peninsula. Instead, the elimination of the Arab principality which lay be-

---

the *limes Arabicus* from Aqaba to Sadaqa, west of Maʿān, is a problem; see *supra*, note 5, for the two opposite views related to this problem. The controversy concerning the important Arab tribal group Thamūd of Ruwwāfa in the Ḥisma region of northern Ḥijāz may be set within the framework of this problem; for Bowersock, Thamūd was *intra limitem*, for Graf it was *extra limitem*. It was through this gap that the Muslim columns sent against the Byzantines by the Caliph Abu-Bakr in A.D. 633 slipped into southern Trans-Jordan and Palestine.

[7]The term is used in this chapter not in the sense of a clear line of defense, as it was used for the *limes* in Europe; see preceding note.

[8]Ḥatra, the other Arab fortress balancing Edessa in Persian territory, had fallen to Shāpūr about this time, ca. 240.

[9]For the campaign of Gordian against the Persians and the peace concluded by Philip, see *CAH*, 12, pp. 87–88.

tween the Romans and the Persians brought the former closer to the latter.[10]

The Palmyrenes.   The last of the three Arab city-states to fall to the Romans in this second phase of Arab-Roman relations was Palmyra, the destruction of which brought about even more important changes in the Roman frontier defense system than that of Petra and Edessa.[11]

Like Petra, Palmyra was a caravan city and a bulwark of frontier defense, but while Petra policed the desert and thus warded off the Arab nomads of the Peninsula, Palmyra's function in the Roman defense system was more complex. In addition to policing the desert for Rome against the raids of the desert nomads, it was Rome's bulwark against the militant Sasanids under the aggressive Shāpūr, who captured Valerian and who in turn was beaten and checked by the Palmyrene Odenathus. The capture of the city by Aurelian in A.D. 272 and its reduction into a mere village the following year produced that vast vacuum which had been occupied by Palmyra's commercial and military presence, internationally ramified. The vastness and complexity of that vacuum may be measured in the following manner.

1. The great desert oasis, caravan city, and fortress controlled from its strategic position the trade arteries that ran from the Land of the Two Rivers, the Arabian Peninsula, and the Persian Gulf to the Mediterranean. All this was at Rome's disposal, mediated to her by the energetic Palmyrene community of traders. The elimination of Palmyra presented Rome with a grave problem, namely, maintaining the prosperity of its trade with the Orient; but how Rome dealt with the problem is not very clear. The rise of the Sasanids, much more aggressive than the decadent Parthians, had made the Mesopotamian trade route unsafe,[12] and it is thus pos-

[10]Just as the conquest of Arab Ḥatra by Shāpūr ca. 240 eliminated that Arab buffer city and consequently brought the Sasanids closer to direct confrontation with the Romans.

[11]The circumstances that led to the destruction of Palmyra are not so obscure as those that led to the annexation of Nabataea. The destruction was forced on Rome by Palmyra's revolt, and the revolt itself was not typical of Roman relations with her Arab clients; these relations were mutually beneficial and consequently harmonious. Whether Rome would have eliminated Palmyra in any case as another instance of "winding up the Republic" remains to be shown, and exactly what Zenobia had in mind when she revolted is not entirely clear.

[12]Although this does not seem to have deterred Palmyra from establishing

sible that the shift from the Mesopotamian to the West Arabian and the Red Sea route began in the third century, accelerated by the fall of Palmyra, and signaling a return to the same trade routes that had been presided over by the Nabataeans.[13]

2. Palmyra had also protected the northern half of the Roman frontier adjacent to the Arabian Peninsula and reaching the Euphrates. All along the Euphrates and in the desert to the south roamed powerful Arab tribes, a source of potential and actual danger to the eastern frontier and the provinces. Palmyra, itself Arab, effectively controlled the desert frontier with its turbulence and transhumance. Now that frontier lay open and presented problems of a special and peculiar nature to Rome. How Rome responded to the new situation created by the elimination of Palmyra is not crystal clear, but what is clear is that its elimination now caused Rome to shoulder herself the responsibility of frontier defense against the Arabs of the Peninsula; and, what is more, it proved to be confrontational, bringing Rome face to face with the Arabs of the Peninsula.[14]

---

trade stations and relations with the regions to the east and south of it. The fact that it was an Arab city must partly explain its success, since the world with which Palmyra traded consisted to a great extent of Arabs whether those of the Peninsula, of the Land of the Two Rivers, or of the Persian Gulf. Thus, in spite of the Roman orbit in which she moved and of the rise of the hostile Sasanids, Palmyra was in a unique position to maintain these trade relations.

[13]D. Graf follows Mayerson in suggesting that the transfer of *legio X Fretensis* from Jerusalem to Ayla "represents Aurelian's attempt to revive the old trade routes from the East in the aftermath of the Palmyrene revolt." And he also follows Ritterling in explaining the appearance of *legio IV Martia* at Betthoro (Lejjūn) as due to Aurelian's reinforcement of the eastern defense system, thus dissociating the two transfers from the Diocletianic reforms; see Graf, *SDAF*, p. 19. The suggestions are attractive, but it is doubtful whether in the aftermath of the fall of Palmyra and on the eve of his departure to the Occident to crush Tetricius, Aurelian would have had the time or the inclination to think of trade routes. However, it is relevant to mention that the South Arabians were represented at Aurelian's triumph in A.D. 274, although reference to the embassy comes from the *Historia Augusta*, "Aurelian," 33.4; see also E. H. Warmington, *The Commerce between the Roman Empire and India*, 2nd ed. (London, 1974), p. 138.

[14]The reference in the *Notitia Dignitatum* to two Arab units of *equites Saraceni* in Phoenicia is tantalizing; it is tempting to connect their appearance in that province with Aurelian's military dispositions after his destruction of Palmyra and his desire to have the Roman frontier protected by these units of *equites* who, moreover, as Saraceni were familiar with the problems of the region and with their fellow Arabs in the Peninsula. For their strategic location on routes leading from Palmyra to Damascus and Emesa, see van Berchem, quoted in Graf, *SDAF*,

3. The defense of the Orient in the sixties had been left to Palmyra, which under Odenathus acquitted itself remarkably well during the period of the imperial crisis. Now the elimination of Palmyra was confrontational not only with the Arabs of the Peninsula but also with the Persians of the Land of the Two Rivers, who were deployed along the other side of the Euphrates. The vacuum created by the fall of Palmyra was a dangerous one since it involved not only the Arabs of the Peninsula but the other, much more important world power, Iran.

II

Aurelian did not stay long enough in the East to be able to effect extensive frontier reorganization and did not live long enough to return to the East for his Persian campaign, having been murdered early in A.D. 275 near Byzantium. If he had, it is almost certain that he would have brought about a thorough reorganization of the oriental *limes*. However, after his destruction of Rome's bulwark against the Arabian Peninsula and Sasanid Persia, it is inconceivable that Aurelian's strategic insight would not have led him to make at least tentative and provisional changes[15] in the frontier defense, called for by the vacuum he himself had created by the destruction of Palmyra, which left a goodly portion of the Orient exposed. He had to hurry back from the Orient to the Occident to deal with Tetricius and his Gallic Empire. How he would have reorganized the defenses of the Orient if he had not been murdered and had fought the projected Persian campaign is difficult to tell. Perhaps the Persian campaign itself was not unrelated to the Arab one against Palmyra, and he may have viewed it as its necessary and natural continuation.

It was therefore left to Diocletian to reorganize the oriental

---

p. 19. Arabs described as Ituraeans and Saracens fought under Aurelian, if the account of the *Historia Augusta* is authentic; see "Aurelian," 11.3. Who these two Saracen units of *equites* were is impossible to tell. It is very tempting to think that they were the ones who fought with him against the Palmyrenes and that they were none other than the Tanūkhids—according to the Arabic sources the inveterate enemies of the Palmyrenes; on these two units in the *Notitia Dignitatum*, see *infra*, p. 59. For the Arabic sources on the Tanūkhids, see the relevant chapters in *BAFOC*.

[15] See *supra*, notes 13–14, and Graf, *SDAF*, p. 17.

limes.[16] He stayed in the Orient long enough and reigned long enough to effect that reorganization. Even before his campaign against the Saracens, ca. A.D. 290, and that of his Caesar, Galerius, against the Persians in 297/8, Diocletian had inherited from his predecessors in the third century both an Arab and a Persian problem, caused respectively by the elimination of Arab Edessa and Palmyra and the rise of the Sasanids, aggressive and expansionist. It is therefore more correct to say that Diocletian's reorganization of the oriental *limes* was a response to both the Persian and the Arab problems rather than to only the former or the latter;[17] and the two problems were related.[18] The following observations on some features of Diocletian's reorganization of the oriental *limes* are restricted to those in which he responded to the challenge from the Arabs.

1. Who the Saracens were that crossed the path of Diocletian, against whom he campaigned and over whom he triumphed, putting them in chains and transplanting them to Thrace, is not clear; but a further reference to them clearly indicates that the *nationes* who were vanquished by Diocletian lived in Syria. This unrest among the Syrian Arabs could possibly suggest some relation to the souring of Arab-Roman relations owing to the destruction of Palmyra by Aurelian.[19]

2. Diocletian is said by Malalas to have constructed *fabricae,* factories of arms, in Antioch, Edessa, and Damascus.[20] Malalas speaks of the raids of the Saracens in connection with the factory con-

[16]The fundamental study is W. Ensslin's "Zur Ostpolitik des Kaisers Diokletian," *Sitzungsberichte der Bayerischen Akademie der Wissenschaften*, Philosophisch-historische Abteilung (Munich, 1942), Heft 1, pp. 7–83. On the problems of this *limes,* e.g., the two *limites, interior* and *exterior,* see "*Limes Orientalis*" in *BAFOC,* Part III.

[17]As Ensslin and Graf have argued in "Zur Ostpolitik des Kaisers Diokletian" and *SDAF* respectively; Graf, however, has in mind the desert Arabs, the tribes of North Arabia (p. 20), while the Arab problem was more extensive and also related to the Arab political structures in the Orient.

[18]Except in the case of the Nabataean Arabs, who, unlike the Palmyrenes, were far from the area of Persian dominance.

[19]On these Arabs against whom Diocletian campaigned, see Ensslin, *op. cit.*, pp. 15, 19.

[20]Malalas, *Chronographia*, ed. Dindorf (Bonn, 1831), pp. 307–8; and Ensslin, *op. cit.*, p. 65.

structed in Damascus, and this suggests that Phoenicia at least was exposed to Saracen raids.

3. Galerius's Persian campaign resulted in the peace of 298, according to the terms of which some five Persian satrapies across the Tigris were ceded to Rome.[21] This clinched the Roman possession of Mesopotamia in its entirety and with it the permanent acquisition, at least until the peace of Jovian in 363, of a large number of Mesopotamian Arabs[22] who were settled on both sides of the Khābūr. Confrontation between the two world powers, to which the elimination of autonomous Edessa and Arab Osroene by Gordian earlier had contributed, was now complete.[23]

4. By far the most important feature of the Diocletianic reorganization of the oriental *limes* as far as the Arabs were concerned is undoubtedly the construction of the *Strata Diocletiana,* that fortified military road which ran from Damascus through Palmyra to Sura on the Euphrates, and the extension of the fortification system of watchtowers and forts on the road which ran from Petra in the south to Circesium on the Euphrates in the north, passing through Palmyra. In so doing, Diocletian gave his own peculiar solution to the problem created by the elimination of Palmyra as Rome's desert fortress and also completed the work of Trajan who, after eliminating Nabataea as a client kingdom, had the *Via Nova Traiana* constructed in the newly created Provincia Arabia.

III

The diachronous treatment of the Arab presence in the Orient and of the various stages whereby Rome finally absorbed its Arabs throughout these four centuries from Pompey to Diocletian provides a clearer background for reexamining the problem of the Arab units

[21]What has been said of Aurelian's projected Persian campaign, *supra*, pp. 24–25, may be said of this peace treaty. It may have been deemed a sequel, and a necessary one, to the elimination of Palmyra, reflecting a desire to gain a strategic advantage over Persia by the possession of Mesopotamia in its entirety for dominating the Sasanid Land of the Two Rivers. It is noteworthy that before his defeat, the Persian King Narse had opened hostilities by invading Syria.

[22]Including "Arabia in Mesopotamia," on the other side of the Khābūr.

[23]Reflected in Diocletian's increasing the number of the legions from eight to twelve.

in the *Notitia Dignitatum*[24] and making further observations within this new context.

The *Notitia Dignitatum* is the prime document which accurately reflects the nature and extent of what might be termed Arab manpower in the service of Rome. Although the period on which it is informative is the Byzantine—the fourth and the early fifth centuries—there is in it the Roman substrate or layer which goes back to the pre-Byzantine period. The foregoing sections have tried to shed some light on the extent of Arab diffusion in the Orient when the Romans brought it under their rule. The application of various designations to the different Arab groups had obscured the extent of that diffusion and, correspondingly, the extent of the Arab contribution to the armies of Rome in both the Orient and the Occident; that contribution was considerable. The principal value of the *ND* to the student of Arab-Roman relations is that it reveals how Rome dealt with the Arab problem in the Orient—how after wearing down, taming, and absorbing the Arabs within the *imperium*, she enlisted them in her service to fight her wars against the Peninsular Arabs as well as other enemies. The *ND* thus documents the success[25] of the Roman experiment in dealing with the Arab problem.

[24]On the Arab units of the *Notitia Dignitatum*, see *infra*, pp. 51–63. In addition to the bibliography on the *ND* cited in that chapter, the following items may be added: E. Demougeot, "La *Notitia Dignitatum* et l'histoire de l'Empire d'Occident au début du Ve siècle", *Latomus*, 34 (1975), pp. 1079–1134; "Aspects of the *Notitia Dignitatum*," ed. R. Goodburn and P. Bartholomew, *British Archaeological Reports, Supplementary Series*, 15 (1976); in spite of the fact that it deals mainly with the Occident, the latter work has some regional studies which are relevant to the study of the Arab units in the East. More relevant and especially important is M. Speidel, "The Rise of Ethnic Units in the Roman Imperial Army," in *Aufstieg und Niedergang der Römischen Welt*, ed. H. Temporini (Berlin–New York, 1975), vol. II, 3, pp. 202–30, and the bibliography, pp. 230–31; see also M. G. Jarrett, "Thracian Units in the Roman Army," *Israel Exploration Journal*, 19 (1969), pp. 215–24.

[25]Just as the *Strategicon* in its own *negative* way documents the success of Byzantium in dealing with the Arabs, to whom there is no reference whatsoever in that military manual of the late sixth century as there is to other peoples hostile to the empire. The silence of the *Strategicon* must be construed as eloquent testimony to the success of the Byzantine experiment of dealing with the Peninsular Arabs. That experiment was so successful that there was no need to mention the Arabs as actually or potentially posing a threat to the empire.

The success of the Roman and the Byzantine experiment (until the reign of

The detailed examination of the Arab units of the *Notitia Dignitatum*, however, presents many problems[26] which are important to the student of Arab-Roman relations and to the general student of the *ND*, but considerable uncertainty attends these problems. The following paragraphs discuss them briefly and present at least a framework within which further discussion of the problems may be conducted.

1. The overwhelming majority of the Arab units in the *ND* were not Peninsular Arabs living *extra limitem*, but belonged to the Arabs whom the Romans had found in the Orient when Pompey appeared in the sixties of the first century B.C. and whom the Romans in the course of the four following centuries absorbed within the *imperium*. Most of the units belonged to the category of *Equites Indigenae*; a few of them are recognizable by their names and gentilic affiliations, such as Palmyrenes, Ituraeans, and Thamudeni. Arabs belonging to these three groups fought in the Roman army both in the Orient and elsewhere in Europe and Africa.[27]

2. The legal status of these units in the Orient can only be inferred, but it is almost certain that they were *cives*. As provincial Arabs living within the *imperium*, they must have acquired citizenship either by virtue of their service in the Roman army or after *civitas* was extended to the provincials in A.D. 212 by the *Constitutio Antoniniana*.

3. Three units in the *ND* are described as *Saraceni*:[28] two in Phoenicia, the *Equites Saraceni Indigenae* and the *Equites Saraceni*,

---

Maurice) contrasts sharply with the failure of Byzantium to deal with the Arabs of the seventh century and thus provides a background for a better understanding of their successes as seen within the perspective of Arab-Roman relations throughout eight centuries.

[26]Notably, the chronology of the service record of the various units—when this or that particular unit was recruited and stationed in a particular post and, in the case of a Palmyrene or an Ituraean one, whether it entered the service before or after the fall of Palmyra or Ituraea.

[27]For Arab archers in the service of Rome, see the important article by Hubert van de Weerd and Pieter Lambrechts, "Note sur les corps d'archers au Haut Empire," in *Die Araber in der alten Welt*, vol. 1, pp. 661–77; the last section, pp. 673–77, describes the rising importance of the cavalry in the Roman army after the battle of Carrhae and the far-reaching changes in armor and tactics which that disaster brought about; the Arabs listed in the *ND* served both as mounted *sagittarii* and *clibanarii*.

[28]On these three units treated in a different context, see *infra*, Chap. V, "*Notitia Dignitatum*," p. 55 notes 20, 23, and p. 59 note 33.

and a third in the *Limes Aegypti*, the *Equites Saraceni Thamudeni*. These references to the Saraceni are the most tantalizing and also the most controversial of all the references to the Arab units in the *Notitia*. A solution to the problem of these three units, designated as Saraceni, could throw much light on the history of Arab-Roman relations and on the problems of the *Notitia* in general. The main questions which these three units pose are: (*a*) their legal status: were they *cives* recruited from within the *imperium* as the other Arab units, or were they Peninsular Arabs; (*b*) does the application of the term *Saraceni* imply that they were nomads, in view of what Ammianus says on the equation of the Saraceni with the Scenitae;[29] and (*c*) do these Saraceni, especially those of Phoenicia, represent the new type of *foederati* who appear in the fourth century in the Byzantine period and who are regularly referred to as Saraceni? These are large questions for which there are as yet no definitive answers. *Saraceni* itself, the fairly recent term which was apparently unknown in the Hellenistic period but which in Roman times started to designate the Arabs or some of them, is still unfortunately attended by many problems which await solution.[30] However, some progress has been made in this direction, and one could advance the study of the problems related to these three units by at least raising the pertinent questions and, methodologically, by disentangling the third unit, the *Equites Saraceni Thamudeni* of Egypt, from the other two, stationed in Phoenicia:

(*a*) The *Equites Saraceni Thamudeni*: the *ND* refers to two units of Thamudeni, one in Palestine and the other in Egypt; but only the one in Egypt is referred to as *Saraceni*, the other as *Equites Thamudeni Illyriciani*. This raises the question why one unit is described as Saracen while the other is not. Since the term *Saracen* is considered late in usage, its application to one of the two units could suggest that it was recruited later than the other; but even this is by no means certain, since the rise of the term *Saracen* may considerably antedate its early extant attestations. According to Ammianus, the term *Saraceni* is equivalent to *Scenitae*, and thus it may have been used of the unit in Egypt to distinguish it from the other unit which was not nomadic. If true, this would be a

[29]Ammianus Marcellinus, *Res Gestae*, XXII.15.2; XXIII.6.13.
[30]On the term *Saraceni*, see *infra*, pp. 123–41.

reflection of the realities of tribal social life in Arabia, where part of one and the same tribe could be sedentary while the other could be nomadic; presumably this applied to the Thamūd, some of whom, such as those of the inscriptions at Ruwwāfa, were sedentary, while the others were nomadic.[31]

(b) Important as the references to the Thamudeni and the Saraceni Thamudeni are, they are less important to the Byzantine period than the reference to the two Saracen units stationed in Phoenicia; but the answers to the pertinent questions about them are as uncertain as those about the former. In addition to what has been said concerning the possibility that they go back to the time of Aurelian, with whom they fought against the Palmyrenes and who stationed them in Phoenicia to occupy the political and military vacuum created by the fall of Palmyra,[32] the following possibility might be entertained, deriving from the fact that the ND is a document that reflects the military realities of the fourth and the early fifth centuries: the stationing of these two units in Phoenicia may go back not to the third but to either the fourth or the fifth century,[33] representing the foederati of these centuries, the new type of Arab allies that the Byzantine period witnessed. If so, they could be the Tanūkhids of the fourth century or the Salīḥids of the fifth; and if the two units did belong to the new type of Arab allies, the foederati, whether Tanūkhid or Salīḥid, the chances are that they were not cives.[34]

IV

Whatever the exact truth about these units, designated as Saracen, may turn out to be, they remain an important group of

---

[31]It is tempting to think that the application of the term Saraceni to the Thamudeni of Egypt implies that that unit was recruited after the fall of Thamūd and its reversion to nomadism; hence the application of the term Saraceni in the sense of Scenitae to it. On the theme of "re-bedouinization," see W. Caskel, "The Bedouinization of Arabia," in Studies in Islamic Cultural History, ed. G. E. von Grünebaum, pp. 36–46, especially pp. 40–41; this article, however, has to be used with great care.

[32]See supra, note 14.

[33]The employment of only the term Saraceni to describe them, without further gentilic qualification such as Thamudeni, could fortify this view. The Arab foederati of the Byzantine period are almost never referred to by specific gentilic designations but simply by the generic term Saraceni.

[34]For different views of these Saraceni, see Graf, SDAF, pp. 17–18.

units in the *ND* since reference to them either reflects the realities of the fourth and fifth centuries of the Byzantine period or the transition to it from the Roman. *Saraceni* became the regular term for designating the Arabs in the Byzantine period, during which developed the system of *symmachoi* and *phylarchoi, foederati* and *phylarchi*. But that system did not emerge suddenly in the Byzantine period; it had its roots in the Roman period, and it remains to make a few observations on those roots as an introduction to the study of the system in the Byzantine period.[35]

1. The system of employing Arab tribal chiefs in the service of Rome antedated the Byzantine period. A variety of terms was used to designate the tribal chief allied to Rome, such as *syndikos, ethnarchēs,* and *stratēgos.*[36] All these were swept away in the Byzantine period by the term *phylarchus*[37] which became towards the end of the fourth century the standard term for designating the Arab tribal chief allied to Rome.

2. In the Roman period, these chiefs and their tribes, allied to Rome, coexisted with much more important Arab groups with whom Rome had to deal—sedentary clients such as the Nabataeans and the Palmyrenes. They were, therefore, relatively unimportant, except in limited spheres of activities as desert patrol units for enforcing law and controlling the transhumance of Peninsular tribes from wandering into Roman territory.[38] But after the elimination of the powerful Arab client kingdoms one after the other in the

[35]On the phylarchal and federate system in Byzantine times, see the relevant chapters in *BAFOC.*

[36]See Graf, *SDAF,* p. 32.

[37]Also used in late Hellenistic and in Roman times; see F. Gschnitzer, "Phylarchos," *RE,* Supplement, 11 (1968), cols. 1072–74.

[38]Perhaps Safaitic ʿAwīd could represent this type of Arab tribe in the Roman period. The history of its checkered relations with Rome can be recovered with the help of Arabic and Greek epigraphy; see Graf, *SDAF,* p. 16. Its *mlk* ("king") was probably no more than a local chief, and thus "lord" would be the more appropriate rendition of *mlk.* Imruʾ al-Qays, who was buried in the same area of Namāra which ʿAwīd roamed, was also *mlk,* but he should be distinguished in almost every sense from the *mlk* of ʿAwīd; on Imruʾ al-Qays, see chap. 1 on the reign of Constantine in *BAFOC.* The difficulty of establishing a chronology for ʿAwīd's activities and relations with the Romans makes drawing conclusions on this tribe rather difficult. Thus the model tribe for the study of Arab-Roman relations must remain Thamūd, whose history is solidly documented by informative Greek and Nabataean inscriptions of the second century A.D. and by references in the *ND.*

Roman period, these Arab *foederati* of the Byzantine period assume a much more important role.

3. In spite of a strong Roman military presence, the desert regions of the Orient and the Arabian Peninsula presented problems of defense and security which could best be met by Arabs accustomed to the geographical conditions of the region and to the warfare techniques peculiar to the desert, depending on mobility, which in turn was related to that of the two desert animals, the horse and the camel, and to the use of the bow and arrow.[39] The Arab desert warrior, Rome's ally, was thus often an *eques sagittarius*. In the Byzantine period, border unrest continued to be one of the important concerns of the Arab *foederati*, especially in areas facing the Arabian Peninsula, but these also had to shoulder perhaps more important responsibilities related to the Persian-Byzantine conflict.

Postscript: Ritterling discussed in *RE*, 12 (1925), 1347 the composition of the army, legionary and auxiliary, which Aurelian led against the Palmyrenes by analyzing the crucial passage in Zosimus, *Historia Nova*, I.52.3–4, and Kenneth Holum has argued that 50,000–60,000 would be a reasonable guess for its size since, according to Zosimus, it was smaller than that of the Palmyrenes, which numbered 70,000.

I should like to thank Professor Holum for some fruitful conversations on Aurelian's army and for drawing the arrows on Map V, which illustrates the advance of the Palmyrene troops into Asia Minor and Egypt during Zenobia's revolt.

[39]On the saddle bow and its adoption by camel riders, see W. Dostal, "The Evolution of Bedouin Life," *Studi Semitici: L'antica società beduina*, 2 (1959), pp. 15–28.

III

The Arab Factor in Roman History in the Third Century

The third century witnessed a considerable surge of Arab self-assertion, through which the Arabs became a factor in Roman history throughout that century. This factor is represented in the first half of it by the Arab members of the Severan dynasty, towards the middle of it by Philip the Arab, and in the second half of it by Palmyra's Odenathus and Zenobia.[1]

I

Septimius was not an Arab but a "Phoenician" from Leptis Magna;[2] his wife, however, was descended from the line of Arab priest-kings[3] that had ruled Emesa in Roman times for a long period after the Settlement of Pompey.[4] It was Julia Domna who provided the Arab element to the Severi, directly as the wife of Septimius Severus and the mother of Caracalla, who was thus half-Arab, and indirectly as the sister of Julia Maesa and aunt of the

---

[1]Volume 12 of *CAH* provides adequate background material against which the discussion of the Arab factor in the third century may be set; for the relevant chapters on the Arabs in the third century, see *ibid.*, pp. 1–72 for the Severi; pp. 87–95 for Philip the Arab; and pp. 169–80, 306 for Palmyra, together with the bibliographies which go with these pages. Although much has been written on the third century since the publication of *CAH*, 12, that volume with its bibliographies is the most convenient single work to which the reader can refer for most of the data on the Arabs included in this chapter.

[2]The term *Semitic* is more accurate and appropriate for describing the Severan dynasty; *Oriental* is too general and not revelatory of the ethnic background of the Severi.

[3]Julia Domna was the daughter of Julius Bassianus, priest of the god Baal, in Emesa.

[4]On the annexation of Emesa by the Romans after a long period of autonomy, see Chad, *Les dynastes d'Émèse,* pp. 103–5, 109–13; this family of Arab priest-kings had ruled Emesa for some time before the Settlement of Pompey.

latter's two daughters, Julia Soaemias and Julia Mammaea, mothers of the Emperors Elagabalus and Severus Alexander respectively.[5]

What the influence of the *mater patriae, mater senatus,* and *mater castrorum* was on the master of the Roman world from 192 to 211, her husband Septimius, who changed the character of the principate and with it the Roman state, is a question that cannot be determined with accuracy. But it was or must have been considerable in view of her endowments and her ambition, and it was possibly exerted also indirectly through such of her countrymen as Ulpian and Papinian, with whom she surrounded her husband. In addition to her involvement in imperial matters, she was the center of a well-known eclectic literary circle and carried on the fight of paganism against Christianity by commissioning the sophist Philostratus to write the *Life of Apollonius of Tyana.*[6]

It was after the death of Severus and during the reign of her son Caracalla that Julia became even more powerful. What matters in this period is the *Constitutio Antoniniana,*[7] the extension of *civitas* to all free inhabitants of the empire and the obliteration of the distinction between Roman and provincial in A.D. 212. It is difficult to believe that the author of the *Constitutio* was only that crude soldier Caracalla and that the talented mother and her lawyers, Ulpian and Papinian,[8] were not also behind the famous edict. Al-

---

[5]Thus the empresses of the Severan dynasty were wholly Arab and its emperors were mostly so: Septimius, the founder of the dynasty, was not, but all the rest were, either wholly or partly. Caracalla was half-Arab; Elagabalus and Severus Alexander were at least half-Arab and probably wholly so.

This striking number of emperors and empresses of Syrian Arab origin was to be paralleled in the seventh and eighth centuries by the equally striking number of Syrian popes in Rome: John V (685–86), Sergius (687–701), Sisinnius (708), Constantine (708–15), and Gregory III (731–41), the second and fifth of whom, Sergius and Gregory, were canonized.

[6]One important feature of her Emesene Arab background may be involved in her stand for paganism and her struggle against Christianity, namely, the pagan cult of the sun-god of Emesa, Baal, of whom her father Julius Bassianus was priest. Contrast with the background of Philip the Arab, who hailed from a region in the Orient where Christianity had spread, the Provincia Arabia; see *infra,* p. 72.

[7]For the *Constitutio Antoniniana,* see A. N. Sherwin-White, *The Roman Citizenship* (Oxford, 1973), pp. 279–87; 380–93.

[8]An Emesene Oriental origin has been suggested for Papinian; if so, it is not clear to which ethnic group of the Semitic Orient he belonged.

though various motives have been assigned to its issue, it is not impossible that the ethnic origin of Julia and her son and the fact that the family hailed from one of the provinces of the East were operative factors.[9]

In addition to the part they played in the civil history of Rome by the issue of the *Constitutio Antoniniana*, these Arab dynasts from Emesa played an important role in its religious history. During the reign of Elagabalus (218–22), the Emesene sun-god, after whom Bassianus was surnamed Elagabalus, was installed in Rome.[10] But more important is the involvement of two of the Arab empresses, Julia Domna and her niece Julia Mammaea, in the religious movements of the time. The first, as has been mentioned, wrote a chapter in the history of the conflict between Christianity and paganism by championing the latter. In contrast to her aunt, Julia Mammaea was favorably disposed to Christianity; Hippolytus dedicated a volume to her, and she was considered almost a Christian by Eusebius, who records her request to converse with Origen and the latter's journey to Antioch where Mammaea happened to be staying. It was her son Severus Alexander who was considered a Christian by the ecclesiastical writers, and there can be no doubt that his "Christianity" must have been to a great extent inspired by his mother.[11]

The deep interest of the empresses and their sons in religion, pagan and Christian, can certainly be related to the religious cult of their city of origin and to their descent from the Arab priests

---

[9]This view might derive some support from what Dio Cassius says on the motive behind the edict, namely, that nominally it was an honor to the non-Romans of the empire; see Dio, *Roman History,* Loeb ed. (1927), LXXVIII.9.5. Perhaps Julia Domna and Caracalla were also influenced by Septimius's own consciousness that he did not belong to the Roman establishment and by his well-known hostility to the Roman aristocracy and the Senate; on Dio's conception of both Caracalla and Julia Domna as crafty "Syrians," see *ibid.*, LXXVIII.6.1; 10.2. On the relation between the edict and the "Syrian, or Semitic, form of solar worship," see *CAH*, 12, p. 46; "Arab" might have been used for "Syrian" and "Semitic"; see *supra*, p. 6.

[10]If the two empresses, Julia Domna and Julia Maesa, were the daughters of the priest of the sun-god, Elagabalus had been himself the priest of that god; thus the year A.D. 218 witnessed the elevation to the principate of an Arab priest of the sun-god of Emesa.

[11]On Julia Mammaea and Alexander, see *infra*, p. 71 and note 17.

of the sun-god of Emesa with its resoundingly Arabic name, El
Gabal.[12] They start, and naturally so, as devotees of the sun-god,
their own native god, but they end up by gravitating towards
Christianity. In so doing they represent the progress made by that
religion at the highest level of Roman life, namely, the court.[13]

II

Unlike the principate of his distinguished Semitic predecessor
Septimius, Philip's had no great significance in the imperial history
of Rome and may be judged rather episodic.[14] However, in the
history of Arab-Roman relations, it is of some importance for the
Arab factor in the third century and for the spread of Christianity.
Within this framework, the following observations may be made
on Philip's principate.[15]

1. Just as the pagan Arab cult of the sun-god of Emesa is a
relevant feature of background for the interest of the Severi in
religion and in the case of Elagabalus for the installation of the
Arab sun-god in Rome itself, so was the spread of Christianity in
the Provincia Arabia the relevant feature of background for the
Christianity of Philip the Arab.[16] The Provincia was *Arabia haeresium
ferax*, as is clear from the accounts of the ecclesiastical historians,
but it was also one of the provinces that witnessed the early spread
of Christianity, and thus its Arabs, for geographical and other
reasons, were among the early converts. Philip must be adjudged
its most celebrated Christian Arab in the history of imperial Rome.
If Severus Alexander was partly Arab and partly Christian, Philip
was wholly Arab and wholly Christian, and thus he represents the
triumph of both Christianity at the highest level and the elevation

[12]The priest-kings of Emesa continued to exercise their sacerdotal functions
even after they ceased to be kings and after Emesa had been annexed by the
Romans; see Chad, *Les dynastes d'Émèse*, p. 121.
[13]For this, see A. Harnack, *The Mission and Expansion of Christianity in the
First Three Centuries*, trans. and ed. James Moffatt (London–New York, 1908),
vol. 2, pp. 42–52; also pp. 64–84 for the spread of Christianity among women,
and prominent ones among them.
[14]Perhaps because of its short duration, which did not give him the chance to
leave his own peculiar imprint on the course of Roman history as his Semitic
predecessor Septimius had done and as his Christian successor Constantine was to
do.
[15]Philip's Christianity is treated in detail, *infra*, pp. 65–93.
[16]See R. Aigrain, "Arabie," *DHGE*, 3, col. 1167.

to the purple of a *princeps* who did not belong to the Roman establishment, but who hailed from the world of the Semitic Orient—
Arabia.

2. Not only the emperor but also his wife, Marcia Otacilia
Severa,[17] brings to mind the Arab empresses of the Severan dynasty—the four of them. Since she is known chiefly because of her
Christianity and Origen's letter to her, she is closest to Julia
Mammaea. If the latter was almost a Christian, the former was, like
her husband, wholly so, and thus Marcia Otacilia Severa and Philip
represent an advance on Julia Mammaea and Alexander in their
relation to Christianity.[18] She accompanied Philip to Rome, and
thus may be added to the list of four empresses of the Severan
dynasty who resided in Rome itself, on the Palatine.

3. Finally, a genetic relationship may be predicated between
the rise of Philip to the principate and that of the Severi. Philip
was born in Auranitis in what later became Philippopolis (al-
Shahbā'), not far from Emesa. It is difficult to believe that the
spectacle of a fellow Arab such as Elagabalus, hailing from Emesa
and attaining to the principate, went unnoticed by Philip, who
was a distinguished officer in the Roman army and was thus closer
to the seat of power as praetorian prefect than the priest of the sun-
god in Emesa, in spite of the latter's good connections, represented
by his grandmother, Julia Maesa. The spectacle of Arab and half-
Arab emperors from neighboring Emesa must have left a deep
impression on Marcus Julius Philippus, and thus the rise to imperial dignity of the Severi must be considered an element in the rise
of Philip himself. Whether the fall of another Arab dynast, the
last Abgarid of Edessa, was also an element is not clear. But it
is noteworthy that the *princeps* at whose murder Philip connived
was none other than Gordian, the one who brought about the
downfall of the last Arab king of Edessa, like Philip both Arab and
Christian.

---

[17]See *infra*, pp. 72–76. The presumption is that she was an Arab who had
adopted a Latin name as the Severan empresses had done.

[18]The connection of both empresses with Origen is another point of comparison between the two; see *ibid.*

III

The Palmyrene Arab chapter in the history of the third century and of Arab-Roman relations is unique.

1. Unlike other cities that the Arabs occupied in the Orient, such as Macedonian Edessa, Palmyra was an ancient Semitic foundation, close to the desert and the Arabian Peninsula. Occupied by the Arabs, it emerged in Roman history with a strong Arab complexion from the very beginning, and this complexion persisted in spite of the strong outside influences to which it was subjected from Iran and from the Graeco-Roman world.[19] Unlike other Hellenized and Romanized Arabs in the Orient, the Palmyrenes kept their Arabic names even when they added a Roman one, as when Ḥayrān added Septimius. The Arab character of Palmyra was stronger than that of the Emesa of the Severi.[20]

2. Palmyra was the Sparta among the cities of the Orient, Arab and other, and even its gods were represented dressed in military uniforms. No Arab group before the rise of Islam reached the degree of military efficiency and power that the Palmyrenes reached in the third century, as is clear from the military career of their most distinguished prince, Odenathus, and this in spite of the fact that they were really a commercial community whose capital was a caravan city.[21]

Both of the above-mentioned facts throw light on the extraordinary military endeavors of Palmyra in the second half of the third century, when it took on none other than the two world powers, Persia and Rome.[22] Its military might enabled it to beat the Sasanid Shāpūr handsomely and thus turn the tide in favor of Rome, while it is probably its strong Arab identity, coupled with a consciousness of its own power, that could explain its war against Rome as either a separatist war or one designed to endow the Palmyrene dynast with the *imperium*.

[19]Relevant material may be found in M. Rostovtzeff, *Caravan Cities* (Oxford, 1932), pp. 90–152, and in the more recent work of H. J. W. Drijvers, *The Religion of Palmyra* (Leiden, 1976).

[20]On this strong Arab character and on the place of Palmyra in the Arab zone in the Orient, see *supra*, p. 15.

[21]Compare and contrast with Mecca, also a caravan city, and with its inhabitants, the Quraysh, also a commercial community.

[22]Muslim Arabia took on the two world powers *simultaneously*.

The dimension of the Palmyrene Arab factor in the history of the third century may be measured by a brief discussion of the two phases of Palmyrene history successively represented by Odenathus and Zenobia.

Odenathus. The two successful counteroffensives by Odenathus in the sixties against Shāpūr, the warrior king of Sasanid Persia, were decisive in reversing the fortunes of the Roman-Persian war, which had had for its somber background the capture of the Emperor Valerian in the fifties. A telling indication or reflection of the high esteem in which he was held by the Romans was the conferment[23] of the highest titles on him, *imperator* and *corrector totius Orientis*, in addition to *rex regum* as a slight to Shāpūr.

In spite of the fact that he learned how to fight in both the Roman and the Persian manner and had archers and mailed cavalry in his tactical units, Odenathus was also the Arab warrior of an Arab desert city, and the desert was his field of operations against Shāpūr. Thus his generalship, manifested in the speed of his movements,[24] had about it something of the style of the desert warrior.

Just as his victories changed the course of Roman history in the East, so did his death change the course of Palmyrene history and that of Arab-Roman relations. His very victories may have made the Romans apprehensive of him and of the rising power of Palmyra, and thus the view that his assassination in Emesa was politically inspired has something to be said for it.[25] His death, however, made possible the political career of his widow Zenobia and the extraordinary events that followed his death until the destruction of the city in 273. Thus he cuts the largest historical figure in the history of Arab-Roman relations, the closest to him being the Idumaean, Herod the Great, in the first century B.C.

Throughout his career, after he gave up negotiating with Shāpūr, he was loyal to Rome. What ambitions he harbored is difficult to tell, and the imperial designs of his widow do not necessarily argue that he had such. However, it is not impossible

[23]However grudgingly. It is not clear whether *rex regum* was bestowed on him or assumed by him.

[24]In the sixth century, the Ghassānid king Mundir, son of Arethas, came closest to Odenathus in his conduct of lightning campaigns against the Persians and their Arab clients, the Lakhmids.

[25]He was deemed *capax imperii* and consequently *rapax imperii*.

that the spectacle of the Severan Arabs from Emesa[26] and of a chronologically closer neighbor, Philip the Arab, from Ḥawrān, attaining the purple could have whetted Odenathus's imperial appetites.
But if these are difficult to predicate with certainty of Odenathus,
they are easy to predicate of Zenobia.

Zenobia.   The death of Odenathus made Zenobia the ruler of
Palmyra—the regent during the minority of her son Wahballāt—
just as his achievements made possible her ambitions and imperial
plans. Out of these ambitions evolved the extraordinary events of
her quinquennium in Palmyra, during which almost the whole of
the eastern half of the empire fell to Zenobia, to be followed by
Aurelian's two dramatic campaigns against Palmyra, which ended
in the destruction of the city.[27] But it was probably the rise to
imperial dignity of Philip and the Emesene Arabs that must be considered motive forces in Zenobia's decision to revolt against Rome,
and it was the empresses of the Severan dynasty that naturally must
have been her models in her imperial aspirations, especially the
first, Julia Domna.[28]

Like her she was called Augusta, and her relation to her son
Wahballāt[29] was not unlike that of Julia to Caracalla after the death
of their respective husbands. It is, however, more in cultural matters that Zenobia must have tried to imitate her Arab precursor:

[26]His own name was *Septimius* Odenathus.

[27]It is interesting to speculate on the outcome of the struggle if Aurelian's
adversary had been Odenathus rather than the mediocre Zabdas. The failure of
Palmyra in its imperial designs against Rome in the third century may be contrasted with the success of another Arab caravan city, Muslim Medina, under the
leadership of Muhammad four centuries later.

[28]It is noteworthy that she looked up to Cleopatra, and this could suggest
that her revolt against Rome was inspired by the example of the Ptolemaic queen;
her imperial ambitions, however, have to be related to those of historical personages closer to her chronologically and geographically, her Syrian countrymen and
almost her contemporaries—the Arabs of Emesa. In this connection, what Dio
Cassius says in his *Roman History*, LXXIX.23.3, on Julia's Domna's ambition "to
become sole ruler and make herself the equal of Semiramis and Nitocris, inasmuch
as she came in a sense from the sames parts as they" is important. If, according
to the historian who knew the members of the Severan dynasty so well, Julia
Domna wanted to emulate her "neighbors"—the Assyrian and the Egyptian
queens—it is not unnatural to suppose that Zenobia of Palmyra wanted to emulate
Julia of Emesa, closer to her in time, space, and ethnic background than either
of the two queens were to Julia Domna.

[29]After the death of another son, Herodianus.

Longinus in Palmyra was the counterpart of Philostratus in the circle of Julia Domna; Neo-Platonism prospered during the reigns of both;[30] and like Julia Domna, Zenobia remained pagan.[31]

Not only under Odenathus and Zenobia but also after its destruction in 273 did Palmyra play a major role in the history of the Roman East. Its elimination was almost immediately followed by vast changes in the imperial defense system in the Orient, which were directly related to the fall of the Arab city.[32]

Appendix

The names of the empresses of the Severan dynasty—Julia Domna, Julia Maesa, Julia Sohaemia/Soaemias, and Julia Mammaea—are noteworthy. The *nomen* of each of these empresses is Latin, Julia, but the *cognomen* is not. Since they were Arab women from Emesa, it is almost certain that their *cognomina* are Arabic:

1. Arabic Dumayna, the hypocoristicon of Dimna, Dumna, or Damna, is the closest Arabic name to Domna.[1] It is an old Arabic personal name attested in the full name of an early Abbāsid Arab poet who, however, is best known by his matronymic—Ibn al-Dumayna.[2]

2. Maesa is most probably the feminine *nomen agentis* of Arabic *māsa*, a verb which signifies walking with a swinging gait. It is especially appropriate as a woman's name, and the verb from which it is derived is often used by Arab poets to describe the figures of the women whom they apostrophize.

3. Sohaemia is recognizable as Arabic Suhayma or Suḥayma, also

---

[30]It was under Zenobia that Aemilius founded the Neo-Platonic school in Apamaea.

[31]Although she lent her support to Paul of Samosata in his attempt to become bishop of Antioch, presumably to win the support of the Christian population.

[32]For this, see *supra,* pp. 24–26.

[1]It is generally accepted that Domna has no relation whatsoever to Latin Domina. On the various significations of Arabic Dimna, related to the color black, see E. W. Lane, *Arabic-English Lexicon*, Book I, Part III, p. 916. What the non-hypocoristic form of this archaic Arab name, Dumayna, really means is not clear.

[2]For the collected poems of Ibn al-Dumayna, see A. R. al-Naffākh, *Dīwān Ibn al-Dumayna* (Cairo); the matronymic of the poet is discussed on p. 11.

related to the color, black. Suḥaym is a well-known Arabic hypocoristic name and Suḥayma is its feminine form.[3]

4. Mammaea is most probably Māma, the closest approximation to it in the Arabic onomasticon. It is archaic, attested in the full name of a pre-Islamic Arab figure, Kaʿb, which, like that of Ibn al-Dumayna, included his matronymic, Ibn-Māma.[4]

The retention by these empresses of Arab names is, of course, significant, and is relevant to the discussion of the problem of the Arab identity of this imperial Arab matriarchy of the third century.

---

[3]On the various significations of asḥam, suḥaym, see Lane, *op. cit.,* Book I, Part IV, p. 1321. It is remarkable that two of these *cognomina*—Domna and Soaemias—are or may be related to the color black, and this brings to mind the black stone of Emesa.

[4]For Kaʿb ibn-Māma, see *Al-Mufaḍḍaliyyāt*, ed. A. M. Shākir and A. Hārūn (Cairo, 1963), vol. I, p. 217.

Roots and names related to those of three of the Severan empresses, Domna, Maesa, and Soaemias, namely, DMN, MYS, SḤM, and SHM respectively, are attested in G. Lankester Harding, *An Index and Concordance of Pre-Islamic Arabian Names and Inscriptions* (Toronto, 1971), pp. 243, 576, 312, 324.

IV

Cultural Contacts and Contributions

The three preceding chapters have perhaps shed enough light on the political and military aspects of Arab-Roman relations in the four centuries or so which elapsed from the Settlement of Pompey to the reign of Diocletian. The treatment, inevitably brief, has aimed at identifying the problems of Arab-Roman relations in these centuries and measuring their range, as an introduction to a better understanding of these relations in the Byzantine period.[1] As the three preceding chapters have concentrated on the political and military aspects of these relations, a few brief observations remain to be made on some of the non-political and non-military aspects involved.

1. In the course of these four centuries Arab historical figures crossed the paths of the Romans,[2] many of them disguised under Graeco-Roman names, but recognizable as Arabs. The most prominent and the best-known figure with whom the Roman period opens is undoubtedly the Idumaean, Herod the Great, known to most because of his association in the Gospels with the Nativity and the Massacre of the Innocents. Had it not been for Josephus, he would have remained shrouded in the notoriety of the Gospel story, but the Jewish historian has preserved from oblivion the record of the extraordinary career of this Idumaean Arab[3] who, in

[1] But it has also aimed at constructing a framework within which the problems of these four centuries and their ramifications may in the future be discussed in a more detailed fashion.

[2] On Germans who crossed the paths of the Romans in the fourth century, see Manfred Waas, "Germanen im römischen Dienst," *Habelts Dissertationdrucke*, Reihe Alte Geschichte, Heft 3, ed. H. Schmitt and J. Straub (Bonn, 1971). There is room for a similar work on the Arabs in the service of Rome.

[3] Loathed, quite understandably, by the peoples of both the Old and the New Testament, Herod does not present an easy task for his historian; see Momigliano's balanced chapter in *CAH*, 10, pp. 316–39; also, A. H. M. Jones, *The Herods of Judaea* (Oxford, 1938), pp. 28ff.

addition to his political sagacity and military competence, was one of the cultural forces in the history of the Orient for a long time. Philhellene and *philorhomaios*, especially the former, he immersed himself in Hellenistic culture and tried to propagate it in his court and in the East in various ways, through the Greek literary circle with which he surrounded himself and through the construction of hippodromes, theaters, and amphitheaters. His benefactions both in Greece and in the Greek Orient were many and he had the distinction of acting as *agonothetes* at Olympia, not inappropriate for one who was himself a great athlete. His more permanent contribution, however, was in Palestine itself, where he was a great city builder and where his name is associated with such cities as Caesarea and Sebaste, and above all with the rebuilding, enlargement, and beautification of the Great Temple at Jerusalem.

In the course of the three centuries that elapsed after Herod the Great, Arab figures continued to contribute to the making of Roman history, and something has been said on these figures of the third century when the Arabs became an important factor in Roman history. But in spite of the importance of the Severan dynasts, Arabs and half-Arabs, and of Marcus Julius Philippus, who attained to the purple, the most important historical figure with whom the Roman period closes is most probably not any of these but Odenathus of Palmyra, who thus balances Herod the Great at the opening of this period and who, in some respects— energy, ruthlessness, and physical strength—was not unlike his Idumaean predecessor and counterpart. Unfortunately no Josephus recorded his exploits, and these have to be extracted from inferior sources. Even so, from the pages of the *Historia Augusta*, in the chapters on the Tyranni Triginta and Aurelian, there emerges the portrait of a great soldier in the service of Rome, a dour and hardy desert warrior who recalls Herod the Great, but who far outdistances him in the range of his military duties and exploits. He seems, however, to have been exclusively a soldier obsessed by wars and campaigns, unlike Herod who was one of the great apostles of Hellenism in the Orient. But what Odenathus omitted to do was made good by his wife and widow Zenobia, who thus succeeded in relieving Palmyra from being merely a fortress and caravan city and made it one of the most flourishing cultural centers in the Orient.

2. The contribution of the Arabs of the Orient to Roman

imperial interests in these centuries was varied. The preceding chapter has outlined their contribution in the military sphere, in the defense of the oriental *limes* against the Arabs of the Peninsula and in Rome's wars with the Parthians and the Sasanids. It has also touched on their contribution in another sphere, the commercial life of the empire, which the two Arab communities—the Nabataeans and the Palmyrenes—promoted.[4]

It remains to give some recognition to the role they played in two other important areas, namely, the urbanization of the region and the religious life of the empire.[5] The references to that role are scattered, and this has obscured it. It is therefore necessary to put together, however briefly, the principal facts that pertain to each of these areas for a better comprehension of the Arab role.[6]

(*a*) The various Arab groups that the Romans found in the Orient in the first century were sedentary groups who either had occupied and then developed the urban centers founded by the Semitic or the Hellenic population or themselves had founded the cities in which the Romans found them established.[7] These Arab or Arabized cities were to be found everywhere—on the Mediterranean, not far from its shores, and in the valleys of the rivers, the Khābūr, the Orontes, and the Jordan.[8] In addition to these urban foundations in the western parts of the Orient, there was the Arab urban establishment of the Nabataean and the Palmyrene Arabs who contributed substantially to the urbanization of the Arabian limi-

[4]For the contribution of the Arabian Ḥimyarites to the commercial revolution in ancient times, see the present writer in "Pre-Islamic Arabia," *CHI*, 1, pp. 9–12, 16–18.

[5]On their possible contribution to an important aspect of civic Roman history, namely, the extension of *civitas* to the provincials, see *supra*, pp. 34–35.

[6]The treatment is not intended to be more than sketchy; it also aims at constructing a framework for a future detailed discussion, as in the case of Arab-Roman political and military relations; see *supra*, note 1.

[7]Thus the Arab urban establishment in the Orient forms part of the larger Semitic one, contributed to by such cognate groups as the Canaanites, Aramaeans, and Hebrews, and should be recognized as such. Although naturally susceptible to Semitic and Hellenistic influences, the Arab city could develop its own distinctive identity, architecturally and otherwise, as Petra did.

[8]The standard work on the cities of the Orient is Jones, *Cities*, in which much material may be found on the Arab cities of the region in the Roman and Byzantine periods. It is especially valuable to the prospective historian of this topic, since the Arab cities are discussed not in isolation but within the larger context of other urban centers, Semitic and Hellenistic.

trophe;[9] but the two Arab peoples who contributed most to the urbanization of the region were the Nabataeans[10] and the Herodians.[11] And yet if one were to single out one city that the Arabs developed into a major cultural center in the Orient, it would be neither Petra nor Bostra nor Palmyra, but Edessa,[12] a city they did not found but which they developed under the Abgarids as the great cultural center[13] of the Semitic Orient, rivaling Greek Antioch.

(b) In the history of paganism in the Roman period, the contribution of the Arabs is important enough. That contribution reached its climax in the reign of the Severan Elagabalus who installed the Arab sun-god in Rome itself. Although the worship of that sun-god did not last long, it witnessed a revival later in the century in the reign of Aurelian.

The same third century witnessed the more important contribution of the Arabs to the fortunes of that religion which was to establish itself as the state religion of the empire in the fourth century. The Severan Empress Julia Mammaea favored Christianity, and so did her son Alexander Severus; with Philip, that religion

---

[9]For Arab caravan cities, see Rostovtzeff, *Caravan Cities*; it may still be used with profit.

[10]Recognition must be given in this context to the achievement of the Nabataeans in revolutionizing technology in their arid or semi-arid region of the Orient; they distinguished themselves as agriculturists and hydraulic engineers and this enabled them to colonize intensively such regions as the Auranitis and the arid Negev. Much light has been thrown recently on the Nabataean achievement in the Negev; see, for example, the useful bibliography of Avraham Nagev in D. Graf, *SDAF*, p. 24. On the favorable view of the Nabataeans taken by Strabo, see *Geography*, XVI.4, 21, 26, and by Diodorus Siculus, see *The Library of History*, XIX.94–97.

[11]On the foundations of Herod the Great, see Momigliano, *CAH*, 10, p. 328, and on those of his sons, see Avi-Yonah, *The Holy Land*, pp. 104–5.

[12]For the standard work, see J. B. Segal, *Edessa, 'The Blessed City'* (Oxford, 1970).

[13]The important urban centers that the Arabs founded in Roman times are in sharp contrast with their urban foundations in the Byzantine period; these were almost exclusively associated with one group of Arabs—the *foederati*; and it was from the *ḥīras*, the military camps of these, that the small Arab towns of the fourth and two following centuries developed. On *ḥīra*, see the present writer in "The Etymology of Ḥīra," *Linguistic Studies in Memory of Richard Slade Harrell* (Washington, D.C., 1967), pp. 163–73. This article has been reprinted for the convenience of the reader in *BAFOC*, Part III. It is noteworthy that, in Islamic times, the Arabs built only one important city in the region, Ramla, in Palestine; it was built by the Umayyad Caliph Sulaymān, A.D. 715–17, who made it his capital.

reached the highest point of its fortunes in the third century when it was confessed by the master of the Roman world and his wife, Marcia Otacilia Severa. Philip was the precursor of Constantine.[14]

And yet the contribution of these imperial dynasts to the fortunes of Christianity was ephemeral and of limited significance, especially when compared to that of Constantine in the fourth century. But what was not so ephemeral and insignificant was the contribution of a provincial dynasty, that of the Arab Abgarids of Edessa.[15] The conversion of Abgar VIII,[16] ca. A.D. 200, to the Christian faith was a matter of the utmost importance to the fortunes of Christianity, especially of Eastern Christianity, and it was to endure throughout the ages. That conversion immediately made of the city of Edessa, the seat of the Arab dynasty of the Abgarids, the great fortress of the Christian faith in the Semitic Orient and the great center for its propagation in Mesopotamia.[17] As such, it long survived the fall of the dynasty towards the middle of the third century; but even as Edessa fell as an independent city, there arose shortly after in the same century on the Lower Euphrates another Arab city, Ḥīra,[18] which for more than three centuries exercised a similar function among the pre-Islamic Arabs,[19] a haven for the persecuted ecclesiastics of the Church in Persia.

[14]The Arabs also contributed their share of martyrs in this Roman period; the best known are the two famous martyrs Cosmas and Damian, buried in Edessa, the *anargyroi*, the "silverless" patrons of physicians. For these and the Greek distichs in the *Menaea* that refer to them and to their brothers as of Arab origin, see *A Dictionary of Christian Biography*, eds. W. Smith and H. Wace (New York, 1974), vol. 1, p. 691.

[15]On some useful *Arabica* pertaining to the Abgarids and Osroene, see Segal, *Edessa*, pp. 17–33.

[16]According to A. R. Bellinger and C. B. Welles, Abgar IX, called the Great, should be the eighth and not the ninth dynast with that name; Segal, *Edessa*, p. 14 note 1.

[17]Thus balancing the other great Christian center in the Orient, namely, Greek Antioch. The association of Edessa as a Christian city with the Abgarids is reflected in Jacob of Sarūj's "Homily on Habīb the Martyr," where Edessa is referred to as "the daughter of Abgar"; see *The Ante-Nicene Fathers* (Grand Rapids, Michigan, n.d.), vol. 8, p. 712.

[18]On Ḥīra, see the present writer's article "Ḥīra," in *EI*, 3, pp. 462–63.

[19]It endured into the Islamic period, during which its most distinguished Christian Arab was Ḥunayn b. Isḥāk al-ʿIbādi in the ninth century; he was the "most important mediator of ancient Greek science to the Arabs"; see G. Strohmaier, "Ḥunayn b. Isḥāk al-ʿIbādi," *EI*, 3, pp. 578–81. Further on Edessa and Ḥīra, see *infra*, p. 112 note 13.

Edessa and Ḥīra were thus, in pre-Islamic times, the two principal Arab urban centers which exercised a far-reaching influence on the Semitic Christian Orient as well as on the Arabs, and in both cases it was Christianity that was the determining factor in the efficacy of their function as centers of cultural radiation. Although the second was not in the Orient but outside it and within the Persian sphere of influence, it did exercise a powerful influence on the course of events—religious and other—which affected the Christian Arab *foederati* of Byzantium in the Orient throughout the three centuries of their existence.

Bust of Emperor Caracalla
Naples, National Museum, Farnese Collection

PART TWO
TOPICAL STUDIES

V

Notitia Dignitatum

I

The *Notitia Dignitatum*[1] is a valuable document for assessing the contribution of the Arabs to the Byzantine armies of the fourth and the fifth centuries. But the earlier Roman substrate in it is recognizable, and, as has been argued, "there is good reason for believing that the armies of the Eastern frontier provinces from the Thebaid to Armenia . . . remain in the Notitia much as Diocletian left them."[2] Thus, in spite of its date of composition and the fact that it reflects conditions that obtained a century or so after the death of Diocletian, it is possible to extract from the *ND* enough data for forming a fairly clear picture of the nature and extent of the Arab contribution in the Roman period and in the early Byzantine period to which this book is partly a prolegomenon.[3] As will be seen in the course of this chapter, the history of most of the Arab units listed in the *ND* goes back to Roman times.

[1]*Notitia Dignitatum*, ed. O. Seeck (Berlin, 1876). On the *ND*, see G. Clemente, *La "Notitia Dignitatum,"* Saggi di storia e letteratura, 4 (Cagliari, 1968). See also the discussion of the *ND* in A. H. M. Jones, *The Later Roman Empire* (Norman, Oklahoma, 1964) (hereafter, *LRE*), vol. 2, pp. 1417–50, and the entry *"Notitia Dignitatum"* (hereafter, *ND*), in *RE*, 17 (1939), cols. 1077–1116. For bibliographical orientation on the *ND*, see Clemente, *op. cit.*, pp. 385–97; also *supra*, p. 27 note 24.

[2]See Jones, *LRE*, vol. 2, p. 1427.

[3]On the army of the Later Roman Empire, the standard work is still R. Grosse, *Römische Militärgeschichte von Gallienus bis zum Beginn der byzantinischen Themenverfassung* (Berlin, 1920) (hereafter, *RM*); for a more recent treatment of the same topic, see *LRE*, vol. 1, chap. 17, pp. 607–86; for the army in the fourth century, see D. Hoffmann, *Das spätrömische Bewegungsheer und die Notitia Dignitatum*, Epigraphische Studien (Düsseldorf, 1969–70), vols. 1–2, with bibliography in vol. 2, pp. 227–38; for the fourth and fifth centuries, see *RM*, pp. 221–58, 259–71, and *LRE*, pp. 97–101, 199–204.

A

The Arab units in the Byzantine frontier army (the *limitanei*) are understandably concentrated not far from the Arabian Peninsula in the Diocese of the Orient and in Egypt.[4] They are not always explicitly referred to as such, and this is one of the problems that the *Notitia* presents. The references to the Arabs fall into the following categories:

1. Some units are clearly referred to by the term *Arab*:
   (a) Ala tertia Arabum in Limes Aegypti (Or. XXVIII.24)
   (b) Cohors quinquagenaria Arabum in Mesopotamia (Or. XXXVI.35)
   (c) Cohors tertia felix Arabum in Arabia (Or. XXXVII.34)
2. Other units are referred to by the term *Saracen*:
   (a) Equites Saraceni indigenae in Phoenicia (Or. XXXII.27)
   (b) Equites Saraceni in Phoenicia (Or. XXXII.28)
3. Some units are referred to by their tribal affiliations:
   (a) Equites Saraceni Thamudeni[5] in Limes Aegypti (Or. XXVIII.17)
   (b) Cohors secunda Ituraeorum in Limes Aegypti (Or. XXVIII.44)
   (c) Equites Thamudeni Illyriciani in Palestine (Or. XXXIV.22)
4. Some units are related to their city:
   (a) Cuneus equitum secundorum clibanariorum Palmirenorum, under the command of the *magister militum per Orientem* (Or. VII.34)
   (b) Ala octava Palmyrenorum in the Thebaid (Or. XXXI.49)

The Arab character of other units in the *Notitia* is inferential and ranges from the possible to the probable to the almost certain:

1. Arab are certain units that are described as *indigenae* ("native"), e.g., those in the province of Arabia (Or. XXXVII.18–20). These can be only Arab, unlike certain units also described as *indigenae*, which are not necessarily Arab.[6]

---

[4]About A.D. 380–82, Egypt was detached from the Diocese of the Orient and became a separate diocese, its *praefectus* receiving the title of *Augustalis*.

[5]The most specific reference to an Arab unit in the *ND*, since it mentions both the generic name, *Saraceni*, and the specific tribal one, *Thamudeni*.

[6]For example, those under the command of the *dux* of the Thebaid: Or. XXXI.25–29.

2. Description of units by function, as (*a*) *Equites* and (*b*)
Sagittarii, often combined with each other[7] and sometimes with
indigenae,[8] makes probable the Arab character of some of these units.
This probability is based on the association of the horse with Arabia
and the Arabs in regions contiguous to the Arabian Peninsula and
in areas, *intra limitem*, whose ethnic complexion was Arab. The
association can also be extended to the bow, for the use of which
the mounted archers of Palmyra were well known.[9] Finally, units
described as (*c*) *Dromedarii* may be Arab, since the camel is a
distinctly Arabian animal.[10] The unit in Palestine (Or. XXXIV.33)
is likely to be Arab and possibly so those in the Thebaid (Or.
XXXI.48, 54, 57).

B

Tactically or functionally, the Arab units in the *Notitia* may
be classified as follows:

1. The *Equites*:[11] so are styled in the *Notitia* the *vexillationes*,
the higher grade cavalry, e.g., *Equites Saraceni* (Or. XXXII.28).
Many of these *Equites* are *promoti*.[12]

2. The units of *Equites* are quite often also *sagittarii*: they are
the mounted archers, e.g., the *Equites sagittarii* (Or. XXXII.24).

3. More complex is the *Cuneus equitum secundorum clibanariorum*

---

[7]E.g., *Equites sagittarii*, as in Syria (Or. XXXIII.21–22).

[8]E.g., *Equites sagittarii indigenae*, as in Syria (Or. XXXIII.18, 20).

[9]For the archers of Palmyra in the service of Rome on the Danube and in
the Sahara, see Starcky, *Palmyre*, pp. 36, 43–52; and Altheim and Stiehl, *Die
Araber in der alten Welt*, vol. 1, pp. 661–77; the latter includes references to
another Arab group as archers, namely, the Ituraeans.

[10]Arab camels and *dromedarii* in the service of Rome are attested: (*a*) a large
train of camels loaded with corn accompanied the army of Corbulo from the
Euphrates to Armenia (Tacitus, *Annales*, XV.xii); these could only have been
Arab camels; (*b*) an *Ala* of Palmyrene *dromedarii* are attested in the second century;
see Starcky, *Palmyre*, p. 43, or Starcky, ed., *Inventaire des inscriptions de Palmyre*
(Damascus, 1949), X.128; (*c*) but the best documentation for Arab *dromedarii* in
the service of Rome comes from the papyri for Cohors XX Palmyrenorum (third
century); see R. O. Fink, "Roman Military Records on Papyrus," *Philological
Monographs of the American Philological Association*, 26 (Cleveland, 1971); see the
index, p. 512, under *dromedarii*, the overwhelming majority of whom belonged
to Cohors XX Palmyrenorum. Many of the names are recognizably Arab, while
the Latin *gentilicia* must have been assumed by these Arab *dromedarii*.

[11]For these, see *RM*, pp. 53–54.

[12]For these, see *ibid.*, pp. 49–50, and H. M. D. Parker, "The Legions of
Diocletian and Constantine," *JRS*, 23 (1933), p. 188.

Palmirenorum (Or. VII.34). The *cuneus*[13] is the new formation, the wedge, and its members are *clibanarii*,[14] the mailed cavalry, specifically the scale or chain armor cavalry, characteristic of the armies of Zenobia.

4. The lower grade *Alae*[15] of cavalry; they are only a few: two in *Limes Aegypti* and the Thebaid (Or. XXVIII.24; XXI.49) and one in Phoenicia, which may have been Arab (Or. XXXII.38).

5. The *Cohortes*[16] of infantry: there are three of them that are definitely Arab: one in *Limes Aegypti* (Or. XXVIII.44), another in Mesopotamia (Or. XXXVI.35), and yet another in Arabia (Or. XXXVII.34).

6. Finally, there is the camel corps, the *Ala dromedariorum*; the one stationed in Palestine is likely to be Arab (Or. XXXIV).

It is clear from an examination of the Arab contingents in the *Notitia* that the overwhelming majority of the Arab tactical units were high-grade cavalry—*Equites*, sometimes *Equites sagittarii*.

C

The extension of *civitas* to provincials by Caracalla in A.D. 212 made of the many Arabs in the Orient Roman citizens, and when these served in the Roman army, they did so as *cives*. The Arab units of the Roman frontier army in the *Notitia* discussed above fall within this category.[17] Whether *cives* of Arab origin were likewise enrolled in the *legiones* stationed in the Diocese of the Orient is not entirely clear.[18]

The employment of the term *Saraceni* to describe some Arab units in the *Notitia* raises a problem. *Saracen* had become the technical term for the Arab allies of Byzantium in the fourth century, best represented in this century by the auxiliary troops of Queen

---

[13]See *RM*, pp. 51–53.

[14]On these, see J. W. Eadie, "The Development of Roman Mailed Cavalry," *JRS*, 57 (1967), pp. 169–73; A. D. H. Bivar, "Cavalry Equipment and Tactics on the Euphrates Frontier," *DOP*, 26 (1972), pp. 273–91.

[15]See *RM*, pp. 45–47.

[16]*Ibid.*, pp. 42–45.

[17]On the Arab origin of the *limitanei* in these regions, see Dussaud, *Pénétration*, p. 157; the whole chapter entitled "Rome et les Arabes," pp. 147–58, is relevant.

[18]The description of "Legio Tertia Cyrenaica" in *Historia Augusta* ("Severus," 12.6) as *Arabica* must refer to its being stationed in the Provincia Arabia and not to its ethnic constitution.

Mavia.[19] The frequent use of the term *Saraceni* in the fourth century in the works of the ecclesiastical historians[20] coincides with the establishment of a new Arab-Byzantine relationship, reflected in the Namāra inscription of Imru' al-Qays, especially in the part that speaks of the Arab tribes as cavalry in the service of Rome.[21] These were certainly *foederati*. But whether the Saracen units in the *Notitia* were *cives* or *foederati* is difficult to tell. The term was probably used in a purely ethnic sense, following fourth-century usage in referring to the Arabs as *Saraceni*, perhaps indicating that these units had been enrolled more recently[22] than those designated *Arab*, who had been in the service of Rome before the fourth century.[23]

[19]For these, see the chapter on Zosimus, sec. III, *infra*, pp. 119–21. *Saraceni* in the fourth century also designated the *Scenitae Arabes* whether or not they were allies of Byzantium with federate status (Ammianus Marcellinus, *Res Gestae*, XXII.15.2; XXIII.6.13), thus designating Arabs who were not *cives*. The term *Arabes* then tended to designate those who were not Scenitae (nomads), whether in the Peninsula, such as the inhabitants of Arabia Felix, or those within the *limes*, the inhabitants of the province of Arabia.

[20]The term *Saraceni* is attested before the fourth century, for which see B. Moritz's article, "Saraka," *RE*, Zweite Reihe, I.A, cols. 2387–90. No entirely satisfactory explanation has been given to the etymology of this term. Its *vogue*, however, in the fourth century, may be related partly to its popularity among the ecclesiastical historians, who conceived of the Arabs as a biblical people descended from Hagar and who consequently often referred to them by the newly coined term *Hagarenoi*, descendants of Hagar. It is possible that they conceived of *Saracenoi* as the negative biblical equivalent of *Hagarenoi*, i.e., not descended from Sarah. But as *Saracenoi* had already been established as a term for the Arabs, the ecclesiastical historians found it convenient to use, thus popularizing it in spite of false etymology. For a detailed discussion of the term *Saracenoi*, see *infra*, Chap. IX and app.

[21]On this inscription, see the present writer in "Philological Observations on the Namāra Inscription," *JSS*, 24 (1979), pp. 33–42.

[22]"Saracen" as an epithet for a military unit in the Roman army is used in the part on Aurelian in the *Historia Augusta*, which speaks of the *Alae Saracenae* (*HA*, "Aurelian," 28.2); Aurelian's *cognomen*, commemorating a victory over the Arabs, was not *Saracenicus* but *Arabicus*, for which, see H. Dessau, *Inscriptiones Latinae Selectae*, 3 vols. (Berlin, 1892–1916), no. 576.

When *foederati*, the Saracens were subordinate to their Arab *phylarchi*, not to the Roman *duces*. But these two units in the *Notitia* appear under the command of the *dux* of Phoenicia, and this could imply that they were considered regular units in the Roman army and hence *cives*. On the other hand, they could have been under their own *phylarchi*, left unmentioned, and only *ultimately* subordinate to the *dux* of Phoenicia.

[23]That *Saraceni* is used in an ethnic rather than federate sense in the *Notitia* may be supported by the fact that the *Notitia* is a list of units whose members

II

The extent of the Arab contribution to the Roman army of the fourth and fifth centuries as reflected in the *ND* can be correctly measured only by a study of the Arab units in each province, where their presence is attested or presumed or suspected.[24] The major problem is to determine the ethnic character of those units in the Diocese of the Orient described in the *Notitia* as *indigenae* and what possibility there is that they were Arab.

The Arab penetration of the Fertile Crescent in ancient times is a well-known fact.[25] With this as a general background, it is proposed here to discuss the ethnic complexion of the *indigenae* of each province by interlocking it with whatever ethnographic discussions there are in the sources on these provinces. Absolute certainty cannot be predicated of these conclusions, and some of these must remain conjectural. The uncertainty derives from the fact that some of the military stations of these units in some provinces have not been definitely identified; this leaves uncertain whether a particular station was situated in the Arab or non-Arab sector of a particular province, a consideration especially important in provinces with a multi-racial complexion, such as Mesopotamia, but not so important in others, such as the province of Arabia.[26]

---

were *cives*, and thus the Arab *foederati* of Byzantium in the fourth and fifth centuries who are attested elsewhere in the sources are not likely to have appeared in this document. This dovetails with the fact that the Provincia Arabia was a major center of the *foederati*, and consequently Saracen units with federate status should have been listed for Arabia and not only for Phoenicia in the *ND*. This reasoning is confirmed by the following observation: Namāra in the Provincia Arabia had been an important Roman military post in imperial times, but it is not even listed in the *ND*; it is conspicuous by its absence, as are other posts for this region and for Trachonitis. The most natural explanation is that these inaccessible regions were left to the custody of the Arab *foederati*, who are known to have been established there since the time of Imru' al-Qays (d. 328); see R. Dussaud, *Topographie historique de la Syrie antique et médiévale* (Paris, 1927), p. 269; and A. Poidebard, *La trace de Rome dans le désert de Syrie* (Paris, 1934), pp. 61–62.

[24]This is especially important since the sources for the fifth century on the Arab *foederati* are exiguous. The *ND* preserves the contribution of those who were *cives*, the provincial Arabs in the Orient.

[25]For the western half of the Crescent, Syria, see Dussaud, *Pénétration,* and for both halves, see the more recent researches in Altheim and Stiehl, *Die Araber in der alten Welt*, vol. 1, pp. 139–80, 268–372.

[26]There is no up-to-date commentary on the *ND* with detailed maps for the

Consequently, there is likely to be a margin of error in the identification of the Oriental *indigenae* as Arab; some may turn out to be non-Arab while other units not included as Arab may turn out to be such. For this reason care has been taken to indicate the degree of certainty or uncertainty that attaches to these identifications in order to keep the margin of error very slim or as slim as possible and thus to enable the generalized result on the Arab military presence to be valid.

Magister Militum Per Orientem: Or. VII

Under the command of the *magister militum*, there was a Palmyrene cavalry *cuneus*[27] entitled:

Cuneus equitum secundorum clibanariorum Palmirenorum (34)

Limes Aegypti: Or. XXVIII

Under the command of the *comes rei militaris*, three recognizably Arab units are attested:

1. Equites Saraceni Thamudeni,[28] Scenas Veteranorum (17)

---

stations of all the units; Hoffmann's work, *Das spätrömische Bewegungsheer*, has useful maps which show the stations of the legions only. The old edition of Böcking has not entirely outlived its usefulness as a commentary; see E. Böcking, *Notitia Dignitatum*, 3 vols. (Bonn, 1839–53). But the student of the *ND* has at his disposal a number of excellent studies on the various provinces and regions of the Orient and these will be laid under contribution.

[27]See *supra*, p. 54 and note 14; on the *cuneus* in the *ND*, see E. Nischer, "The Army Reforms of Diocletian and Constantine," *JRS*, 13 (1923), p. 29, and also p. 17, where the author infers the existence of another *cuneus* of Palmyrene *clibanarii*, the cuneus equitum primorum clibanariorum Palmyrenorum.

[28]For this important tribal group, see A. van den Branden, *Histoire de Thamoud* (Beirut, 1966); and Böcking, *ND*, vol. 1, p. 295. The Thamudeni appear elsewhere in the *Notitia*, assigned to Palestine, but there they are not referred to as *Saraceni* (Or. XXXIV.22). The application of the term *Saraceni* to the Thamudeni of Egypt could suggest that they entered the service of Rome more recently than those in Palestine, not described as such. Attractive is the identification of *Tendunias* in John of Nikiou with *Thamudenas*, suggested in Altheim and Stiehl, *Christentum am Roten Meer* (Berlin, 1971), vol. 1, p. 360 note 28; cf. the Coptic etymology suggested by A. J. Butler, *The Arab Conquest of Egypt* (Oxford, 1902), p. 217 note 1. See also Altheim and Stiehl, *Christentum,* p. 368 note 82, on the association of the Arabs and their tent-camps with the names of localities and garrison towns in the *ND* that begin with *scenas*, such as Scenas Mandrorum, Scenas extra Gerasa, Scenas Veteranorum. This unit and the other two in the *Limes Aegypti* were under the command of the *comes rei militaris*. All the Arab

2. Ala tertia Arabum,[29] Thenemuthi (24)
3. Cohors secunda Ituraeorum,[30] Aiy (44)

Thebaid: Or. XXXI

One definitely Arab unit is attested, entitled:

Ala octava Palmyrenorum,[31] Foinicionis (49)

Other units that may have been Arab:[32]

---

units in the other provinces of the Orient, namely, the Thebaid, Palestine, Arabia, Phoenicia, Syria, Euphratensis, Osroene, and Mesopotamia were under the command of *duces*.

[29]The use of the term *Arab* rather than *Saracen* could imply that this unit was an old one in the service of Rome. On the unit and its station, see Böcking, *ND*, vol. 1, pp. 297–98.

[30]The Ituraeans are a well-known Arab group who served in the Roman army; see *supra*, note 9. Another cohort of Ituraeans is attested in the *ND* for the Occident, under the command of the Comes Tingitanae (Or. XXVI.16). Both are infantry units. On Ituraea and the Ituraeans, see Böcking, *ND*, vol. 1, p. 309, and vol. 2, Pars Posterior, pp. 540–41; *RE*, 9, cols. 2377–80; Dussaud, *Pénétration*, pp. 176–78; A. H. M. Jones, "The Urbanization of the Ituraean Principality," *JRS*, 21 (1931), pp. 265–75.

[31]The presence of this unit in Egypt may go back to the time of Zenobia or to that of Diocletian, who may have transferred it there for his Egyptian campaign.

[32]Arabs lived in Egypt in pre-Islamic times and so these six units or *Equites* could have been Arab, but they could also have been non-Arab, belonging to one or more of the peoples of Upper Egypt and Nubia. The Arabs in Egypt lived in the well-known Arabian nome halfway between Pelusium and Memphis, across the Nile in Arsinoites (Fayyūm), and in the Thebaid with the Blemyes between the Nile and the Red Sea. Marcian of Heraclea in the second century speaks of the Arabs between the Nile and the Red Sea and refers to them as Ἀραβαιγύπτιοι, *Périple de Marcien d'Héraclée* (Paris, 1839), p. 18; while Dionysius of Alexandria in the third century refers to them as Saracens and mentions the Arabian Mountain in his letter to Fabian, Bishop of Antioch, *PG*, 10, col. 1305. For a succinct account of the Arab presence in pre-Islamic Egypt, see Altheim and Stiehl, "Araber in Ägypten," *Lexicon der Ägyptologie*, vol. I, 3, 360–61.

As for the three *alae* of *dromedarii*, these are not described as *indigenae*, and so they must have been brought from elsewhere; in view of the association of the Arabs with camels, the proximity of Arabia, and the presence of Arab troops in Egypt, it is likely that they were Arab. It is of interest to note that as early as A.D. 156 *dromedarii* are attested in the Thebaid; a small detachment of them formed part of Cohors I Augusta praetoria Lusitanorum; for the 19 *dromedarii* in this cohort, one of whom carried the Semitic-sounding name of Barbasatis, see Fink, "Roman Military Records on Papyrus," p. 232. Mommsen assigns the formation of these three *alae* to the time of Diocletian; see Mommsen, *Gesammelte Schriften* (Berlin, 1913), vol. 8, p. 561. Camel-breeding by the Arabs of the Arabian nome was famous; see Altheim and Stiehl, "Araber in Ägypten," *ibid*. See also the entry Ἀραβικός for a reference to the ἀραβικὸν χάραγμα in F. Preisigke, *Wörterbuch der griechischen Papyrusurkunden* (Berlin, 1931), p. 269.

1. Equites sagittarii indigenae, Tentira (25)
2. Equites sagittarii indigenae, Copto (26)
3. Equites sagittarii indigenae, Diospoli (27)
4. Equites sagittarii indigenae, Lato (28)
5. Equites sagittarii indigenae, Maximianopoli (29)
6. Equites promoti indigenae (30)
7. Ala tertia dromedariorum, Maximianopoli (48)
8. Ala secunda Herculia dromedariorum, Psinaula (54)
9. Ala prima Valeria dromedariorum, Precteos (57)

Phoenicia: Or. XXXII

Two definitely Arab units[33] are:

1. Equites Saraceni indigenae, Betroclus (27)
2. Equites Saraceni, Thelsee (28)

Units that are possibly[34] or likely to have been Arab:

1. Equites promoti indigenae, Saltatha (20)
2. Equites promoti indigenae, Auatha (22)
3. Equites promoti indigenae, Nazala (23)
4. Equites sagittarii indigenae, Abina (24)
5. Equites sagittarii indigenae, Casama (25)
6. Equites sagittarii indigenae, Calamona (26)
7. Equites sagittarii indigenae, Adatha (29)

[33]These two units of *Equites* are described as *Saraceni*. The first is described as *indigenae*, while the second is not. The difference in description may not have any significance, but it could imply that the second unit was moved to Phoenicia from some other province. Since these units were stationed in Phoenicia, they could have been Palmyrene Arabs who entered the service of Rome after the fall of Palmyra. For the two stations, see A. Musil, *Palmyrena*, American Geographical Society, Oriental Explorations and Studies, 4 (New York, 1928), pp. 252–53; and Dussaud, *Topographie*, p. 270.

[34]The seven units of *Equites* described as *indigenae* are likely to be Arab, since the ethnic complexion of this region is Arab; it was in this region that the Arab principalities of Palmyra, Emesa, and Ituraea had flourished, all of which had lent their military service to the Romans. Four of these units were *sagittarii* and as mounted archers they suggest a former Palmyrene or Ituraean connection. Whether or not the eighth unit, the Ala Prima Foenicum, is Arab is not clear. Its members may have been Aramaicized Arabs who thus were described territorially rather than ethnically, but they could have been non-Arab inhabitants of Phoenicia. On the stations of these units, see Böcking, *ND*, vol. 1, pp. 376–84, but more authoritatively, Musil, *Palmyrena*, pp. 252–53, and Dussaud, *Topographie*, pp. 268–71.

Syria: Or. XXXIII

Units that are likely to have been Arab:[35]

1. Equites sagittarii indigenae, Matthana (18)
2. Equites promoti indigenae, Adada (19)
3. Equites sagittarii indigenae, Anatha (20)
4. Equites sagittarii, Acadama (21)
5. Equites sagittarii, Acauatha (22)

Euphratensis: Or. XXXIII

Troops in Euphratensis were also under the command of the *dux* of Syria, and one unit in Euphratensis may have been Arab,[36] namely, the one stationed at Rusafa:

Equites promoti indigenae, Rusafa (27)

Palestine: Or. XXXIV

One unit is definitely Arab:

Equites Thamudeni Illyriciani,[37] Birsama (22)

[35]What has been said of the Arab complexion of Phoenicia may with equal truth be said of Syria extending to the Euphrates; this Arab complexion would have been enhanced and militarized by the rise of Palmyra in the third century to a position of dominance in the whole region. Classical authors attest to the strong Arab element in the Syrian region, and of these Strabo may be singled out; he places the Arabs of Syria to the south of the Apameians and to the east—across the Orontes, in Parapotamia, and also in Chalcidice; see Strabo, *Geography*, XVI.ii.11. For the stations of these units, see Musil, *Palmyrena*, pp. 253–55; Böcking, *ND*, vol. 1, pp. 387–88; and Dussaud, *Topographie*, pp. 274–75.

[36]On the Arab tribes along the Euphrates, see Strabo, *Geography*, XVI.i.27–28; XVI.ii.1; XVI.iii.1; Pliny, *Natural History*, V.xxi.87. For Rosapha, see Musil, *Palmyrena*, pp. 260–72, and Dussaud, *Topographie*, pp. 253–55, 275, and the map in V. Chabot, *La frontière de l'Euphrate* (Paris, 1907), opposite p. 408.

[37]On the Thamudeni, see *supra*, note 28. The Thamudeni are enrolled in the unit of the Illyriciani just as the Mauri of unit No. 21 in Palestine. In this connection, Parker's views on the Illyriciani may be quoted: "Again, in Aurelian's army against Palmyra, Dalmatian and Moorish horsemen are found side by side with German legionaries, and it is not improbable that the cavalry contingents called 'Illyriciani' which in the *Notitia* are found in the provinces of Phoenicia, Syria, Palaestina, Osroene, Mesopotamia, and Arabia, date back in origin to Aurelian's resettlement of the eastern provinces"; see Parker, "Legions," pp. 187–88. It is interesting that Illyriciani units or troops remained in Palestine until the reign of Heraclius in the seventh century; see *Acta M. Anastasii Persae*, ed. H. Usener (Bonn, 1894), p. 26, lines 12–13, and W. Kaegi, "Notes on Hagiographic Sources for Some Institutional Changes and Continuities in the Early Seventh Century," *Byzantina*, 7 (1975), pp. 65–67.

Units that are possibly or likely to have been Arab are:[38]

1. Equites promoti indigenae, Sabaiae (23)
2. Equites promoti indigenae, Zodocathae (24)
3. Equites sagittarii indigenae, Hauanae (25)
4. Equites sagittarii indigenae, Zoarae (26)
5. Equites sagittarii indigenae, Robatha (27)
6. Equites primi felices sagittarii indigenae Palaestini, Sabure sive Veterocariae (28)
7. Equites sagittarii indigenae, Moahile (29)
8. Ala Antana dromedariorum, Admatha (33)

Osroene: Or. XXXV

Units that are possibly or likely to have been Arab are:[39]

1. Equites promoti indigenae, Banasam (18)

---

[38]What has been said in notes 34–35 on the Arab ethnic constitution of certain parts of Syria and Phoenicia is likewise true of the southern desert of Palestine inhabited, before the region was incorporated into the empire, by the Idumaean and Nabataean Arabs; it is, therefore, quite likely that these units described as *indigenae* were Arab. What has been said of the territorial term *Foenices* above in note 34 may be said of the Palaestini unit No. 34. As for the *Ala Dromedariorum*, this, too, is likely to have been Arab for the same reasons advanced in connection with the three *alae* in the Thebaid in note 32 above. In the *apparatus criticus* of the *ND*, the description of the *Ala* as *Antana* is questioned and *Antoniniana* is suggested instead.

The Arab character of these units is corroborated by the Arab military presence represented by the phylarchs. These were enlisted in the service of Byzantium in southern Palestine and are attested in the Nessana Papyri and in the Edict of Beersheba, both of which will be discussed in detail in *BAFIC*. For the stations of the units of *Equites* and the *Ala Dromedariorum*, see Böcking, *ND*, vol. 1, pp. 345–48, 351–52. Abel's discussion of *all* the units of the *Notitia* in Palestine is valuable and so is his map; see F. M. Abel, *Géographie de la Palestine* (Paris, 1938), vol. 2, pp. 178–84, and map 10.

[39]The Arab complexion of the Trans-Euphratesian provinces—Osroene and Mesopotamia—was as strong as that of the Cis-Euphratesian ones, Syria and Phoenicia. The western part of the region was even referred to as "Arabia" in the classical sources (Pliny, *Natural History*, V.xx.85), while the eastern part was called Bēth-ʿArabāyē in the Syriac sources; in Islamic times these regions were called Diyār Muḍar and Diyār Rabīʿa, for which see *EI*, *s.vv.* In addition to these significant designations in the classical and the Syriac sources for the region in pre-Islam, both these sources testify to the strong Arab element in the northern half of the Land of the Two Rivers; for the classical sources, see Strabo, *Geography*, XVI.i.26; and Pliny, *Natural History*, V.xx–xxi; the latter is more specific as he identifies Osroene with "Arabia" and speaks of the Arab tribe of Praetavi in Mesopotamia, whose capital was Singara. For the Syriac sources on the Arabs in

62   ROME AND THE ARABS

2. Equites promoti indigenae, Sina Iudaeorum (19)
3. Equites sagittarii indigenae, Oraba (20)
4. Equites sagittarii indigenae, Thillazamana (21)
5. Equites sagittarii indigenae, primi Osroeni, Rasin (23)

Mesopotamia: Or. XXXVI

Units that are definitely Arab:
Cohors quinquagenaria Arabum, Bethallaḥa (35)
Units that are possibly Arab[40] are:

1. Equites promoti indigenae, Constantina (24)
2. Equites sagittarii indigenae Arabanensis, Mefana Cartha (25)
3. Equites sagittarii indigenae Thibithenses, Thilbisme (27)
4. Equites sagittarii indigenae, Thannuri (28)

Arabia: Or. XXXVII

Units that are definitely Arab:
Cohors tertia felix[41] Arabum, in ripa Vade Afaris fluvii in castris Arnonensibus (34)

---

this region, see J. B. Segal, "Mesopotamian Communities from Julian to the Rise of Islam," *Proceedings of the British Academy*, 41 (1955), pp. 119–20. (The distinction between the ʿArab and the Ṭayāyē in Segal's article must be only social not ethnic and corresponds to the distinction sometimes made in classical writers between Arabs and Scenitae; the former were considered more sedentary and developed than the latter but both were considered Arab.) The two most important Arab kingdoms of the Trans-Euphratesian region were Edessa and Ḥatra. The first, the kingdom of the Abgarids, became the Roman province of Osroene. Pliny (*Natural History*, VI.117) and Tacitus (*Annales*, XII.12) refer to the Edessenes simply as *Arabes*.

On the stations of these five units of *Equites* in Osroene, see Böcking, *ND*, vol. 1, pp. 398–400, and Chabot, *Frontière*, pp. 275, 320. See also the map in Chabot, opposite p. 408.

[40]On the Arab element in Mesopotamia, see *supra*, note 39. This region was to become, in Islamic times, Diyār Rabīʿa, and it is almost certain that the Rabīʿa group was represented in the Trans-Euphratesian regions in pre-Islamic times. On the stations of these four units, see Böcking, *ND*, vol. 1, pp. 411–12, 414; and Chabot, *Frontière*, pp. 303, 310. On the second unit, described as *Arabanenses*, and its two stations, see *ibid.*, p. 299, and Dussaud, *Topographie*, pp. 483–85, 487, 489, 491–92, 521; see also the map in Chabot, *Frontière*, opposite p. 408, and the map in Poidebard, *La trace de Rome*, atlas vol.

[41]"Felix" is attested for another Arab unit in Palestine, the Equites felices primi sagittarii indigenae Palaestini (Or. XXXIV.28).

Units that are most likely to have been Arab[42] are:

1. Equites promoti indigenae, Speluncis (18)
2. Equites promoti indigenae, Mefa (19)
3. Equites sagittarii indigenae, Gadda (20)
4. Equites sagittarii indigenae, Dia-Fenis (23)

[42]The basic work on the province of Arabia is still the monumental work by R. E. Brünnow and A. von Domaszewski, *Die Provincia Arabia*, 3 vols. (Strasbourg, 1904–9); for the *castella* of the *limes Arabicus*, see R. E. Brünnow, "Die Kastelle des Arabischen Limes," *Florilegium ou recueil de travaux d'érudition dédiés à Monsieur le marquis Melchior de Vogüé* (Paris, 1909), pp. 65–77, which supplements Domaszewski's article in Kiepert's *Festschrift* on the chapters in the *ND* on Arabia and the relevant part of chap. XXXIV on Palestine. For the employment of native troops, see Brünnow, "Die Kastelle," p. 76. More accessible and recent is Abel's *Géographie*, vol. 2; for the stations of the four units of *Equites* and that of the *Cohors*, see pp. 187–91 and map 10. But these works on the Provincia Arabia are being overtaken by the recent researches of Glen W. Bowersock ("A Report on Arabia Provincia") and of a group of younger scholars such as M. Speidel, David F. Graf, S. Thomas Parker, D. L. Kennedy, and Henry I. MacAdam.

VI

The First Christian Roman Emperor:
Philip or Constantine?

E cclesiastical authors in the fourth and fifth centuries were
united in their judgment that the first Roman emperor to
adopt Christianity was Philip the Arab. It was only in modern
times that the question of Philip's Christianity has been called into
question, and critical opinion has remained divided. There are those
who maintain that Philip both professed and practiced Christianity
and those who deny that he even embraced it. The most balanced
account of this controversy is that of R. Aigrain, who harbors no
doubts whatsoever concerning Philip's Christianity, but when he
wrote his account, which was published in 1924, he apparently did
so unaware that some distinguished scholars such as Stein and
Gwatkin had declared and argued for the opposite view.[1] The arguments of these scholars, especially Stein, cannot be ignored, and
they must be examined before the truth about Philip's religious
persuasion can be determined. As Philip's Christianity is of some
importance to ecclesiastical, Roman, and Arab history, it is proposed here to give this problem a detailed treatment which will
take into account all its dimensions and ramifications.

I

The ecclesiastical sources that vouch for the Christianity of
Philip the Arab may be classified into three sets:
1. The main and the earliest source is, of course, Eusebius,

---

[1]For Aigrain's account, see "Arabie," *DHGE*, 3, cols. 1166–67; for a more
recent and enthusiastic affirmation of Philip's Christianity, see H. Grégoire, *Les
persécutions dans l'empire romain* (Brussels, 1964), pp. 9–10 and the long note 3 on
pp. 89–91; the affirmation is even more enthusiastic in the earlier edition of the
work (1950); see pp. 11–12 and note 3 on pp. 90–91.

who in the *Historia Ecclesiastica*[2] refers to Philip explicitly and implicitly in some five passages, the first three of which express Philip's Christianity, while the remaining two imply it. The first (*HE*, VI.xxxiv) describes the famous scene in Antioch on Easter Eve, 13 April, A.D. 244, when the emperor wanted to participate in the paschal vigil but because of his sins was prevented from doing so by the bishop and could participate only after he had confessed; the second (*HE*, VI.xxxviii) tells of a letter written by Origen to Philip and another to his spouse, Marcia Otacilia Severa; the third (*HE*, VI.xxxix) speaks of the persecution unleashed by Decius out of enmity towards Philip; the last two are given on the authority of Dionysius, bishop of Alexandria (A.D. 247–65): in the first (*HE*, VI.xli.9), reference is made implicitly to the tolerant rule of Philip in contrast with that of Decius which followed, and in the second (*HE*, VII.x.3), also implicitly, to both Severus Alexander and Philip as being openly Christian.

The first reference is the most explicit; it is also detailed and thus leaves no doubt whatsoever that Philip was a Christian. Besides, it is not isolated: four other references, three of which involve contemporaries of Philip, namely, Origen and Dionysius, testify explicitly and implicitly to his Christianity, and no one who reads these passages in the *HE* with an open mind will doubt their tenor or clear implication. Why Eusebius chose to express himself the way he did is a problem, but the difficulty it poses is a perfectly negotiable one.[3]

2. Three important Latin writers, Jerome, Orosius, and Vincent of Lérins, are unanimous in their verdict on Philip's Christianity, and that verdict is also reflected strongly in their use of the term *primus*, his being the first Roman emperor to adopt Christianity.[4] These are not late but early authors who lived in the

---

[2] Eusebius, *Historia Ecclesiastica*, ed. E. Schwartz, *Eusebius Werke*, *GCS*, 9 (Leipzig, 1903–9): part I (1903) contains Books I–V; part II (1908) contains Books VI–X and the Latin translation of the *HE* by Rufinus.

[3] See *infra*, pp. 77–79.

[4] The term *primus* appears in two different works of Jerome, the *Chronicon* and the *Liber de viris inlustribus*; for its occurrence in the first, see *Die Chronik des Hieronymus*, ed. R. Helm, *GCS*, 47 (1956), p. 217; for *primus* in the second, see *Liber de viris inlustribus*, *TU*, 14 (Leipzig, 1896), p. 32, line 33. For *primus* in St. Vincent, see *Commonitorium primum*, *PL*, 50, col. 662; in Orosius, see *Historiae adversum paganos*, *CSEL*, 5 (Vienna, 1882), p. 478, line 13. For more on these three authors in connection with Philip's Christianity, see *infra*, pp. 78–83.

latter part of the fourth and the early part of the fifth century. Of the three, Jerome is the most important; he is the closest to Eusebius, the chief source, chronologically, and he is the translator of his *Chronicon*, wherein the explicit statement on Philip's Christianity occurs. That statement admits of one of two interpretations: Jerome either found it in the Greek *Chronicon* of Eusebius or he arrived at it independently, basing it on sources available to him. In either case, it is a clear and strong affirmation of, and an important testimony to, Philip's Christianity.

3. The third and last set of sources on Philip's Christianity is represented by John Chrysostom[5] and by Leontius,[6] bishop of Antioch ca. 350. Both are early writers who were removed by only a century from the period of Philip's principate and, what is more, lived in Antioch itself, the scene of Philip's humiliation and repentance. Both are naturally more interested in St. Babylas, the Antiochene bishop and martyr who barred Philip from participation in the paschal vigil, than in the emperor himself. This together with the fact that Babylas is not mentioned in Eusebius (*HE*, VI.xxxiv) and the further fact that the two writers were Antiochenes all suggest that they represent an independent tradition based on local accounts that had survived in Antioch itself—the scene of the humiliation—and not on Eusebius of Caesarea. This Antiochene local tradition may even be more important than the other one, the Caesarean, from which Eusebius derived his account of Philip's Christianity. It is local, possibly oral in part, prevalent in Antioch itself, while the other is distant, entirely written, with which Eusebius was acquainted through the documents of his library at Caesarea. But the two regional accounts dovetail and in so doing they corroborate each other.

II

In recent times, the most determined opponent of the view that Philip was the first Christian Roman emperor has perhaps been Ernst Stein. He devoted to the investigation of this problem three columns of his article on Philip in *RE*,[7] in which he (*a*) dis-

[5]John Chrysostom, *De S. Babyla contra Julianum et gentiles*, PG, 50, cols. 541–42; the apologetic treatise was composed ca. 382 when John was still a deacon; see Quasten, *Patrology* (Westminster, Md., 1960), vol. 3, pp. 467–68.
[6]*Chronicon Paschale*, ed. L. Dindorf (Bonn, 1832), vol. 1, pp. 503f.
[7]See *RE*, 10, 1 (1918) cols. 768–70, followed by G. Downey in *A History of Antioch in Syria* (Princeton, 1961), pp. 306–8, especially note 140.

missed the three Latin sources—Jerome, Orosius, and Vincent of Lérins—as derivative from Eusebius and the two Greek ones— Leontius and John Chrysostom—as not representing a second independent source; (*b*) examined the various statements in the principal source, Eusebius, dismissing them as founded on rumors; (*c*) appealed to various facts taken from the career of Philip to prove his paganism; and finally (*d*) tried to explain how the "legend" of Philip's Christianity arose and acquired vogue. As (*a*), the three Latin and the two Greek sources he dismissed, has been discussed in the preceding section,[8] it remains to examine (*b*), (*c*), and (*d*) in his argument.

1. Stein opens his argument by pointing out that Eusebius introduces his account of Philip's Christianity and the scene at Antioch (*HE*, VI.xxxiv) reservedly, with the words κατέχει λόγος, which Stein chooses to interpret as *Gerüchte*. But λόγος admits of interpretations other than "rumor"; Eusebius was not recording contemporary history but the reign of a third-century Roman emperor, for which he used records and documents, and, indeed, κατέχει λόγος may be translated, as in fact it has been, by "it is recorded" or at least "it is reported."[9] Furthermore, κατέχει λόγος is likely to refer to the details of the scene at Antioch rather than to the fact of Philip's Christianity expressed in Χριστιανὸν ὄντα; the details of that scene were of extraordinary interest and Eusebius may have wanted to remind his possibly startled readers that his information comes from records at his disposal from which he was quoting.[10]

A close examination of this first reference in Eusebius to Philip's Christianity (followed by four others)[11] yields the conclusion that Eusebius did vouch for Philip's Christianity, but it also reveals some detachment or lack of enthusiasm—rather surprising, coming

[8]For more on these Latin and Greek sources, see *infra*, pp. 71 and 79– 83.

[9]By J. E. L. Oulton in the English translation of the *HE* in the *Loeb Classical Library* (London and Cambridge, Mass., 1938), vol. 2, p. 89, and by A. C. McGiffert in *A Select Library of Nicene and Post-Nicene Fathers* (1890; reprinted Grand Rapids, Michigan, 1971), vol. 1, p. 278. In his Latin version of the *HE*, Rufinus renders κατέχει λόγος as *traditum est*; see *Historia Ecclesiastica, GCS*, part II, p. 589, line 27.

[10]For the view that λόγος refers to Origen's letter to Philip, see *infra*, p. 76.

[11]On this, see *supra*, pp. 65–66.

as it does from the father of ecclesiastical history, especially in view
of the fact that he was noticing the *first* Christian Roman emperor.
It is this lack of enthusiasm, reflected stylistically in lack of emphasis, that could explain the employment of κατέχει λόγος.
Consequently, the problem that faces the student of this chapter in
the *Historia Ecclesiastica* is not whether Eusebius vouched for Philip's
Christianity but why he did not emphasize it as much as he might
have done.[12]

2. Stein considers the details of the scene at Antioch unhistor-
ical. He does this first by dismissing Eusebius's account as belonging to the same order of *Gerüchte* as that of the two Greek sources,
Leontius and Chrysostom; he then states that it is inconceivable
that a Roman emperor of the third century, immediately before
prejudice against the Christians found bloody expression in the
Decian persecution, would have subjected himself to a humiliation
that would have been a greater affront to the dignity of the Roman
state, still pagan at the time, than even the one which took place
a century and a half later in Milan, involving Theodosius and
Ambrose, and which created such a sensation even in a world
already won to Christianity.

As far as the relation of Eusebius to the other two Greek
authors is concerned, it has been pointed out that the latter represents an important and independent local Antiochene source and
that far from diminishing the authenticity of Eusebius's account,
they actually enhance it.

As to the account's incredibility, deriving from its being an
affront to the Roman state, it may be pointed out that the account
does not sound as incredible as Stein suggests; one may cite precisely the case Stein himself cited, namely, that of Theodosius and
Ambrose, as a parallel, and a more remarkable one since it involved the self-abasement of a more illustrious Roman emperor
than Philip. Moreover, Stein is oblivious to the fact that the scene
in Antioch was not as humiliating as that in Milan and thus would
not have constituted such an affront to the dignity of the Roman
state; it simply involved the quick repentance of the emperor on
his way back from the Persian front and on his way out to Rome,
and thus the episode was extremely local in character. The one

---

[12]On this, see *infra*, pp. 77–79.

involving Theodosius was entirely different since it had for its background the massacre of some seven thousand at Thessalonica, the excommunication of the emperor for some eight months, and a dramatic dialogue between bishop and emperor that was extremely humiliating to the latter.[13]

It is not out of place in this connection to refer to Gwatkin's views[14] on this scene in Antioch. His is the more sober appraisal of the account, which, unlike Stein, he does not "entirely reject." However, he starts from the premise that Philip was not a Christian and consequently argues that it was curiosity that may have led him to the church at Easter and that "his exclusion from the more solemn parts of the service" is explicable by the fact that he was not baptized.

Gwatkin's views are open to the following objections: (1) His interpretation begs the question since he starts from the premise that Philip was not a Christian and the premise is based on his interpretation of Eusebius's account of Origen's letter to Philip.[15] But it is the account of the scene at Antioch that is the crucial passage in Eusebius for Philip's Christianity while Origen's letter to him is far from being a ground for rejecting his Christianity. (2) As to Philip's going to the church on Easter, it is impossible to accept the explanation offered by Gwatkin. The churches of those days were not exactly tourist attractions—they were humble structures that could not possibly have attracted the attention of a *princeps* and, what is more, one in a hurry and anxious to reach Rome. (3) The explanation for Philip's exclusion from participating in the more solemn parts of the service, namely, that he was not baptized, has to be rejected.[16] Eusebius adds that after his repentance he was allowed to participate in the service, and this clearly indicates that he was a Christian who had been excluded from the service only

[13]For this, see Theodoret, *Historia Ecclesiastica*, ed. L. Parmentier, GCS, 19 (Leipzig, 1911), V.17.

[14]See H. M. Gwatkin, *Early Chruch History to A.D. 313* (London, 1927), vol. 2, pp. 152–53.

[15]On the possible contents of this letter of Origen, see *infra*, p. 75.

[16]Since there is no evidence for it. Even if he was not baptized, this would not invalidate the case for his Christianity; Constantine himself postponed his baptism till the very end of his life, and this was not uncommon in those days; for further on Constantine's baptism, see *infra*, note 60.

because he had been in a state of sin. The student of the *HE* cannot dismiss all these details as unrevelatory of Philip's Christianity and instead think of his visit to the church in terms of tourism motivated by curiosity.

3. Eusebius quotes Dionysius, bishop of Alexandria (A.D. 247–65), on the tolerant Valerian (253–58) before he launched his persecution. Dionysius describes him as so friendly to the Christians that he even surpassed "those who were said to be openly Christians" (οἱ λεχθέντες ἀναφανδὸν Χριστιανοὶ γεγονέναι). The reference is clearly to Severus Alexander and Philip and it is a valuable testimony to Philip's Christianity. Stein, however, dismissed it outright as evidence that Severus Alexander was a Christian. The text, however, cannot be dismissed without further ado, and if what it says is untrue or inaccurate concerning Alexander, it is not so concerning Philip. Arguing as Stein did reflects a failure to dissociate the genuine from the spurious, while a close examination of the text reveals that it is only a hyperbole on the part of Dionysius as far as Severus Alexander is concerned, which can be made to appear intelligible when it is remembered that Severus Alexander had statues of Abraham, Christ, and Orpheus among others in his chapel and that he worshiped them devoutly every morning.[17] Severus Alexander was a Christian in this very restricted sense within the eclectic system which he adopted, and thus his description by Dionysius as a Christian admits of something being said for it. The quotation from Dionysius thus turns out to be a valuable source for Philip's Christianity, independently of others in Eusebius, and, what is more, so close to the reign of Philip as to be a contemporary one.

4. It is also inconceivable, according to Stein, that an emperor of the third century would have converted to Christianity without the fact's being mentioned in the contemporary Christian literature that has survived. But Stein assumes, quite erroneously, that Philip was converted during his principate, which is not the case. The

[17]On this, see *Historia Augusta*, "Vita Alex.," 29. 2. On Alexander's religion, see Gwatkin, *Early Church History*, pp. 148–49. In this connection, reference should also be made to Alexander's mother, Mammaea, a religious woman who summoned Origen to her in Antioch and who may have been responsible for the spread of Christianity in the house of Alexander; see Eusebius, *HE*, VI.xxi, xxviii.

presumption is that he was already a Christian when he was elevated
to the purple,[18] and it is simply as a Christian, not as a convert,
that two of his contemporaries remembered Philip—Dionysius and
Origen. This is important to remember about Philip's Christianity.
He was a Roman soldier hailing from the Provincia Arabia, where
Christianity had spread quite extensively, and he was one of those
Romanized Arabs who grew up in a Christian environment. He
had thus been a Christian before he became an emperor, unlike
Constantine, who was converted during his reign and in that well-
known manner. There is no *in hoc signo vinces* in Philip's career,
and it was the celebration of the thousandth anniversary of the
foundation of Rome—the pagan festival—not anything Christian,
that made his reign memorable.

     5. Stein went on to argue that if Philip had been a Christian
he would not have consecrated his father, Marinos, nor made his
son Philip *pontifex maximus*, nor celebrated the Saeculum and the
Millennium according to the pagan rites.[19]

     All these are unacceptable objections. Like his predecessors
and successors, he behaved officially as a pagan emperor, as indeed
he had to if he was to survive. Even the "Thirteenth Apostle"
himself could not but burn incense to many a pagan rite, including
the worhsip of *Sol Invictus*.

     6. The preceding objections led Stein to share the conclusions
of J. Neumann on the evidential value of Origen's letters to Philip
and his wife, Marcia Otacilia Severa (*HE*, VI.xxxvi); Neumann had
argued that Origen was informed about the faith of the royal
couple and must have mentioned it in his letters. Eusebius, who
read these letters, must also have been informed about whether or
not Philip was Christian; since he is silent on the point, his silence
is decisive in yielding the conclusion that Philip was not Christian,
neither baptized nor catechumen.

     This reasoning cannot be accepted and it is open to the fol-
lowing objections.

     (*a*) It rests on the false assumption that the crucial chapter in
Eusebius (*HE*, VI.xxxiv) on Philip's Christianity does not reflect

---

[18]See Aigrain, "Arabie," col. 1167.

[19]What pertains to his father and his son—the consecration and the pontifi-
cate—apparently idiosyncratic on the part of Philip, may be related to his search
for legitimacy and to his dynastic policy respectively.

the former's conviction that the latter was Christian, the assumption itself resting on a peculiar interpretation of the words κατέχει λόγος which introduce the chapter.[20] Furthermore, if Eusebius had not been convinced of Philip's Christianity—which must have been of considerable interest to the biographer of Constantine—and if he had felt that the letters of Origen contained some evidence to support this view, he would certainly have expressed himself clearly on the point.

(*b*) In *HE*, VI.xxxvi, Eusebius was not speaking primarily about Philip but about Origen and his extensive correspondence with various personages. Making statements on the *contents* of the two letters to the royal couple would have been irrelevant to his purpose in that chapter. So his silence cannot be construed as decisive evidence for the view that Philip was not Christian. After referring to Philip's Christianity in *HE*, VI.xxxiv, two chapters earlier, Eusebius probably found it superfluous to repeat the reference.

(*c*) Eusebius does not state categorically that he read these letters of Origen to Philip and his wife. He merely says that he brought Origen's letters together and arranged them. So the question must remain open, but the chances are that he did read them and found nothing in them to make him doubt Philip's Christianity; if he had, he would certainly have recorded it, and as the biographer of Constantine he would have had special interest in doing so.

(*d*) The letters of Origen, now lost, were, however, still extant in the latter part of the fourth and the first part of the fifth centuries. They were seen and evidently read by two distinguished churchmen, Jerome and Vincent of Lérins, and both of them refer to these letters and to Philip's Christianity.

Jerome, the earlier of the two, speaks in his chapter on Origen in the *Liber de viris inlustribus* as follows: *et ad Philippum imperatorem, qui primus de regibus Romanis Christianus fuit, et ad matrem eius litteras fecit quae usque hodie extant.*[21] Noteworthy in this sentence is the fact

---

[20]On this, see *supra*, p. 68.

[21]*Liber de viris inlustribus*, chap. 54, p. 32, lines 33–35; *matrem* in the above citation is a slip on the part of Jerome, who must have been thinking of Mammaea, Alexander's mother, when he wrote that sentence; it was Philip's wife, Severa, who received Origen's letter, not his mother; P. Nautin noted Jerome's mistake in his *Origène* (Paris, 1977), p. 217 note 99; p. 218.

that the letters were extant when Jerome wrote as well as the explicit, emphatic statement on Philip's Christianity. Surely the clear implication of *quae usque hodie extant* is that the learned Jerome read these letters and either found evidence for Philip's Christianity in them or at least found nothing to make him doubt it. If this had not been the case, he would not have referred to these letters while speaking of Philip's Christianity since such reference would only have invalidated his strong affirmation of it. In *HE*, VI.xxxvi, Eusebius did not speak of Philip's Christianity while discussing Origen's letter to him, and this has inclined some scholars to disregard this correspondence as evidence for Philip's Christianity. But Jerome brings the two together[22]—the correspondence with Origen and Philip's Christianity—and this suggests, even indicates, that Jerome found evidence for Philip's Christianity in these letters.

St. Vincent of Lérins is the other churchman who brings Origen's letter to Philip and the latter's Christianity together in his chapter on Origen in the *Commonitorium primum*.[23] In so doing he may have followed Jerome, but some independence from Jerome is reflected in the text of his statement on Origen and Philip.[24] Of the letters he says: *quos ad Philippum imperatorem, qui primus Romanorum principum Christianus fuit, Christiani magisterii auctoritate conscripsit.*[25] While Eusebius is silent on the contents of these letters and while Jerome refers to their being extant, Vincent is not so entirely silent, since he adds that they were written *Christiani*

----

[22]Apparently the first to do so, and this suggests—contrary to what Stein thought—that he evinced some independence from Eusebius in this matter. Perhaps after reading Eusebius's account of Philip's Christianity and Origen's letter to him, Jerome's curiosity was aroused and so he decided to read these letters to which Eusebius referred.

[23]See *Commonitorium primum*, cols. 662–63.

[24]As may be seen from the quotation that follows when compared with that of Jerome: (*a*) he conceives of Philip as *princeps*, not *rex* as Jerome does; (*b*) he speaks of the *auctoritas* he displayed in the writing of those letters; and (*c*) he refers to them as *epistolae*, not *litterae* as Jerome does.

[25]It is noteworthy that he speaks of letters in the plural, while Eusebius speaks of one letter addressed to Philip and another to his spouse. Vincent must have been thinking of both these letters when he used the plural. In the text of *PL*, the last word in the quotation, *conscripsit*, is erroneously written *conscripsi*. It should, of course, read *conscripsit*, as is clear from the Stephanus Baluzius edition of the *Commonitorium* from which the text in *PL* was taken; see *Sanctorum Presbyterorum Salviani Massiliensis et Vincentii Lirinensis Opera* (Paris, 1684), p. 343.

magisterii auctoritate, and the clear implication is that he read these letters since he would not have made that statement without having done so.[26]

Thus Origen's letter to Philip turns out to be quite decisive in establishing Philip's Christianity, after some scholars have thought that it is decisive for establishing the contrary. The precious references in the *Commonitorium* and the *Liber de viris inlustribus* to the letter have made it possible to trace it to the times of Jerome and Vincent, the two churchmen who read it.

When Origen wrote in 244, he did so to an emperor who was already Christian. A further question may be raised about the contents of this letter, and these can only be surmised.

(*a*) Philip hailed from Arabia, the *provincia* known as *haeresium ferax*, and Origen himself went to Arabia when he cured Beryllos, the bishop of the Arabs in Bostra, of his heretical views. It is not unnatural to suppose that the letter may have been written with a view to seeing to it that the Christian Arabian emperor held doctrinally correct views.

(*b*) Origen came from a family that had had a taste of pagan Roman imperial indisposition towards Christians; his father Leonidas had died a martyr in the persecution unleashed by Septimius Severus in 202, and Origen himself was to be imprisoned and subjected to torture in the one unleashed by Decius in 250. The spectacle of a Christian as the head of the Roman state is likely to have excited Origen, whose letter to Philip may thus have been related not to orthodoxy but to the meaning of Philip's principate to the fortunes of Christianity and the Christian Church.

(*c*) The letter must have been written in 244 when Philip was still in the East before his departure for Rome. It was then that Babylas, the bishop of Antioch, prevented him from taking part in the divine mysteries, and it is tantalizing to think that it was this

[26]Furthermore, Vincent of Lérins, like Jerome, had a special interest in Origen; the author of the Vincentian Canon most probably read as much as he could of the work of one who, like Tertullian, was for him a heretical defector. This is confirmed by what he says in the first part of his chapter (XVII) on Origen; especially relevant is his judgment on his eloquence: *eloquentiam vero quid memorem cuius fuit tam amoena, tam lactea, tam dulcis oratio ut mihi ex ore ipsius non tam verba quam mella quaedam fluxisse videantur?* Set against this, Vincent's reference to Origen's *auctoritas*, displayed in writing his letter to Philip, is thus likely to have been the result of his having read those letters.

that occasioned Origen's letter to Philip, possibly to commend the emperor for his humility.[27] Origen was at the time in Caesarea, and if the letter was indeed about Philip's repentance at Antioch,[28] it is almost certain that this letter was the source on which Eusebius drew for writing his account of the scene at Antioch in *HE*, VI.xxxiv. If so, the λόγος in *HE*, VI.xxxiv, would be none other than the ἐπιστολή of *HE*, VI.xxxvi.

7. Finally, Stein turns to explaining what he calls the legend of Philip's Christianity and relates its rise to the fact that Philip fared well with the ecclesiastical historians because of his friendly attitude towards Christians and Christianity, in contrast to those that followed him in the purple, especially the one who immediately did so, Decius.[29]

Stein's conclusion on how the "legend" arose rests, of course, on his interpretation of the crucial passage in Eusebius (*HE*, VI.xxxiv), which, according to him, does not reflect the fact of Philip's Christianity. His interpretation has been analyzed and rejected, and with it may be rejected his conclusion on the rise of the "legend." But two more observations on texts relevant to the "legend" in Eusebius may be made.

(*a*) In *HE*, VI.xli.9, Dionysius of Alexandria speaks of the kindly rule of Philip the Arab to be followed by that of the hostile Decius. This alone does not prove that Philip was Christian, but Dionysius refers elsewhere (*HE*, VII.x.3) to Philip as such; and so this statement in VI.xli.9 has to be understood in relation to the one in *HE*, VII.x.3, which clearly refers to Philip's Christianity.

(*b*) And so is the passage that gives an explanation of Decius's persecution, namely, his animosity towards Philip. The natural interpretation of the passage is that Philip was Christian and that

---

[27]The biblical scholar in Origen might have been aroused to preach in the letter on the biblical parallel of David and Nathan.

[28]It should be remembered that Origen was not unknown personally in Antioch—the scene of Philip's humiliation—whither he had been summoned ca. 218 by Alexander's mother Mammaea. Philip's repentance in Antioch may have inspired some Christians of Antioch who remembered Origen's visit to the city to write to him about it, and this in turn may have inspired Origen to write to Philip.

[29]Ensslin rests much of his argument against Philip's Christianity on this! Most of his views on this problem are derivative and superficial; see his chapter on "The Senate and the Army," *CAH*, 12 (1939), pp. 94–95.

his successor and enemy, Decius, gave vent to his animosity by persecuting the sect that shared the religious persuasion of the emperor he detested. What Eusebius says on Decius's motive in launching the persecution may or may not be true, and in this context it is relatively unimportant; what is important is the implication of the passage, namely, that Eusebius considered Philip a Christian, a view expressed twice in his work, when he recited the account of his exclusion from the church service in Antioch (*HE*, VI.xxxiv) and when he quoted Dionysius of Alexandria on Philip's Christianity (*HE*, VII.x.3).

III

The examination of the various relevant passages in Eusebius on Philip undertaken in the preceding section yields the conclusion that Eusebius does vouch for Philip's Christianity. However, the fact remains that critical opinion in modern times is divided on the interpretation of these passages in Eusebius; this division in the critical camp must be accounted for, and the accounting will throw more light on both Eusebius and Philip.

A

The genesis of the problem may be sought in Eusebius himself and the manner in which he expressed himself on Philip's principate and Christianity. The ecclesiastical historian is clearly not as emphatic as he might have been, and this lack of emphasis has contributed to a certain vagueness in phraseology that inclined some modern scholars to argue as they did. This lack of emphasis in the *Historia Ecclesiastica* is a reflection of a lack of enthusiasm in Eusebius himself, and this, too, has to be accounted for. The answer why the first ecclesiastical historian lacked some enthusiasm in describing the Christianity of the first Christian Roman emperor may be sought in the realization that Eusebius was in a very special relationship to Constantine. Not only is the *Laudes Constantini* an encomium but such also is the *Vita* itself since the extraordinary turn in the fortunes of Christianity brought about by Constantine naturally made of Eusebius a panegyrist of the instrument of that turn. When Eusebius wrote his *Historia Ecclesiastica*, he based his chronological system on the reigns of Roman emperors and he presented the events of ecclesiastical history as related to each reign. It is not difficult to see how the encomiast of Constantine could see something miraculous in his reign, coming as it did after a period of great persecution and tribulation to the Church. In full conformity with the rules of panegyrical art, he conceived the last reign in his *Historia Ecclesiastica*—that of Constantine—which witnessed the triumph of Christianity, as the climax of the long trials of the Church throughout the preceding three centuries. Without suppressing the facts about the reign of Philip, the first Christian Roman emperor, he presented the reign of Constantine in glowing colors that obscured that of Philip and almost made historians forgetful or even doubtful of the fact that the latter was the first Christian Roman emperor, an honor many modern historians have consequently accorded to Constantine.

Whether Eusebius viewed Philip as an Ishmaelite or a sedentary Saracen, ethnically related to the Herods of New Testament times and to the heresiarchs of later times, remains to be shown. If so, the image of the Arabs would have been an element in Eusebius's reluctance to give Philip the credit of being the first Christian Roman emperor.[30]

But it is not only Eusebius in his capacity as a panegyrist of Constantine that is responsible for obscuring Philip's Christianity. Philip's Christianity itself and the circumstances of the reign could also make intelligible that lack of enthusiasm which characterizes Eusebius's account of Philip. The following facts and features of Philip's Christianity may be mentioned for comparisons and contrasts with that of Constantine: (1) Philip was not a convert who adopted Christianity under dramatic circumstances such as are associated with the conversion of Constantine and which impressed all his biographers, future as well as contemporary, starting with the principal one, Eusebius. (2) In all probability, Philip's Christianity—unlike Constantine's—remained a personal, private affair, although not a secret one, while his friendly gestures towards Christians and the amelioration of their condition,[31] important as these were, cannot be compared with those of Constantine, such as the declaration of Christianity as a *religio licita* and the end of the

---

[30]For Eusebius's perception of the Arabs, see *infra*, pp. 95–109. Especially relevant in this connection is his silence on Abgar VIII, the first Christian ruler of Edessa and of any Near Eastern state; see *infra*, pp. 109–12.

[31]Instances of this are enumerated by Aigrain in "Arabie," col. 1167.

persecutions, the foundation of the new Christian capital, the convocation of the Council of Nicaea, and the magnificent building program in the Holy Land and elsewhere. (3) Unlike Constantine's, Philip's reign was short in duration, lasting for only five years; what he might have done for Christianity if it had been given him to reign as long as Constantine remains an open question. Thus his principate must be judged relatively non-significant to the progress of Christianity[32] and to its conquest of the pagan *imperium*—a marginal victory—and the transformation of the ancient world or the *imperium romanum* is rightly related to the conversion of Constantine.

Thus the truth about Eusebius's account of Philip's Christianity has to be sought in two circumstances: the role of Eusebius as a panegyrist of Constantine and the relative non-significance of the short reign of Philip to the fortunes of Christianity. The one without the other might have made some difference, but it is the combination of the two that explains Eusebius's account in tone and substance.

B

A return to the three Latin authors discussed above—Jerome, Orosius, and Vincent—is now necessary. As has been pointed out, the three not only vouched categorically for Philip's Christianity but also emphatically when they referred to him as the first, *primus*, of all Roman emperors to be Christian. The most important as far as Eusebius is concerned is, of course, Jerome, who lived for a long time in Palestine, was the translator of his *Chronicon*, was the older contemporary of the other two, and thus closer to the times of Eusebius.

Jerome refers to Philip as *primus* twice, in the *Chronicon* and in the *Liber de viris inlustribus*:

1. Two explanations have been given above[33] for this strong affirmation of Philip's Christianity in Jerome, one of which is that it is a faithful reflection of Eusebius's thought and an equally faith-

---

[32]Made even more so by the return of the principate to the very pagan Decius and after him to other pagan rulers. The fact seems to have been appreciated by Orosius who notes that with the exception of Julian, all Constantine's successors were Christian; see *Historiae adversum paganos*, VII.28.

[33]See *supra*, pp. 73–74.

ful reproduction of the original text of the *Chronicon* in Greek.[34] This is the most likely explanation for the appearance of the term *primus* in the Latin version of the *Chronicon* which Jerome translated in 380, and in support of this view the following may be adduced: the original version of the *Chronicon* was written about 303, while the revision of this version took place in the twenties since it continues to the *vicennalia* of Constantine, the twentieth year of his reign, in 325. The chances are that *primus* appeared in the early version of the *Chronicon*, written about 303 before the extra-ordinary events of the second and the third decades, during which Constantine was converted and Eusebius became his panegyrist. In 303, Eusebius was not in a special relationship to any Roman ruler but belonged to a persecuted religious sect. In these circumstances it is quite likely that he would have been warm or warmer towards Philip and referred to him as *primus*. Whether he changed the wording of his account of Philip's reign when he revised the *Chronicon* in the twenties is not clear. In any case, Jerome would have translated *primus* either from the original version or from the revised one, if *primus* was kept in the latter.

2. Jerome repeated *primus* twelve years later in 392 in his reference to Philip in chapter 54 of his *Liber de viris inlustribus*. That chapter is on Origen and the term appears in the context of Origen's letter to Philip; Jerome refers again to Philip's Christianity in the same chapter in connection with the Decian persecution. That Philip is referred to in a chapter written on Origen suggests that Jerome, who leans heavily on Eusebius in his *Liber de viris inlustribus*, may have had the latter's *HE* before him when he wrote the chapter on Origen, since it is in the *HE*, not in the *Chronicon*, that Origen's letter to Philip is mentioned. Unlike Eusebius's *Chronicon*, the Greek original of the *HE* had survived, and the reference to Philip in the *Liber de viris inlustribus* and in the *HE*, which latter work most probably was Jerome's source, raises the question of whether Eusebius revised his account of the reign of Philip in the later stages or editions of the *HE*. Jerome could have taken *primus* from the *Chronicon*, which he had translated twelve

[34]It is noteworthy that the events of the reign of Philip belong to the *Chronicon* as written by Eusebius himself and not to the continuation which Jerome wrote for the years 325–78.

years before,[35] but, as has just been argued, the reference to Origen suggests a different provenance—the *HE*. What has been said about the two versions of the *Chronicon* in 303 and in 325 may be said about the *HE* and its references to Philip and his Christianity. The *HE* passed through various stages and Eusebius made additions to it as extraordinary events followed one another in the second and third decades of the century dominated by Constantine.[36] It is noteworthy that references to Philip appear in Book VI, which belongs to the group of books that was written either in 312 or before, even before the outbreak of the persecution of Diocletian in 303, that is, before Constantine appeared as a Christian and protector of Christianity and before the bishop of Caesarea became his panegyrist. If the term *primus* appeared in the *HE*, it would have done so at this stage, and it is quite likely that it did appear or at least a strong affirmation of Philip's Christianity was expressed.

The final version of the *HE* does not have the term *primus*, and the lack of emphasis in Eusebius's account of Philip's Christianity in it raises the question of a rehandling of the original account as Eusebius was adding to the *HE* in the second and third decades Books IX and X, and possibly VIII, with their account of the reign of Constantine. Such a rehandling is understandable, coming as it could have done from a panegyrist of Constantine who wanted to present the reign—the climax of his work—as the triumph of Christianity. That such a rehandling of the reign of Philip did take place may derive some support from the rehandling of the reign of another figure to whom Constantine was related as a contemporary, namely, his co-Augustus Licinius. It has been argued that the fourth stage of the *HE* is represented by "removing the passages inconsistent with the *damnatio memoriae* of Licinius and replacing them with an account of his downfall, in 325, at the time of the Council of Nicaea."[37] In the case of Philip, the account of his Christianity may have been rewritten with a view to belittling it or making it seem insignificant in order to enhance that of Constantine.

---

[35]On the possibility that the account of Philip's reign in the Latin version of the *Chronicon* may have been influenced by the *HE*, see *infra*, Chap. VII, note 16.

[36]See Quasten, *Patrology,* vol. 3, p. 315.

[37]*Ibid.*, argued by E. Schwartz and summarized by Quasten.

It is noticeable that in the *HE* Eusebius does not refer to his hero Constantine as the first Christian emperor, which would have been expected from a panegyrist and a historian of the Church who had based his chronological system on the reigns of Roman emperors, most of whom had been non-Christian or anti-Christian. This is indirect evidence that Constantine was not the first; Eusebius could not very well have presented him as such in a work that had referred to one of his predecessors, namely, Philip, if not as *primus*, at least as Christian. But the problem of giving the palm to Constantine must have been on the mind of Eusebius. In 325, all he could do was to rehandle the *HE* by toning down Philip's Christianity lest it should diminish the glory of Constantine. But ten years later, in a work that was devoted exclusively to Constantine and in which there is naturally no reference to Philip, Eusebius comes close to using the term *primus* and as an encomiast does not find it difficult to do so when in chapter 3 of the *Vita*[38] he refers to Constantine, "who alone (μόνος) of all that ever wielded the Roman power was the friend of God, the Lord of all, and has appeared to all mankind so clear an example of a godly life."[39] The judgment on Constantine, especially its second part, is patently untrue. The biographer who forgets the crimes[40] attributed to Constantine and writes on his being the exemplar of a godly life is only a panegyrist who is carried away by enthusiasm and whose statements must be construed as rhetorical exaggeration. Nevertheless, the judgment is significant in this discussion of the problem of the first Christian Roman emperor and represents the last stage[41] in Eusebius's handling of the pair—Philip and Constantine—which began with the revision of the *Chronicon* and the *HE* in the twenties.

C

If Eusebius left the question open or vague as to who the first Christian Roman emperor was and if the Latin authors, Jerome

---

[38]See *Vita Constantini*, ed. F. Winkelmann, *GCS* (Berlin, 1975), pp. 16–17.

[39]It is noteworthy that in this quotation he uses the term μόνος, not πρῶτος, and makes no explicit reference to Constantine's *Christianity*, as if aware that πρῶτος would be noticeably untrue.

[40]For further on this, see *infra*, p. 87.

[41]It is noticeable that in the same year in which he composed the *Vita* (335),

and Vincent of Lérins, declared for Philip without any reference
to Constantine in their explicit and strongly worded judgments,
there was one Latin author who paired the two together in one
single statement, declaring that with the exception of Philip, Constantine was the first Christian Roman emperor, *primus imperatorum
Christianus, excepto Philippo.*[42]

The author, Orosius,[43] was sent by Augustine to Palestine
where he visited Jerome at Bethlehem in 415, and it is reasonable to suppose that his views on who the "first" was derive from
Jerome, who must be credited with the strong affirmation of
Philip's Christianity. Though derivative, Orosius's judgment is
important since it is the considered judgment of Christian antiquity
on this question, expressed by one who, unlike Eusebius, was not
in any special relationship to either emperor, as Eusebius had been
to Constantine.[44] It is a measured and, what is more, an interpretative judgment in that it presents Philip's Christianity in its
true light and significance in the history of Christianity and the
Church—namely, that it was precursory to that of the "Thirteenth
Apostle."[45]

Perhaps even more important than Orosius's pairing of Philip
and Constantine together is the possibility that Philip was asso-

---

he spoke in rather pejorative terms of the Arabs in the *Laudes Constantini*; see
infra, p. 101.

[42]Orosius, *Historiae adversum paganos*, VII.28.

[43]On Orosius, see B. Altaner, *Patrology*, trans. Hilda C. Graef (New York,
1960), pp. 280–81.

[44]"In the Middle Ages, [Orosius's *Historiae*] was much used as a manual of
universal history" (*ibid.*). Thus medieval Europe, partly through him, accepted
the fact that Philip was the first Christian Roman emperor. When it did so, it
took over the judgment of an author who, although secondary, derived from
Jerome and Eusebius.

[45]Orosius's passage on Constantine and Philip is echoed almost verbatim by
the anonymous author of *Origo Constantini Imperatoris*, the first part of the so-called
Anonymus Valesianus. That that discriminating author, described by Mommsen as
Ammiano neque aetate neque auctoritate inferior, chose to quote Orosius on Constantine
and Philip is significant. He was a biographer only of Constantine in his *Origo*
(unlike Orosius, who wrote in his *Historiae* on both Philip and Constantine in
the third and fourth centuries) and thus did not have to refer to Constantine's
Christianity together with that of Philip. But he did, and this could suggest that
there may have been conflicting claims advanced on behalf of one or the other of
these two to be the first Christian Roman emperor and that the question was
settled in favor of Philip. For the section on Constantine and Philip in the *Origo*,
see Th. Mommsen, *Chronica Minora I, MGH*, 9 (Berlin, 1892), p. 10.

ciated with Constantine by none other than the latter himself. In spite of the fact that the two Philips, father and son, are not referred to as *divi* on inscriptions and that the erasure of their names is frequent, there is the statement in Eutropius[46] that both were deified, which now cannot be dismissed lightly, especially as none other than Stein himself, the determined opponent of Philip's Christianity, had suggested an elegant solution to the problem posed by this statement.[47] He persuasively argued that the consecration of Philip could not have taken place before the reign of Constantine and, what is more, that it was the latter who, as a Christian influenced by Eusebius's account of Philip as the first Christian emperor, must be credited with his consecration.[48] If Stein's reasoning is valid, it will conclusively corroborate the testimonies of the three Latin authors.

Philip's Christianity is also relevant to a discussion of another statement that involves Constantine's co-Augustus Licinius. At the end of the *Vita* of the three Gordians in the *Historia Augusta*,[49] it is stated that Licinius derived his descent from Philip.[50] The claim, possibly a counter-claim to Constantine's "descent" from Claudius Gothicus, is certainly fictitious, but the motive behind it deserves some attention. That Licinius chose to derive his descent from Philip rather than some other emperor may be related to the fact that Philip was Christian and to the possibility that it was Constantine who was responsible for his consecration. This could afford the key to understanding an otherwise surprising and fictitious claim on the part of Licinius. Licinius was no Christian but he did issue conjointly with Constantine the Edict of Milan in 313. Perhaps in order to win over the large number of Christians in the *pars orientalis* over which he was Augustus or to cultivate good relations with his co-Augustus, he circulated the claim that he was descended from the first Christian emperor, Philip the Arab.

---

[46]*Breviarium*, ed. F. Rühl, Bibliotheca Teubneriana (Leipzig, 1887), IX.3.

[47]E. Stein, "Kleine Beiträge zur römischen Geschichte," *Hermes*, 52 (1917), pp. 571–78.

[48]Noteworthy is the possible numismatic support for this view, namely, that the head of Philip appears on two medallions of the arch of Constantine; for the controversy on the interpretation of the two medallions, see *ibid.*, p. 578.

[49]*Historia Augusta*, "Vita Gord.," 34.5.

[50]The statement, of course, could be fictitious, coming as it does from the *HA*, for which, see R. Syme, *Ammianus and the Historia Augusta* (Oxford, 1968), and *idem, Emperors and Biography* (Oxford, 1971).

D

It remains to discuss the other party involved in the imperial-
ecclesiastical confrontation in Antioch on 13 April 244—the bishop
who denied Philip access to the church and who received him
only after the latter had done penance. Unlike the other parallels
to this confrontation—in Milan, Constantinople, and Canossa—
this one in Antioch is relatively unknown and so is the bishop who
was involved in it, Babylas. The intensive examination of the evidence relative to Philip's Christianity and of the crucial passage in
Eusebius on the penance at Antioch (*HE*, VI.xxxiv) makes it necessary to return to Babylas and to the scene of that penance.

1. This most celebrated of the bishop-martyrs of Antioch after
Ignatius in the Roman period deserves to be better known[51] because
in addition to his martyrdom his name is associated with that
imperial-ecclesiastical confrontation in Antioch, parallels to which
have made even better known the names of Ambrose, Nicholas
Mysticus, and Gregory. Many factors have contributed to the relative obscurity which has been the lot of Babylas: (*a*) the earliest
source, Eusebius, is not expansive on the confrontation and does
not even mention his name, which has either to be inferred or to
be supplied from other sources; (*b*) the two translations of his relics
in the fourth century ordered by the caesar, Gallus, and by the
emperor, Julian, for two different reasons provided his *passio* posthumously with miraculous elements,[52] which were further enhanced
after they were given literary expression by the eloquence of John
Chrysostom, who preached two panegyrics on him.[53] All this has
operated to his disadvantage in that it has inclined scholars to view
with suspicion the unadorned facts of his life given by the earliest
and most trustworthy source, Eusebius, and to forget that in spite
of rhetorical embellishments and exaggerations, fully understandable in an apologetic treatise, Chrysostom was reflecting an im-

[51]See the short article on St. Babylas in *DHGE*, 4 (1932), col. 33; more
extensive is the article which appeared in *Bibliotheca Sanctorum*, valuable also for
representations of St. Babylas in art; see *BS*, 2 (1962), cols. 679–81.

[52]See *BHG*, 1, pp. 74–75; *BHL*, 1, p. 138; for critical scholarship on St.
Babylas, see "Les deux saints Babylas," *AB*, 19 (1900), pp. 5–8; and H. Delehaye
in various works, such as *Les passions des martyres et les genres littéraires* (Brussels,
1921), pp. 209–10, 232; "Les origines du culte des martyres," *Subsidia Hagiographica*, 20 (1933), pp. 193–95 *et passim*.

[53]See Quasten, *Patrology* vol. 3, pp. 467–68.

portant local Antiochene tradition on the imperial-ecclesiastical confrontation, independent of Eusebius of Caesarea and corroborative of it.

2. A close examination of the passages in Eusebius that refer to Babylas (*HE*, VI.xxxiv) suggests that the former might have been more expansive and explicit on the latter than he was: (*a*) in this crucial passage that describes the encounter with Philip, Babylas is left anonymous, and although Eusebius certainly knew who the confessor bishop of the imperial penitent was, since he refers to his episcopate in Antioch twice elsewhere,[54] he chose to refer to him not by his name but through a circumlocution which describes him as the one who was then presiding over the church in Antioch; (*b*) when he mentions him by name he does so only twice and fleetingly, although after Ignatius he was the most celebrated bishop of Antioch in Roman times.[55] Ignatius was, of course, more important than Babylas, but the latter did cut a relatively large figure in ecclesiastical history. Even if considerations of space and relative importance were operative in the composition of the *HE*, Eusebius might at least have mentioned him by name rather than by a circumlocution while describing his encounter with Philip in Antioch. The anonymity to which Babylas was consigned is suspect.

Eusebius's account of Philip and the conclusions drawn in the preceding sections on why Eusebius was not sufficiently enthusiastic in telling the story of Philip's Christianity come to mind and may be drawn upon. It is not impossible that he deliberately left Babylas's name out lest the name of the bishop, made famous by his subsequent martyrdom, should give prominence to the penance at Antioch and with it the fact of Philip's Christianity as anterior to that of his hero Constantine.[56] Alternatively, and perhaps more plausibly, Eusebius avoids mentioning Babylas and his ecclesiastical rank as bishop possibly because such an explicit mention of name

---

[54]*HE*, VI.xxix, xxxix.

[55]Cf. the two very short notices of Babylas with Eusebius's expansive account of Ignatius in *HE*, III.xxii, xxxvi.

[56]It is not impossible that Babylas held theological views unacceptable to Eusebius and consequently the latter, who felt strongly about heresies (*HE*, I.i.1), did not quite approve of Babylas; hence the indifferent reference to him in *HE*, VI.xxxiv. If Babylas wrote anything, nothing of it has survived.

and rank would have drawn attention to the fact that bishops of the reign of Constantine, Eusebius included, had not the courage of Babylas to accord Constantine himself a similar treatment for the crimes the latter committed and compared to which those of Philip were not serious.[57] The fact that Eusebius does not specify Philip's crime against Gordian could corroborate this view, since specification would have invited further comparison with those of Constantine, also of the same order but much more heinous.[58] This alternative explanation is rather important and may be added to what has been said above[59] on why Eusebius was not so enthusiastic about advertising Philip's Christianity; this had been associated with an imperial-ecclesiastical confrontation which might have been repeated in the reign of Constantine if there had been bishops of the moral and spiritual stature of Babylas, and if repeated, would have advertised the crimes[60] of the emperor on whose Christian virtues Eusebius enthusiastically expatiated.

3. The defense of the authenticity of the crucial passage in Eusebius on the imperial-ecclesiastical encounter makes possible the drawing of the following conclusions on the bishop-martyr of Antioch: (a) This was Babylas's finest hour before his martyrdom some six or seven years later in the Decian persecution. The episode

[57]Philip only connived at the murder of Gordian by the troops, who clamored for a man to lead them, not a child.

[58]These, too, consisted of murders, which included such close relatives as his eldest son Crispus and his own second wife, Fausta. These, of course, took place in 326, after the supposed completion of the final version of the *HE* in 325; but although the *HE* comes to an end with the year 325 it may have been revised later in the twenties; besides, there had been other crimes committed before 325, such as throwing prisoners to wild beasts in the amphitheaters of Trier and Colmar.

[59]For this, see *supra*, sec. III.B. This alternative explanation, presented in this section, could thus shed light on the serious omissions in this passage in *HE*, VI.xxxix, namely, the name of the bishop and the nature of the crime committed by Philip.

[60]Constantine postponed his baptism till the end of his life because, according to him, he wanted to be baptized in the Jordan; but he may also have done this because baptism would have entailed an embarrassing confession of post-baptismal sins. It is noteworthy that the bishop who administered the last rites to Constantine was not Eusebius of Caesarea but Eusebius of Nicomedia, who thus would have been the best-informed source on these sins if Constantine confessed them. Thus historiography possibly suffered from the fact that the Eusebius who administered the last rites was not the ecclesiastical historian, who might have revised what he had written on Constantine in the *HE*, the *Vita*, and the *Laudes*, if he had heard his hero's confession.

reveals a stern ecclesiastic,[61] the stuff of which martyrs are made, and it represents the first of two encounters with Roman emperors over both of whom Babylas triumphed: Philip, whom he challenged in an Antioch church, and Decius, whom he defied with martyrdom in an Antioch prison.[62] (*b*) The encounter itself is of considerable importance in the history of imperial-ecclesiastical relations. Babylas appears as the first after the prophet Nathan of Old Testament times to throw a challenge to a Christian ruler, and thus he preludes the series of three subsequent encounters in the Christian period which represent the theme of "the repentance of the emperor"—at Milan in 380 between St. Ambrose and Theodosius, at Constantinople in 906/7 between the patriarch Nicholas Mysticus and the Emperor Leo VI, and at Canossa in 1077 between Pope Gregory VII and the Emperor Henry IV. Although these three were more dramatic, the one in Antioch had no precedent in the Christian period and consequently Babylas appears without a predecessor; furthermore, it took place before the triumph of Christianity in the fourth century, when that religion was still persecuted and was leading a precarious existence, all of which makes Babylas's courageous stand even more remarkable as an example of the triumph of the *sacerdotium* over the *imperium*.[63]

[61]It is reported that before his martyrdom he asked to be buried in his chains.

[62]He was to triumph posthumously over a third emperor, Julian, for which, see the articles cited *supra*, note 52.

[63]Perhaps the foregoing discussion has restored the historicity of the crucial passage in Eusebius (*HE*, VI.xxxiv), which has been under a cloud as far as both Philip and Babylas are concerned. The imperial-ecclesiastical confrontation in Antioch has to be accepted as a fact, and consequently the journey of the student of such confrontations, which usually takes him to Milan and Canossa, must now include Antioch, indeed must begin with it. Of late, Nicolas Oikonomides has made better known the imperial-ecclesiastical confrontation in Constantinople, and thus the four confrontations are equally divided between East and West; see N. Oikonomides, "Leo VI and the Narthex Mosaic of Saint Sophia," *DOP*, 30 (1976), pp. 153–72.

Appendix

After this chapter on the first Christian Roman emperor had been written, my attention was drawn to an article on Philip the Arab,[1] which in turn led me to an earlier one on the same topic.[2] Both are important contributions to a better understanding of the reign, and it is necessary to discuss briefly their relevance to the argument of this chapter.

A

York's aim is to rehabilitate Philip. His own words are the best summary of his views: "Succeeding generations have distorted the image of Philip in the interests of his successor Decius and, ironically, of the Dynasty of Constantine. Despite the hostility of most extant accounts of his reign, there is evidence that Philip the Arab was an excellent ruler whose career deserves rehabilitation. If, as is probable, the emperor was a Christian, the role of Philip in Roman history acquires new significance."

York successfully analyzed the sources unfavorable to Philip.[3] *Inter alia*, he drew new conclusions on his involvement or rather lack of it in the death of Gordian[4] and on the manner of Philip's death.[5]

Less successful is his attempt to solve the problem of Philip's Christianity and matters related to it:[6]

1. He did not realize that there is a transcriptional error or a *lapsus calami* in Jerome's account of the correspondence of Origen with Philip.[7] As a result, York thought that it was the younger Philip who was the recipient of Origen's letter and the first Christian Roman emperor.[8] This partly explains why, in the quotation from his article cited above, York thinks that the elder Philip's Christianity was only "probable."

2. More important is his view on the *logos* in Eusebius, the crucial passage that establishes Philip's Christianity. He put forward the unacceptable view that "Eusebius had probably received this anecdote of Philip as a verbal tradition from the See of Antioch in which the events

---

[1]See H. Crouzel, "Le christianisme de l'empereur Philippe l'Arabe," *Gregorianum* (1975), pp. 545–50 (hereafter, "Christianisme"). I am grateful to Professor T. D. Barnes for drawing my attention to this article.

[2]See John M. York, Jr., "The Image of Philip the Arab," *Historia*, 21 (1972), pp. 321–32 (hereafter, "Image").

[3]*Ibid.*, pp. 321–26.

[4]*Ibid.*, pp. 325–26.

[5]*Ibid.*, p. 332.

[6]*Ibid.*, pp. 326–32.

[7]On this, see *supra*, note 21.

[8]"Image," p. 329.

had occurred."[9] His view that Origen's letter was addressed to Philip the younger, not the elder, must account for his failure to see in the letter of Origen the source of the *logos* and for his view that it represents a verbal Antiochene tradition rather than a solid evidence for Philip's Christianity coming from Origen himself.

In spite of these criticisms, York's article has gone a long way to rehabilitate Philip,[10] even if it left the question of his Christianity an open one.

B

Crouzel's article is an important corrective of York's on Philip's Christianity; its relevant points are the following:

1. There is indeed an Antiochene tradition of Philip's Christianity represented by the sermons of John Chrysostom and the *Chronicon Paschale,* but that tradition is more concerned with St. Babylas than with Philip.[11]

2. Eusebius does not know this Antiochene tradition; had he known it, he would have mentioned the name of the bishop involved in the encounter with Philip, namely, Babylas, and the scene of the encounter, namely, Antioch.[12]

3. The letters of Origen to Philip and to his wife, Severa, are most probably the source of Eusebius when he wrote the section on Philip's Christianity in the *HE.*[13]

The most relevant to this chapter on the first Christian Roman emperor is the third point. Crouzel qualifies his conclusion on Origen's letters as the source of Eusebius's *logos* with the phrase "très probable," while I have argued that it is more than that. In so doing, I have drawn on evidence from Jerome and Vincent of Lérins,[14] who read those letters of Origen the loss of which Crouzel lamented and which prevented him from promoting the probability to certainty.[15]

---

[9]*Ibid.,* p. 327.

[10]For the Εἰς βασιλέα addressed to Philip and for his laws with Christian connotation, see *ibid.,* p. 331. Also noteworthy is the solemn interment in Rome during his reign of Pope Pontianus, who had been exiled by Maximinus Thrax; see Grégoire, *Les persécutions,* p. 90 note 3.

[11]"Christianisme," pp. 546–47.

[12]*Ibid.,* p. 547. It would have been strange if Eusebius had not been informed about the identity of the bishop (Babylas) or of the city (Antioch); the two facts were known, according to the *Chronicon Paschale,* to the Emperor Decius! See *ibid.,* p. 546. I have given an alternative explanation for Eusebius's silence on both; see *supra,* p. 86.

[13]"Christianisme," p. 547.

[14]See *supra,* pp. 73–75, 79–80.

[15]Apparently Crouzel accepted York's views on Jerome's account of Origen's letter to the younger Philip, and so could not use the precious reference in Jerome

In addition to the foregoing three points, Crouzel does not see in Origen, as York does, a teacher of Philip, nor can he see in certain acts of the latter the influence of the Alexandrine doctor.[16] But something may be said for York's view on the universalism of Origen which Philip might have inherited,[17] if only because it could explain or makes easier to understand the fact that Christian Philip celebrated the millennium of Rome's legendary foundation as a pagan emperor.[18]

Two years after the publication of Crouzel's "Christianisme" in 1975 appeared P. Nautin's *Origène*, in which the author adopted a position of extreme scepticism concerning Philip's Christianity,[19] in spite of Crouzel's perceptive and persuasive analysis. Perhaps this was due to the fact that Crouzel did not examine the *logos* in Eusebius at length and consequently could conclude that its derivation from Origen's letter was only very probable.[20] Thus the *logos* has remained haunted by the ghosts of authenticity, and Philip's Christianity, already strongly rejected by Stein in his authoritative article in *RE*, has remained uncertain. The two related problems can be definitively solved only by an intensive analysis of the crucial *logos* in Eusebius and a direct confrontation with all the arguments of the one who mounted the most devastating offensive against Philip's Christianity—Ernst Stein.[21]

C

The two distinguished Oxford scholars who read the manuscript of this book in its entirety have made an important contribution to the discussion of the crucial phrase in Eusebius, κατέχει λόγος. In the

---

to Origen's letter in definitively solving the problem of the source of the *logos* in Eusebius; see *supra*, note 21.

[16]"Christianisme," pp. 548–49, and summarized in the final paragraph, p. 550.

[17]The possibility must be entertained that the emperor did not fully comprehend the universalism of the theologian.

[18]However, what was said on the "paganism" of the Thirteenth Apostle himself, Constantine, is enough by way of analogy and could make unnecessary an appeal to Origen's universalism (*supra*, p. 72). Moreover, what was involved was an extraordinary event, the Millennium, and this could have been celebrated only according to the rites of the pagan empire, even though the emperor was a Christian.

[19]Especially pp. 91, 375f.

[20]Perhaps Nautin missed Crouzel's article. There is a reference to Crouzel's work in Nautin's introduction, p. 7 note 1, but it is to a work that appeared in 1971, four years before the publication of "Christianisme" in 1975.

[21]Crouzel refers to Stein's article once and only to mention his establishment of the date of Philip's birth as A.D. 204; see "Christianisme," p. 550 note 23.

wake of the discussion of the phrase in this appendix, it is necessary to incorporate their contribution.

1. Mr. C. H. Roberts wrote, "I agree with you that the words Χριστιανὸν ὄντα would be naturally taken not as part of the λόγος but as a comment of Eusebius." This encourages me to separate these words from the *logos* as another indication that Eusebius did, in fact, vouch for the Christianity of Philip the Arab. I had not emphasized the importance of these two words before while discussing the *logos* for the first time, having been occupied more with the *logos* and with answering Stein's argument that it means "rumor."[22]

2. He suggested that the phrase κατέχει λόγος might be translated "there is a wide-spread report" and said "it would be useful to establish whether Eusebius uses the expression elsewhere and, if so, in what context."

The decisive argument is whether or not Eusebius ever used it in the sense of written document or only of oral tradition. Mr. Sherwin-White drew my attention to the fact that Eusebius does in fact use λόγος ἔχει in the sense of a written document or a literary source. In his account of the Thundering Legion in *HE*, V.5, where the phrase occurs, there is positive proof that it can refer to literary sources.

3. That the phrase can refer to a written document and does in *HE*, VI.xxxiv, is also corroborated by the fact that Eusebius composed his work not in Antioch but in Caesarea. If he had written his *HE* in Antioch, it is conceivable that the *logos* he refers to might have been a local oral account which could have survived, and very naturally so, in the city in which Philip's humiliation took place. Eusebius, however, wrote not in Antioch but in faraway Caesarea and, consequently, the *logos* is far more likely to have been a written account such as Eusebius might have had at his disposal in Caesarea.

I am, therefore, even more convinced that the λόγος of *HE*, VI.xxxiv, is none other than the ἐπιστολή of Origen mentioned in *HE*, VI.xxxvi, or a written account based on it.[23]

D

The latest to treat Philip's Christianity is Hans A. Pohlsander in an article entitled "Philip the Arab and Christianity."[24] It is a welcome addition to the growing corpus of studies on Philip and includes items that make the bibliography on his Christianity more comprehensive.[25]

---

[22]*Supra*, p. 68.
[23]*Supra*, p. 76.
[24]*Historia*, 29 (1980), pp. 463–73.
[25]He apparently missed Crouzel's article discussed in sec. B of this appendix.

The author reaches conclusions contrary to those of York,[26] who has tried to rehabilitate Philip, and he reverts to the position that he was not a Christian. Unfortunately, he devotes most of his arguments to details[27] which are peripheral to his Christianity and does not come to grips with the central and crucial piece of evidence for it, namely, the *logos* in Eusebius, to which he devotes only two paragraphs.[28] But it is on this *logos* that the truth about Philip's Christianity must stand or fall, and it is for this reason that it has been intensively analyzed in this chapter and its appendix in which all the dimensions of the problem posed by it have been explored.

[26]*Supra*, p. 89.

[27]These have been discussed while Stein's arguments were being examined (*supra*, pp. 67ff). However, Pohlsander's views on Origen's letters to Philip and his wife (pp. 468f) should be commented upon in this footnote; they are unacceptable and are pure guesswork. The analogy with Melito's letter to the philosopher-emperor Marcus Aurelius is invalid; even those who argue against Philip's Christianity do not say that he was hostile to it, and so he does not fall in the category of "hostile emperors" to whom Christian apologists wrote; besides, it should be noted that Origen addressed the letter not only to the emperor but also to his wife, which is significant.

[28]Pp. 466–67, while he devotes so many pages to the reburial of Pope Pontianus (pp. 469–73). The discussion, however, is valuable.

VII

Eusebius and the Arabs

The Arabs are mentioned several times in various works of
Eusebius.[1] In addition to the well-known and tantalizing
reference to the Christianity of Philip the Arab in the *Historia
Ecclesiastica*, there are other less-known references to them in the
Chronicon, in the *Praeparatio Evangelica*, and in the *Laudes Constantini*. These references are of considerable importance to understanding the image of the Arabs in the perception of Eusebius and
to the persistence of this image in the work of the ecclesiastical
historians who came after him.

I

Chronicon. With the exception of one reference to Ishmael, all
the others in the *Chronicon*[2] are to the Arabs and to Arab figures in
the political history of the first three centuries of the Roman period.

(*a*) *Abraham ex ancilla Agar generat Ishmael, a quo Ishmaelitarum
genus, qui postea Agareni et ad postremum Saraceni dicti.*[3] This entry

---

[1]For Eusebius and his work, see Quasten, *Patrology*, vol. 3, pp. 309–45.

[2]*Ibid.*, pp. 311–14. Save for some excerpts and fragments, the Greek original
of the *Chronicon* has not survived, but a Latin and an Armenian version have. The
first was done by Jerome in 380, the second is a work of the sixth century,
and both are based on a revision of the original; for the former, see *Die Chronik
des Hieronymus*, ed. R. Helm, *GCS*, 47 (1956), hereafter cited as *Chronik*; for the
latter, see *Die Chronik*, trans. J. Karst, *GCS*, 20 (1911).

The analysis of the data on the Arabs undertaken in this chapter is based on
the Latin rather than on the Armenian version, since the latter has hardly anything
on the Arabs with the exception of a reference to Philip. It remains to be shown
that the references in the Latin version were later insertions by Jerome which
had not been part of the *Chronicon* in its original Greek form. However, the
reference to the Saraceni, assigned to A.D. 357 (*Chronik*, p. 240), is patently
an entry for which Jerome is responsible as the continuator of Eusebius; the
Chronicon stops in A.D. 325 and Jerome brought it down to the death of Valens
in A.D. 378; for this reference, see chap. 8, sec. II on Jerome and the Arabs in
BAFOC.

[3]*Chronik*, p. 24a.

makes clear that Eusebius/Jerome identified the Saraceni of the fourth and preceding centuries with the Ishmaelites of the Bible;[4] the Saracens are then a biblical people, from the seed of Abraham, but Ishmaelites, descendants of the handmaid.[5]

(b) Herod the Great is mentioned as the son of an Arab mother.[6] The semi-Arab origin[7] of that most unattractive figure in the Gospels could not have endeared the Arabs, already under a cloud as Ishmaelites, to ecclesiastical historians.

(c) Other references are to the Arabs of Mesopotamia and to the wars of Trajan and Septimius Severus against them;[8] in the entry on Trajan's campaign against them, there is also reference to the *Osroenos*, over whom the Abgarids of Edessa ruled. The distinction drawn between the *Arabas* and the *Osroenos*, presumably in the sources Eusebius used, could explain why Eusebius does not conceive of the Abgarids as Arabs.

(d) *Abgarus vir sanctus regnavit Edessae, ut vult Africanus*.[9] The entry on Abgar VIII, the Arab king of Edessa, who had the distinction of being the first ruler of a Near Eastern state to adopt Christianity, is noteworthy.[10] It is made on the authority of one who visited Abgar in Edessa, Julius Africanus,[11] on whose work the *Historia Ecclesiastica* of Eusebius is based; and yet there is no reference to Abgar VIII in the *Historia*, while his ethnic identity is not mentioned in the *Chronicon*. Besides, *ut vult* in the entry is striking: "as Africanus would have it" suggests that Eusebius is reluctant to vouch for the truth of the statement on Abgar VIII and gives it only the authority of Africanus; this is consonant with his omission of any reference to Abgar VIII in the *Historia Ecclesiastica*.

---

[4]For other authors who came before and after Eusebius and made the same identification, see *ibid.*, p. 283, and *infra*, note 62.

[5]The point is driven home by the following entry in the *Chronicon* (*ibid.*, p. 24a) on the birth of Isaac from the freewoman.

[6]*Ibid.*, p. 160.

[7]According to Josephus, his father was an Idumaean, but an Ascalonite according to Julius Africanus; if the former, Herod would have been entirely Arab, since the Idumaeans were an Arab tribe; on Herod's descent, see Eusebius, *HE*, I.vi.2–3; vii.11.

[8]*Chronik*, pp. 194, 211.

[9]*Ibid.*, p. 214; also p. 428 for other authors on Abgar VIII, the Christian king of Edessa.

[10]On Abgar VIII, see *RE*, 1, 1, col. 95.

[11]*Ibid.*, 5, 2, col. 1936, *s.v.* Edessa.

(e) Important are the references[12] to Philip the Arab, who in the Latin version of Jerome is described as *primusque omnium ex Romanis imperatoribus X̃Pianus fuit.*[13] In view of the controversy over Philip's Christianity,[14] which, according to some, is not crystal clear from references to it by Eusebius in the *Historia Ecclesiastica*, this explicit statement in the *Chronicon* is noteworthy.[15] Although it is not certain whether the statement in its Latin form is a literal reproduction of the original Greek of Eusebius or an expansion of it, nevertheless the statement remains valuable. If the former, then Philip's Christianity is established beyond doubt; if the latter, the statement implies that this was Jerome's understanding of what Eusebius had written of Philip and his Christianity in the *Chronicon* and the *Historia Ecclesiastica*[16] or what he himself had established from other sources.[17]

(f) There are references to Odenathus and Zenobia of Palmyra.[18] Odenathus is referred to not as Arab but as *Palmyrenus*, as in other sources.

[12]*Chronik*, pp. 217–18; also pp. 431–32 for other authors on Philip.

[13]*Ibid.*, p. 217, lines 13–14.

[14]For which, see *supra*, pp. 68–71.

[15]Jerome prepared his Latin version in A.D. 380; this is an early date and his is the earliest extant explicit statement on Philip's Christianity. The Armenian version is late, a sixth-century one; it does not refer to Philip's Christianity explicitly and omits all references to the Arabs in the *Chronicon* listed in this section. For Philip in the Armenian version, see Karst, trans., *Die Chronik*, pp. 225–26, where his celebration of the thousandth anniversary of the foundation of Rome is recorded and his Christianity is only implied in the entry on the persecution launched by Decius.

[16]The three items relevant to Philip's Christianity mentioned in the *Chronicon*—the conspiracy against Gordian, his Christianity, and the Decianic persecution—are the same as those mentioned by Eusebius in his *HE*. The Latin version of Jerome which emphatically vouches for Philip's Christianity could suggest that Jerome (if he was responsible for the explicit statement on Philip's Christianity) drew the conclusion on the basis of the three items in the *HE*. And he was not the only early Christian writer who was close to Eusebius's time to do so; for the list, see *RE*, 10,1 (1918), cols. 768–69.

[17]It is noteworthy that he repeats the statement on Philip's Christianity and on his being the first Christian Roman emperor elsewhere in his work (*ibid.*, col. 768). If Jerome had not been convinced of Philip's Christianity, he would not have vouched for it, since he took a dim view of the Arabs, for which, see "St. Jerome and the Arabs" in *BAFOC*, chap. 8, sec. II.

[18]*Chronik*, pp. 221–23. Of interest is *hodieque* in his final statement on Zenobia: *a qua hodieque Romae Zenobiae familia nuncupatur*; it could suggest that this was an observation made by one to whom Rome was personally known, namely, Jerome.

Praeparatio Evangelica. References to the Arabs and Arabia may be found in Books II, IV, VI, IX, and X of the *Praeparatio*,[19] but only the significant ones[20] will be discussed.

(*a*) Book II: Eusebius speaks of the "robbers of Arabia"[21] while discussing the theology of the Egyptians. Although he was quoting Diodorus Siculus,[22] it is practically certain that he vouched for the truth of the descriptive phrase.[23]

(*b*) Book IV: there are two references[24] to the Arabs in chapters 16 and 17, which treat human sacrifice and evil demons in the religious systems of the ancient peoples, including the Arabs. The more detailed is the first, which speaks of the sacrifice of a boy every year to an evil demon and his burial under the altar.[25] These references come in the context of a discussion, with a strong disapproving tone, of the religious beliefs and practices of the pagans.

(*c*) Book VI: there are five references to the Arabs,[26] four in chapter 10 and one in chapter 11: (1) the first is on the custom prevailing in Arabia and Osroene of putting adultresses to death and punishing those who are even suspected of adultery; (2) the second is on the various nations to whom such arts and sciences as painting, architecture, geometry, and the performance of dramatic

---

[19]For the Greek text, see K. Mras, Part I, *GCS*, 43, 1 (1954); Part II, *GCS*, 43, 2 (1956); the references to the Arabs all occur in Part I, cited hereafter as *Praeparatio*; since 1956 the *Praeparatio* has been published in *SC*, but only three volumes have so far appeared, containing Books I, II, III, and VII; the important references to the Arabs are not in these books, and so E. H. Gifford's old commentary may be consulted, *Eusebii Pamphili Evangelicae Praeparationes, libri XV, ad codices manuscriptos denuo collatos recensuit, Anglice nunc primum reddidit, notis et indicibus instruxit* (Oxford, 1903), Tomus IV (hereafter, Gifford, *Praeparationes*). For studies on the *Praeparatio*, see Quasten, *Patrology*, vol. 3, pp. 330–31.

[20]Other references are biblically related ones which provide no new or significant data on the Arabs; *Praeparatio*, pp. 518, 521–22, 541, 553, 595; on p. 576 occurs an interesting reference (deriving from Clement of Alexandria) to the Arabs as having perfected ornithomancy; for this art among the pre-Islamic Arabs, see T. Fahd, *La divination arabe* (Leiden, 1966), pp. 432ff.

[21]*Praeparatio*, p. 65. The same term, *robbers*, is used by Julian for the Arabs; see chap. 3, sec. III on Julian and the Arabs in *BAFOC*.

[22]*Praeparatio*, p. 58.

[23]Cf. his own phrase, "the barbarian Saracens," in *HE*, VI.xlii.

[24]*Praeparatio*, pp. 201, 202.

[25]No particular author is cited for this datum on the Arabs; ὡς φασι (p. 201, line 8) introduces the paragraph on human sacrifice in Laodicaea, Libya, and Arabia. In *Laudes Constantini*, these Arabs are identified as Dumateni; see *infra*, note 46.

[26]*Praeparatio*, pp. 339, 340, 342, 357–58.

poetry were unknown, and among those listed are the Arabs, referred to by two designations, *Tayenoi* and *Saracenoi*;[27] (3) the third
is on the laws of Arabia[28] viewed as those of barbarians; it was the
Romans who, after their conquest of the country, changed those
laws; (4) the fourth pertains to the practice of circumcision in
Osroene and its abolition by King Abgar VIII of Edessa;[29] (5) the
fifth speaks of the rite of circumcision among the Ishmaelites, who
subject their children to it at the age of thirteen.[30]

[27]This is a valuable extract from Bardaiṣan: (*a*) the collocation of two designations for the nomadic Arabs in the eastern and western halves of the Fertile
Crescent, *Tayenoi* and *Saracenoi*, is important to the discussion of the etymology of
the term *Saracenoi*, for which, see *infra*, pp. 123–31; (*b*) the Syriac original of
these extracts from Bardaiṣan has survived and thus it is possible to compare
the two versions; of special interest is the phrase "actor of dramatic poetry,"
ὑποκριτὴν ποιημάτων, which in the Syriac appears simply as "poets"; for the
Syriac version, see Bardaiṣan, *The Book of the Laws of Countries*, Semitic Texts with
Translations, trans. H. J. W. Drijvers (Assen, 1965) (hereafter, Bardaiṣan, *Laws*),
p. 50, line 18; (*c*) in view of Eusebius's familiarity with Bardaiṣan and his *Laws*,
the question arises why there is no mention in the *Historia Ecclesiastica* of the conversion of Abgar VIII, the Arab king of Edessa; see *infra*, notes 29, 54.

[28]The Arabia mentioned here is Mesopotamian Arabia, reduced by Septimius
Severus in A.D. 197–98.

[29]And yet not a word on the conversion of Abgar VIII to Christianity, especially striking since the fact is mentioned in Bardaiṣan, Eusebius's source, and
comes in the context of Abgar's abolition of the practice of castration after his
conversion (Bardaiṣan, *Laws*, p. 59); it is noteworthy that Bardaiṣan ascribes the
abolition of circumcision not to Abgar but to the Romans (*ibid.*, p. 57).

[30]Τοῦτο γὰρ ἱστόρηται περὶ αὐτῶν (*Praeparatio*, p. 358) follows and sup-
ports the statement on circumcision at the age of thirteen. Eusebius is excerpting
from Origen on Fate, from the latter's *Commentaries on Genesis*, and the datum on
circumcision at the age of thirteen may simply be an echo of Gen. 17:25; on the
other hand, the plural pronoun περὶ αὐτῶν is used in the above-quoted statement
with reference to the Ishmaelites, and this could suggest that it is not an echo of
Gen. 17:25, which refers only to Ishmael. If the latter, the datum becomes valuable
since it could point to the survival of the Ishmaelite tradition of circumcision at
the age of thirteen in post-biblical times, possibly the third century, when Origen,
Eusebius's source, wrote on this subject. Origen's thirteen books of *Commentaries
on Genesis* have not survived; if they had, the question might have been settled.
Sixteen of his homilies on Genesis, however, have survived in Rufinus's Latin
translation, but the two relevant ones, III and VII, do not inform on this question;
for these two homilies, see W. A. Baehrens, *GCS*, 29 (1920), pp. 39–50, 70–77.
On the practice of circumcision among the Arabs at the age of thirteen, Origen
was probably following Josephus; the latter is informative on the circumcision of
Ishmael and speaks in clear terms of the Arab practice of deferring circumcision
until the age of thirteen when their ancestor was circumcised; see *Jewish Antiquities*,
vol. 1, pp. 193, 214. This is valuable for tracing the persistence of the custom
among the Ishmaelites in the first century A.D.

The first four references to the Arabs all come from Bardaiṣan,[31] while the fifth comes from Origen.[32] With the exception of the first, all are uncomplimentary.

(d) Book IX: there are two important references to the Arabs in Book IX, which treats what Greek historians had to say on the Jews:

1) In chapter 19, Eusebius excerpts from Molon[33] on Abraham and his two sons, the first from the Egyptian handmaid and the second from his lawful wife; by the first he begat twelve sons,[34] who went off to Arabia, ruled there, and were indeed the first to rule the Arabs; this circumstance explains the fact that the kings of the Arabians of Molon's[35] day are twelve in number and bear the same names as the first twelve.[36]

The excerpt from Molon is of considerable importance, coming as it does from a writer of the first century B.C. If its data are historical, then the Ishmaelite tradition must have been politically still alive in Arabia after the centuries that had elapsed since the composition of the Book of Genesis—that the political system of the Arabs in the first century B.C. was duodecimal in structure,[37] a continuation of the old Ishmaelite one described in Genesis, and not only structurally, but also onomastically.[38]

2) Much less important is a reference to the Arabs[39] in chapter 23, an extract from Polyhistor[40] on Joseph, which tells of the

[31]*Praeparatio*, p. 334.

[32]*Ibid.*, p. 344.

[33]*Praeparatio*, p. 505; Molon is the surname of Apollonius of Alabanda, who flourished in the first century B.C., for whom, see Gifford, *Praeparationes*, pp. 202–3; the excerpt is from his collection, *Against the Jews*.

[34]More correctly, the twelve were Abraham's grandsons through his firstborn, Ishmael.

[35]χαθ᾽ ἡμᾶς (*Praeparatio*, p. 505, line 13).

[36]For the names of the twelve sons of Ishmael, see Gen. 25:13–15.

[37]It would be exciting indeed if this were a contemporary reflection of the "provinces" of which the "empire" of the Nabataeans is suspected to have been composed; see F. E. Peters, "The Nabataeans in the Hawran," *JAOS*, 97 (1977), p. 263; also *infra*, note 42.

[38]The data provided by Molon are important for tracing the Ishmaelite tradition among the Arabs in pre-Islamic times, a subject which will be treated in a later volume of this series.

[39]*Praeparatio*, p. 516.

[40]The surname of Cornelius Alexander of Miletus, who flourished in the first century B.C. Polyhistor is here quoting Artapanus from the latter's book, *Con-*

neighboring Arabs who took him across to Egypt; furthermore, the kings of the Arabs are sons of Abraham and brothers of Isaac. The extract is, of course, based on the account of Ishmael,[41] his descent and his twelve sons, in Genesis. However, what is important is the first-century Greek historian's identification of the kings of the Arabs with the Ishmaelites of the Bible.[42]

Laudes Constantini. There are two references to the Arabs in the *Laudes Constantini.*[43] Both occur in chapter 13, that is, in the second part of the *Laudes*, the treatise presented to Constantine at the dedication of the Church of the Holy Sepulchre.[44] The first pertains to the Arab worship of two deities, Dusaris and Obodas;[45] the second to human sacrifice—the annual burial of a boy beneath the altar by the Dumateni Arabs.[46]

Both references are uncomplimentary. They come in a chapter that is devoted to exposing the absurdity of pagan religious practices such as setting up mortals as gods and indulging in human

cerning the Jews; for both, see Gifford, *Praeparationes*, pp. 298–99; for Artapanus, see also Emile Schürer, *A History of the Jewish People in the Time of Jesus Christ*, trans. S. Taylor and P. Christie (Edinburgh, 1886), Second Division, vol. 3, pp. 206–8, where it is argued that he was an Egyptian Jewish author, a predecessor of Alexander Polyhistor.

[41]For Ἰσραήλ of *Praeparatio*, p. 516, line 20. Ἰσμαήλ of the *apparatus criticus* may be accepted as the better reading.

[42]An identification also made by the ecclesiastical historians, who often use the terms *Ishmaelite* and *Arab* interchangeably; Eusebius identified Ishmaelite with Saracen in the *Chronicon*; *supra*, p. 95. The data deriving from Molon and Polyhistor, the two Greek historians of the first century B.C., on the Arabs and the biblical background of their history, may also be found in Josephus, more authoritative than both in view of his Jewish background and his intimate knowledge of the Arabs and the Arabian scene; see *Jewish Antiquities*, vol. 1, pp. 220–21; and vol. 2, p. 213. The first reference makes clear that in Josephus's day in the first century A.D. the "empire" of the Nabataeans extended from the Euphrates to the Red Sea, that the whole area was called Nabatene, and that it was duodecimal in structure, as it had been when Molon wrote in the the first century B.C. What Josephus says is important to the problem of the "provinces" of the Nabataean "empire" and its Ishmaelite nature; see *supra*, note 37.

[43]For the text, see I. A. Heikel, *GCS*, 7 (1902), pp. 193–259.

[44]For the *Laudes* and the two parts into which it is divisible, the tricennial oration (chaps. 1–10) and the treatise (chaps. 11–18), see Quasten, *Patrology*, vol. 3, pp. 326–28.

[45]*Laudes*, p. 237; for Dusaris, see T. Fahd, *Le panthéon de l'Arabie centrale à la veille de l'Hégire* (Paris, 1968), pp. 71ff.

[46]*Laudes*, pp. 238–39. The Dumateni are the Arabs of Dūmat al-Jandal in northern Arabia; according to Gen. 25:14, Duma is one of the sons of Ishmael.

sacrifice to appease the gods; the Arabs shared with the nations such practices.[47]

Historia Ecclesiastica. There are references in the *Historia Ecclesiastica*[48] to the Herods of Judaea, Abgar of Edessa, the Provincia Arabia, and Philip the Arab.

(*a*) Herod and his family receive mention several times, but references to only three of them are relevant: (1) Herod the Great (37–4 B.C.), whose name is associated with the Massacre of the Innocents and the manner of whose death is described and interpreted as a punishment for his crime; (2) Herod Antipas (4 B.C. to A.D. 39), who married Herodias and beheaded John the Baptist; (3) Agrippa I (A.D. 37–44), who put to death St. James the Apostle and whose death is also described and interpreted as a punishment for what he had perpetrated.[49]

Thus the name of the Herods is associated with crimes against Jesus himself, against the Precursor, and against one of the Twelve Apostles. Moreover, Eusebius is not silent on the ethnic origin of the founder of the dynasty, Herod the Great, whom he describes as Arab through his mother.[50]

(*b*) Eusebius relates the apocryphal story of the exchange of letters between Christ and Abgar (4 B.C. to A.D. 50) and the mission of Thaddaeus, one of the Seventy, who succeeds in healing Abgar and converting him together with many of the Edessenes.[51]

Eusebius vouches for the truth of the account and speaks of the archives of Edessa[52] but does not refer to the ethnic origin of

[47]Philip the Arab's ethnic background, which associated him with a people such as the one described above, may have been one factor which disinclined Eusebius to state the ethnic origin of Philip or to speak unequivocally on his being the first Christian Roman emperor, as he spoke enthusiastically of Constantine; perhaps it is consonant with this reasoning that he chose to include these uncomplimentary references to the Arabs in a panegyric on Constantine, thus sharpening the contrast between the background of the two.

[48]For the *Historia Ecclesiastica*, see Quasten, *Patrology,* vol. 3, pp. 314–17; the critical edition is by E. Schwartz, in *GCS,* 9: Part I (1903), Part II (1908); Part III (1909) contains the introduction and indexes; this edition will be cited hereafter as *HE*.

[49]For these members of the family, see *HE*, I.viii, x–xi; II.viii–x, respectively.

[50]On the authority of Josephus; Julius Africanus gives him a different descent; see *HE*, I.vi.2–3.

[51]*Ibid.*, I.xiii.

[52]*Ibid.*, I.xiii.5; on the exchange of letters, see Altaner, *Patrology,* pp. 77–78.

Abgar, who was an Arab.[53] It is also strange that he does not make any mention of the conversion of Abgar VIII (179–218), which is beyond doubt and closer to his times.[54]

(c) The Provincia Arabia and its Arabs are referred to in three chapters of Book VI: (1) the error of Beryllos, bishop of Bostra,[55] and his restoration to doctrinal orthodoxy by Origen is described in chapter xxxiii; (2) the heretical views of a group in Arabia[56] concerning the soul, also corrected by Origen, are discussed in chapter xxxvii; (3) the heresy of Helkesaites[57] is described in chapter xxxviii.

The chances that these provincials involved in the theological controversies of the third century were Arabs are good. If so, then the Arabs are presented in the *HE* in a new, unfavorable light, that of heretics, a conception of them that was to find fuller expression in the work of later ecclesiastical historians.[58]

(d) It is in the midst of his discussion of these heresies in the Provincia that Eusebius gives his account of Philip the Arab in chapters xxxiv, xxxvi, and xxxix of Book VI.

Philip's Christianity and Eusebius's account of it have been treated separately.[59] Suffice it to say here that the subdued tone with which Eusebius wrote this account did not materially improve the image of the Arabs and Arab rulers in the ecclesiastical history of the first three Christian centuries, nor did the fact that he either

---

[53]Eusebius may not have been aware that the Abgarids of Edessa were Arab.

[54]Especially as he quotes extensively from Bardaiṣan, who mentions the conversion of Abgar VIII explicitly in his *Laws* (p. 58, lines 21–22), and as he based his *HE* on the work of Julius Africanus, who visited Abgar's court. The omission is due to the fact that Eusebius had accepted the account of the conversion of Abgar V, ʿUkkāmā, Christ's contemporary, and thus must have considered the conversion of Abgar VIII non-significant in the history of a city that had been Christian for two centuries since apostolic times; alternatively, he may have been motivated by a desire to present Constantine as the first ruler in history to adopt Christianity. On the Abgarids, their Arab names and conversion to Christianity, see *RE*, 1, 1 (1893), cols. 93–96, *s.v.* Abgar and 5, 2 (1905), cols. 1933–38, *s.v.* Edessa.

[55]On Beryllos, see the notes of G. Bardy in the edition of the *HE* in *SC*, 41 (Paris, 1955), pp. 135–36.

[56]In the table of contents, Eusebius speaks in the heading of chap. xxxvii of "the dissension of the Arabs"; on this group, see *ibid.*, p. 139.

[57]On this heresy, see *ibid.*, p. 140.

[58]E.g., Epiphanius; on the image of the Arabs as heretics, see the discussion in *BAFOC*.

[59]See *supra*, pp. 68–82.

forgot or cared not to inform the reader on Philip's ethnic origin, a striking omission, especially as the epithet "the Arab" often follows the name of Philip.

II

Eusebius is the first Christian writer out of whose work there emerges a coherent and significant Christian view of the Arabs. The foregoing pages have analyzed the various references to the Arabs in four of his works and the results of that analysis may now be put together and related to the standpoints from which these works were written.

A

Chronicon. Of the six references to the Arabs in this work, analyzed above,[60] those that matter are (*a*) and (*b*) on Ishmael and Herod because the Arab character of both is explicitly stated. The rest could have neutralized the uncomplimentary image created by (*a*) and (*b*) since (*c*) and (*f*) present the Arabs not as nomads but as sedentaries, while (*d*) and (*e*) present two Arab rulers as "firsts," namely, Abgar VIII, the first Christian ruler of any state in the Near East, and Philip, the first Christian Roman emperor; however, these references fail to correct the impression created by (*a*) and (*b*) since the referents are presented without their ethnic affiliation. Hence the reader is left with only the impression created by the two entries on Ishmael[61] and Herod.

Eusebius derives from the Old Testament the view that the Ishmaelites are descended from Hagar, the handmaid, and thus are outcasts, outside the promises. To the classical writers, the same people—the Ishmaelites—are known by the name Saracens, and Eusebius does not hesitate to identify the one with the other.[62] Thus the Saracens of the secular writers become regularly identified with the Ishmaelites of the Old Testament, and with the identification of the two terms, *Ishmaelites* and *Saracens*, the two pejorative

---

[60]See *supra*, pp. 95–97.

[61]Only Ishmael is treated in this section; for Herod, see *infra*, p. 107.

[62]The identification may go back not only to Josephus but also to pagan authors who had written on the Jews and the Arabs, e.g., Alexander Polyhistor, for whom, see *supra*, p. 100. Thus all these terms—Arabs, Saracens, Ishmaelites, and Hagarenes—came to be used interchangeably.

connotations of the terms, outcasts and *latrones* respectively, fortify each other and form the basis of the image of the Arabs in ecclesiastical history.[63]

Thus the Arabs do not come off well in the stream of world history presented in the *Chronicon*. That work was written with the aim of showing the antiquity of the Jewish religion, of which the Christian religion was the legitimate continuation. The point of view from which the *Chronicon* was written might have improved the Arab image or even presented the Arabs in a favorable light, especially as Eusebius departed from his model Julius Africanus by his refusal to begin with Adam or the Fall, and began with what seemed to him to be chronologically certain, namely, the events of the time of Abraham. And yet the Arabs as Ishmaelites, who were the sons of Abraham from his firstborn, did not benefit from the new framework within which Eusebius cast his *Chronicon* since, unlike the sons of Abraham through Isaac, they were outside the promises and thus their antiquity and descent from the first patriarch availed them not.

Praeparatio Evangelica. Unlike references in the *Chronicon*, those in the *Praeparatio* are not to individual Arab historical figures but to the Arabs in general. These references project an unattractive[64] image of the Arabs as a people: they appear as pagans and polytheists who indulge in the repulsive practice of human sacrifice

---

[63]The pejorative connotation already attaching to the secular term *Saracens* (barbarians, nomads, robbers) experienced further deterioration with the new biblical etymology given to the term and involving Sarah, from whom the Arabs are said to have falsely claimed descent in order to hide the opprobrium of their origin from Hagar, the handmaid; for this etymology, see Jerome's commentary on Ezekiel, *Corpus Christianorum*, Series Latina, 75, p. 335, and Sozomen, *Historia Ecclesiastica*, ed. J. Bidez, *GCS*, 50 (Berlin, 1960), Book VI, chap. 38, p. 299. False as the etymology is, it is important as a reflection of the new image of the Arabs formed under the influence of theology such as developed in the *Praeparatio*. This etymology does not appear in any of the extant works of Eusebius, but it may well have done so in his lost work, "Interpretation of the Ethnological Terms in the Hebrew Scriptures." This was known to Jerome, who refers to it in the preface of his Latin version as follows: ". . . *diversarum vocabula nationum, quae quomodo olim apud Hebraeos dicta sint, et nunc dicantur, exposuit.*" For another etymology of *Saracens* involving Sarah, see John of Damascus, *De Haeresibus Compendium*, *PG*, 94, col. 764A; this one dissociates them from Sarah.

[64]For these uncomplimentary references and their analysis, including the one or two exceptions, see *supra*, pp. 98–101.

in order to propitiate their evil demons;[65] they are also barbarians in their habits and customs, and the higher forms of civilized life are unknown to them.

Although this picture of the Arabs is not unfamiliar to pagan classical historians, it takes on a special significance in the *Praeparatio* because it is a theological work. Written by Eusebius as an apologist, it was composed with the view of refuting paganism and of demonstrating the superiority of Judaism. The Arabs who as a people share with the Jews an antiquity going back to Abraham fare as badly in the *Praeparatio* as they do in the *Chronicon*, since their association with Abraham is vitiated by the fact that they were Ishmaelites and Hagarenes, that is, outside the Covenant, and thus do not partake of the very religion, Judaism, that the *Praeparatio* extols at the expense of polytheism. In addition to being outside the Covenant from the beginning, they have since Abrahamic times[66] adopted all the habits, customs, and religious practices of the heathens, and consequently they are included in the arguments of the *Praeparatio* directed against these. Thus in the thought of the *Praeparatio*, developed against polytheism and in defense of Judaism, the Arabs are allied to the former and have, in spite of their Abrahamic descent, no share in the latter. This view of the Arabs was further clinched by the new etymology which was given to the term that came to designate the Arabs in the fourth century, namely, *Saracen*.[67] The new etymology reflected the theological view of the Arabs as conceived by Christian writers, who had given them a very humble niche in the complex of the Divine Dispensation.[68]

---

[65]The references to the Arabs in the *Laudes Constantini* are to their pagan religion and practices; see *supra*, p. 101. Hence they do not merit a separate treatment in this context but are referred to in this section on the *Praeparatio*.

[66]The reference to the Dumateni in the *Laudes Constantini* is valuable in that it is not a general term for the Arabs but a specific one which, moreover, relates that particular Arab group to Abraham through one of his grandsons, Duma; see *supra*, note 46.

[67]See *supra*, note 63.

[68]Whether Eusebius said anything on the Arabs in the second part of his apologetic work, the *Demonstratio Evangelica*, of which only half has survived, is not clear; it is unlikely that he did, because if he had, it would have been in the first two books, which, among other things, deal with the Christian rejection of the Mosaic legislation and with the calling of the Gentiles; but there is nothing on the sons of Ishmael in these two books; for the *Demonstratio Evangelica*, see Quasten, *Patrology*, vol. 3, pp. 331–32.

Historia Ecclesiastica. There are four main groups of references to the Arabs in the *HE* pertaining to (*a*) the Herods of Judaea, (*b*) Abgar of Edessa, (*c*) the Provincia Arabia, and (*d*) Philip the Arab.[69] Three of these groups of references are to Arab rulers, while the fourth is to the provincials of Arabia; of the three groups of references to the rulers, only the one pertaining to the Herods speaks explicitly of their Arab or half-Arab origin, while the other references, the ones on Abgar and Philip, are silent on their ethnic affiliation.

Set against the apologetic aim of the work—the victory of the Church guided by God in three centuries over the pagan state—and within the framework of the various themes that constitute the *HE*,[70] the image of the Arabs that it reflects is not a bright one and may be summarized as follows:

(*a*) The importance of the ruler, whether king of a Near Eastern state or emperor of the Romans, cannot be overestimated in a period when the fortunes of Christianity (and, in the period of the persecutions, its very survival) were affected by the attitude of the ruler. Eusebius is silent on the Arab origin of Abgar V and altogether on Abgar VIII, and thus he obscures the Arab contribution to the fortunes of Christian Edessa. He is also silent on the ethnic origin of the first Christian Roman emperor, Philip, who at least gave the Church a respite of five years and, if he had lived longer, might have served the cause of Christianity in a much more substantial way. But he is not silent on the Arab origin of Herod the Great, and thus the Arab image is tarnished by his account of three members of that family: Herod the Great, the would-be *theoktonos* who purposed to kill Jesus himself but who succeeded only in murdering the Innocents; his son and his grandson, Antipas I and Agrippa, who killed the Precursor and one of the Twelve respectively.

(*b*) One of the major themes of the *HE* is heresy and heretics and Eusebius expressed himself strongly on the matter.[71] After the last explicit mention of the Arabs (the Herods) in the *HE*, the first such references occur in Book IV connected with the heresies that

---

[69]For these references, see *supra*, pp. 102–4.

[70]See the introduction to *HE*, Book I, I; also Quasten, *Patrology*, vol. 3, pp. 314–15.

[71]On heretics and heresiarchs as wolves who ravaged the flock of Christ, see *HE*, I, I.1.

sprung up in the Provincia Arabia. Thus long after the ignominious reigns of the Herods, the Arabs adopt Christianity in the third century, but when they do it is as heretics who introduce into the body of the Church false doctrines. Thus to their image as Herods—anti-Christian rulers in the first century—there is now added that of the heretics and heresiarchs in the third, and it is these two facets of their image—Herods and heresiarchs—that the *HE* succeeds in transmitting.

B

Eusebius had no direct knowledge of or contact with the Arabs,[72] since Caesarea in Palestina Prima was the place of his training, his literary activity, his episcopal see, and apparently his birth as well. His knowledge of the Arabs must have been almost exclusively bookish, deriving from authors who may be divided into two classes: (*a*) Graeco-Roman writers who projected a well-known image of the Arabs as *latrones*, raiders of the Roman *limes*, and as nomads and tent-dwellers (*scenitae*), the barbarian Saracens, addicted to unattractive social and religious practices such as human sacrifice; (*b*) biblical authors of Genesis and the Gospels, who conceived of the Arabs as uncovenanted Ishmaelites in Old Testament times and as Herods in the world of the New Testament. The two images from these two different sets of sources were fused even before the time of Eusebius with the identification of the Ishmaelites of the Bible with the Saracens of the Graeco-Roman writers,[73] but he took over the fused image and presented a comprehensive view of various aspects of it in three of his major works: in the annals of the *Chronicon*, in the theology of the *Praeparatio Evangelica*, and in the stream of Christian history in the *Historia Ecclesiastica*.

---

[72]If he encountered any Arabs at all, these must have been "Saracens" whom he might have met in the Thebaid in Egypt after his flight thither from Tyre; for him, these Arabs were barbarians, such as the ones he mentioned in *HE*, VI.xlii.4, when he was describing the plight of Christians who had fled during the persecution unleashed by Decius to the Arabian Mountain, where they were enslaved by the Saracens. After reading this chapter, T. D. Barnes suggested in his letter of 27 March 1979 that Eusebius might have visited Arabia.

[73]To these Graeco-Roman writers, Josephus may be added. He has important material on the Arabs both in biblical and post-biblical times, especially the first century A.D. (*supra*, notes 30, 42), and was one of the chief sources of Eusebius's *HE*, although the latter does not explicitly cite him on the Arabs.

In the last work there are some serious omissions. Since New Testament times the Arabs had made important contributions to the cause and progress of Christianity when some of their rulers were converted such as Abgar VIII of Edessa and Philip the Arab; and yet these third-century figures do not appear as Arab in the *HE* and the significance of their Christianity is not dwelt upon. Instead, a new facet of the Arab image—that of heretics—is projected for the third century, and it persists for a long time in the consciousness of later ecclesiastical historians.

Eusebius cannot be accused of prejudice in the account he gave of the Arabs and their place in the history of Christianity. His chapters on heresy in Arabia are objectively written, while his attitude to Philip is understandable in view of the fact that he was a panegyrist of Constantine, whom he was anxious to present as the first Christian emperor and whose reign thus formed the climax of the *HE*. Furthermore, it was unfortunate for the Arabs that Eusebius's literary *floruit* was not in the second but in the first half of the fourth century. If it had been in the former, he would have witnessed the rise of the new Christian Arab, represented by a figure such as Queen Mavia—the Arab ruler Christianized and dedicated to the promotion of the cause of Christianity and, what is more, not heretical in theological persuasion but very orthodox.

Appendix

The references to Abgar VIII, the Great, in Eusebius call for a short discussion of his conversion to Christianity, to which most writers on the subject subscribe, but which the most recent calls into question.[1]

1. The case for the conversion of Abgar the Great has been well stated by E. Kirsten in his article on Edessa,[2] in which he gives a succinct critical appraisal of all the relevant sources, including the *Liber Pontificalis*. However, since Eusebius left his conversion only implied, it is necessary to make a few observations on Eusebius's omission, which has been seized upon by those who have rejected the account of the conversion

[1] See H. J. W. Drijvers, *Cults and Beliefs at Edessa* (Leiden, 1980), p. 14.
[2] See *RAC,* 4, col. 570; before him, vouched for by B. Kötting, *ibid.*, 2, col. 1142; and after him by G. M. Sanders, *ibid.*, 8, col. 1029.

of Abgar the Great, and to restate and put together the various observations on the problem scattered in the body of this chapter.[3]

(*a*) Eusebius enthusiastically accepted the Abgar-legend, the conversion of the ruler of Edessa in the first century A.D., Abgar ʿUkkāmā, and his correspondence with Jesus, to which he devotes an entire chapter in his *HE*.[4] Consequently, he must have assumed that the Abgarids had already been converted and that Edessa had been a Christian city and continued to be so ca. A.D. 200 when Abgar the Great was converted. Thus Eusebius had no choice but to remember Abgar the Great's Christianity only in passing and, what is more, refer to it on the authority of Julius Africanus. In so doing, he repeated what he did when he wrote his section on Philip the Arab in *HE*, VI.xxxxiv; he did not give Philip's Christianity the prominence that it deserved because he wanted to reserve his superlatives for Constantine.[5]

(*b*) The testimony of Julius Africanus is decisive as a primary source and an eyewitness who visited Edessa and spent some time at the court of Abgar. In writing his *Chronicles*, he may have "lacked the critical attitude towards his sources," and in writing his *Kestoi* he may also have been "uncritical in his studies," but on such a matter as the religious persuasion and conversion of the ruler whom he knew and at whose court he resided there can be no question of the decisiveness of his witness.[6]

(*c*) His testimony makes certain that the well-known, explicit, simple, and unadorned statement on Abgar's conversion in Bardaiṣan's *Book of the Laws of Countries* is authentic. And surely Abgar's abolition of the practice of emasculation in honor of Tarʿata (Atargatis), the Dea Syra, is a significant detail which should corroborate the statement on Abgar's conversion since it could easily point to Christianity as the inspiration behind such legislation; and the same could be said of his abolition of another practice, namely, circumcision.[7] These details coming from another contemporary, Bardaiṣan, confirm Julius Africanus and make certain that the conversion of Abgar VIII was a historical fact.

[3] See *supra*, p. 96.
[4] *HE*, I.xiii.
[5] See the chapter on Philip, *supra*, pp. 65–93.
[6] On Julius Africanus, see Quasten, *Patrology*, vol. 2, pp. 137–40.
[7] On this well-known passage in Bardaiṣan, involving Abgar's conversion and his abolition of castration, see Drijvers in Bardaiṣan, *Laws*, p. 58. On the problem of whether it was the Romans (as in Bardaiṣan) or Abgar (as in Eusebius's version of Bardaiṣan's work) that abolished circumcision, see *supra*, note 29. Perhaps the two collaborated, and the abolition was accomplished by one party with the approval of the other, but for two different reasons. On Eusebius and Bardaiṣan's work, see Drijvers in Bardaiṣan, *Laws*, pp. 61–62 and 68–70; on castration in the judgment of Christians, see G. M. Sanders, "Gallos," *RAC*, 8, cols. 1028–31, especially col. 1029 on Christian Abgar and his abolition of

2. The question arises why this conversion, so well attested, has been viewed with suspicion by some scholars. The answer lies in the rise of the Abgar-legend, with its patently fictitious account of Abgar's correspondence with Jesus, described in the *HE* by Eusebius and in the *Doctrina Addaei*. But the two conversions must be separated from each other, the authentic one of Abgar the Great, the case for which rests on unassailable contemporary sources, and the fictitious one of Abgar ʿUkkāmā, which rests on such a legendary account as that of the *Doctrina Addaei*.[8] The further question of how the Abgar-legend arose must surely be related to the conversion of his namesake around A.D. 200, and the search for apostolicity furnishes the key. The Church of Edessa, like many other Christian Churches, tried to antedate its inception to apostolic times; hence the Abgar-legend, the popularity of which even with the Father of Church History has operated to the disadvantage of the authentic and contemporary accounts that told of the historical conversion of Abgar the Great[9] around A.D. 200.

---

castration. Drijvers does not deny that Abgar introduced a law for the abolition of emasculation, but he rejects the view that it was due to his conversion to Christianity. However, he does not give an alternative explanation for the introduction of the law, and Abgar's Christianity remains the most convincing explanation; see his *Cults and Beliefs*, p. 77; see also *infra*, note 9. For more literature on Abgar's conversion involving Eusebius, Julius Africanus, and Bardaiṣan, see Kirsten, *RAC*, 4, col. 570.

[8]As was done by J. B. Segal in "Pagan Syrian Monuments in the Vilayet of Urfa," *Anatolian Studies*, 3 (1953), p. 118; but later the same author became sceptical of Abgar the Great's Christianity; see his *Edessa*, pp. 70–71, where no cogent reasons are given for his scepticism.

[9]As happened with Drijvers in an otherwise valuable book; see his *Cults and Beliefs*, pp. 14, 77. Nowhere does he give a reasoned argument for his rejection of the conversion of Abgar VIII around A.D. 200. Neither Nau in his *Praefatio* nor Nöldeke in his *Annotationes*, his distinguished predecessors in the study of Bardaiṣan and his book, suspected that the account of the conversion is unauthentic; see their *Liber Legum Regionum, Patrologia Syriaca*, 2 (1907), pp. 492–535, 606. He himself did not suspect it in his own doctoral dissertation—his edition of *The Book of the Laws of Countries*, which appeared in 1965—and in his study, *Bardaisan of Edessa*, which appeared in 1966. In the latter work, he states that "in how far the BLC had a history, received additions for instance, we cannot tell" (p. 75). However, in *Cults and Beliefs*, p. 77, he speaks of "a (later?) revision of Bardaisan's dialogue on Fate," but without elaboration, while his two articles (cited on p. 77 note 4) do not offer much support for this view. Perhaps he has been unduly influenced by the theme of his book, which deals with *pagan* Edessa. Drijvers's *Cults and Beliefs*, however, is important to the concerns of this book since he recognizes the strong Arab factor in Edessa's life, especially the share of the Arab gods in the making of Edessa's pagan pantheon, and so is his other work, *The Religion of Palmyra* (Leiden, 1976), which also has an up-to-date select bibliography on that other Arab city of this Roman period—Palmyra.

Edessa thus remains the first Christian kingdom[10] in the world, the inception of which may be dated around A.D. 200 when the conversion of the royal house made Christianity the state religion, long before Christianity assumed that status in Armenia, in Ethiopia, or in Byzantium itself.[11] Even before their conversion, the Abgarids had made a contribution to the fortunes of early Christianity. They had ruled their city tolerantly for some three centuries and in so doing enabled Edessa to emerge as a major Christian center in the second century,[12] in much the same way that the Lakhmids of Ḥīra, the other Arab foundation on the Lower Euphrates, were to enable that city to become the major center of Arab Christianity in the three centuries before the rise of Islam.[13]

[10]On Adiabene, which lay outside the *imperium romanum* in Arsacid Parthia, and its "Christianity," see Harnack, *Mission and Expansion of Christianity*, vol. 1, p. 1 note 1.

[11]On Edessa, see the old work of R. Duval, *Histoire politique, religieuse et littéraire d'Édesse jusqu' à la première croisade* (Paris, 1892), and most recently, Segal, *Edessa, 'The Blessed City'*. These two works, especially the latter with its comprehensive bibliography, should be an adequate guide to all aspects of Edessa's life and history touched upon in this book.

[12]The two literary monuments of that century are the Peshitta, the Syriac version of the Bible, and that early recension of the text of the Gospel, called the Diatessaron of Tatian, which most scholars associate with Edessa of the second century. Both works, however, are the subject of controversy; see Segal's *Edessa*, index, *s.vv.*

[13]For Ḥīra, see "Cultural Contacts," *supra*, pp. 47–48. Edessa of the Arab Abgarids moved first in an Aramaic then in a Syriac cultural ambience and with the fall of the dynasty moved even further from the Arab orbit and became associated, even identified, with Syriac Christianity. Ḥīra, on the other hand, was an Arab foundation very close to the Arabian Peninsula, where Arabic had no serious rivals, all of which enabled it to emerge as the main center of Arab Christianity in pre-Islamic times. On the Abgarid-Lakhmid filiation, see U. Monneret de Villard, "Il Tāğ di Imru' l-Qais," *Atti della Accademia Nazionale dei Lincei, Rendiconti,* Classe di scienze morali, storiche e filologiche, 8 (1954), p. 228, and the earlier work of W. Seston, *Dioclétian et la tétrarchie* (Paris, 1946), vol. I, pp. 152, 156; for the important role of the Arabs in the propagation of Manichaeism in the Roman Empire, see *ibid.*, pp. 148–66.

VIII

Zosimus and the Arabs

The Arabs figure in the work of a later pagan historian, Zosimus,[1] who like Ammianus was also an analyst of Roman decline. The occasions on which he mentions them are all memorable in Roman history, two during the imperial crisis of the third century, involving Philip the Arab and the Palmyra of Odenathus and Zenobia, and a third in the Gothic War of Valens's reign.[2] These accounts of the Arabs in the *Historia Nova* supply important historical data and are valuable both for the image of the Arabs and for illustrating Zosimus's view of the process of Roman decline.

I

Philip does not fare well with Zosimus, and his unfavorable judgment is generally that of most Roman historians.[3] What is

---

[1]The standard edition is that of L. Mendelssohn, *Historia Nova*, Bibliotheca Teubneriana (Leipzig, 1887). On Zosimus, see M. E. Colonna, *Gli storici bizantini* (Naples, 1956), vol. 1, pp. 142–44; G. Moravcsik, *Byzantinoturcica* (Berlin, 1958), vol. 1, pp. 577–79. See also W. Kaegi, "Zosimus and the Climax of Pagan Historical Apologetics," in *Byzantium and the Decline of Rome* (Princeton, 1968), pp. 99–145; W. Goffart, "Zosimus, the First Historian of Rome's Fall," *American Historical Review*, 76 (1971), pp. 412–41.

[2]There are two other passing references to the Arabs: (1) as Scenitae, in connection with Severus's campaign against Arabia after his capture of Ctesiphon, I.8 (Arabia here can be only Arabia in Mesopotamia); and (2) as Saraceni who fight the Persians during Julian's Persian campaign, III.27. On the sources of Zosimus, see the chapter in F. Paschoud's introduction to his *Zosime: Histoire Nouvelle*, Budé (Paris, 1971), pp. XXXIV–LXIII. Dexippus is most probably his source for Philip the Arab and Eunapius for Zenobia and Mavia.

[3]Philip lasted in the purple longer than many of the emperors of the imperial crisis. With the exception of his involvement in the conspiracy that brought about the death of Gordian, his career does not seem to call for such adverse judgments as have been passed on him; see the chapter on Philip, *supra*, pp. 65–93.

relevant in this connection is to note that Zosimus's account[4] of the reign of Philip (I. 18–22) is surprisingly detailed, out of all proportion to its importance. This is significant and suggests that the account is written not so much to record the facts of the reign as to use the facts as illustration of the point of view that Zosimus was presenting to the reader on the process of Roman decline. The account calls for the following observations.

1. Zosimus's strong views on the barbarization of the empire and the imperial government must be the first explanation for his intense dislike of Philip, whose condemnation is expressed in superlative terms which unmistakably carry strong racial overtones.[5] For Zosimus, the elevation of Philip to the purple must have represented barbarization at the highest level conceivable, especially as Philip had been preceded by a Roman, Gordian, whose downfall he had brought about, and followed by Decius, who is described in strong, approving terms which sharply contrast with those that describe Philip.

Even so, Zosimus's intense hostility towards Philip is not fully explicable in this way.[6] Philip's complicity in the overthrow of Gordian does not seem sufficient ground in a century that witnessed so much bloodshed, violence, and intrigues, nor does his barbarian origin either. Towards the turn of the century Rome had had a "barbarian" emperor, Septimius Severus, an African born at Leptis in Libya, whose native language was Phoenician, and who was married to a provincial from Emesa, Julia Domna. Some of his "un-Roman" activities could have given offense to one who held such views as Zosimus[7] did, and yet he fares well with him (I.8).

2. Zosimus's hostility towards Philip becomes more explicable when it is remembered that the latter was, in Christian tradition, honored as the first Roman emperor to adopt Christianity[8] before

---

[4]It takes up five sections of Book I, while the reign of Severus, much more important than that of Philip, takes up only one half of a section, I.8.

[5]Philip is described as ὁρμώμενος γὰρ ἐξ ᾿Αραβίας, ἔθνους χειρίστου, I.18. On anti-Semitism in the Roman world, see A. N. Sherwin-White, *Racial Prejudice in Imperial Rome* (Cambridge, 1967), pp. 86–101.

[6]He reverts to Philip when reflecting on the Peace of Jovian, and speaks of Philip's disgraceful peace with the Persians (III.32).

[7]Severus's humiliation of the Senate may be contrasted with Philip's deferential attitude to it as described by Zosimus himself.

[8]There has been no cogent refutation of the Christian tradition that Philip was the first Christian emperor; arguments may be found in E. Stein's article in

Constantine. Zosimus's views on Christianity as a factor in Roman decline are well known, and thus Philip's Christianity would have been a major ground for hostility towards Philip, who presented to Zosimus the spectacle of one who, as both barbarian and Christian, was the then ruler of the Roman world. And yet, there is not a single word in the *Historia Nova* on Philip's Christianity, which must have been known to Zosimus from the Christian tradition that mentioned it.[9] In view of his hostility to both Philip and Christianity, one might think that Zosimus would have hastened to include a denunciation of him as the first Christian emperor.

The key to understanding the suppression of anything about Philip's Christianity must be related to Zosimus's suppression of another important fact about him, namely, his celebration of the Secular Games. It is only when his account of the *Ludi Saeculares* is examined that the relationship between the two omissions can be established and the full implication of the two omissions becomes clear.

Zosimus's account is the most detailed extant account of the *Ludi Saeculares* (II. 1–7). He gives them much prominence and contends that the prosperity of the empire was related to the observance of the old religious rites, in which the *Ludi Saeculares* were central; he mentions the names of the emperors who celebrated these Games since Augustus revived them—Claudius, Domitian, and Severus; and finally he takes Constantine, the Christian emperor, to task for having discontinued the practice, and relates this to the disasters that befell the empire since then. Set against the background of Zosimus's views on the Games, his silence[10] on Philip's Christianity becomes intelligible. Philip was the last emperor to celebrate the Games,[11] which he did as an alternative series,[12] coinciding with his

---

RE, 10, 1, cols. 768–70, but they are unconvincing, as has been shown in the chapter on Philip, *supra*, pp. 65–93.

[9]For Christian authors on Philip's Christianity, see *ibid*.

[10]Which must have been deliberate because of the detailed account of both the reign of Philip and of the *Ludi Saeculares* and the importance he attached to the latter.

[11]The fact did not escape the attention of ecclesiastical writers who noted both Philip's Christianity and the fact that the celebration of the thousandth anniversary of Rome's foundation fell to a Christian emperor; for these ecclesiastical writers, see Stein's article cited *supra*, note 8. To these may be added *Anonymous Valesianus* (Pars Prior), VI.33.

[12]This could not have discouraged Zosimus from mentioning Philip's celebra-

celebration of the one thousandth anniversary of the foundation of Rome.

Thus Zosimus's silence on Philip's Christianity and his celebration of the Games is related to (a) the central thesis of the *Historia Nova* and (b) his attack on Constantine.

(a) Philip's celebration of the Secular Games seemed to invalidate the thesis he was propounding for Roman decline: Philip's Christianity[13] did not prevent him from observing the rites of the old Roman religion so important to Rome's prosperity, while his celebration of the Games contributed nothing to the prosperity of the empire in the period immediately following;[14] in fact, that period was the bloodiest and most anarchical in the whole history of the empire.

(b) Philip's Christianity and his celebration of the Secular Games bore directly on the main object of Zosimus's attack in the *Historia Nova*, the emperor who started the process of barbarization and Christianization—Constantine—and, what is more, the Christian emperor who neglected the celebration of the Games, thus opening a disastrous period in Roman history. But here was a third-century emperor who was both Christian and not neglectful of celebrating the old pagan rite and, furthermore, whose celebration of the Games was not followed by the imperial prosperity alleged to attend such celebrations.[15]

Thus Zosimus's antipathy to Philip is complex; in addition to what has been said on its being induced by Philip's Christian faith and his barbarian origin, it is derivative from that which Zosimus developed towards Constantine.

II

Zosimus's attitude to the Palmyrene Arabs is ambivalent, induced in him by the curious twist in the history of Palmyrene-

---

tion of the Games since he records Claudius's celebration of the Games in the same manner (II.4).

[13]Even if Philip was not Christian, the tradition that he was must have been known to Zosimus.

[14]The argument is independent of whether or not Philip was Christian and, if Christian, whether or not Zosimus was aware of his Christianity.

[15]Zosimus's favorable judgment on Septimius Severus becomes clearer when it is realized that for Zosimus he was the last pagan emperor to celebrate the Secular Games (I.8; II.4).

Roman relations, a drama in two parts successively enacted by Odenathus and Zenobia. He does justice to the former as one who protected Roman interests in the East and saved the *pars orientalis* (I.39), but he is hostile to the latter after she revolted against Rome. It is the Palmyra of Zenobia that he expatiates upon, devoting to it an inordinately long account that takes up twelve sections of Book I (I.44, 50–61). In addition to its being valuable for the data it supplies, this account is as important for the theme "Zosimus and the Arabs" as his account of Philip, perhaps even more so.

1. What he thought of the Palmyrenes[16] is clearly expressed and implied, put in the mouth of the oracle of Apollo at Seleucia in Cilicia (I.57); they are described as "deceitful, baneful men." The second verse in the *responsum* smacks of some racialism, as it speaks of the revolt of the Palmyrenes against the "race of the Gods."

Zenobia herself comes in for blame by implication[17] (I.56); after her capture by Aurelian she denounces her friends, including Longinus, as the instigator of the revolt who had led her astray, the unfavorable implication being that she courted her friends in prosperity but betrayed them in adversity.

2. Important as his account is for Arab history and for Arab-Roman relations because of the data he supplies, it is perhaps even more important to a study of Zosimus himself and the point of view from which he wrote his work.

(*a*) This account is clearly written in order to illustrate the author's thesis on the process of Roman decline; and his views are *explicitly* stated and not only implied as in his account of the reign of Philip: (1) *pronoia* protects the empire because in this period the ancient rites are observed, and the issue of Rome's safety is determined before the battle with the Palmyrenes is joined; (2) the agent

[16]He does not designate them Arabs, whether Saraceni or Scenitae, as he designates the Arabs of Mavia or those whom Severus vanquished. He distinguishes them clearly from the barbaroi in I.44, and he could not have done otherwise, in view of the splendor of the Palmyrene urban establishment and the cultured circle around Zenobia, a member of which he refers to, namely, Longinus (I.55).

[17]Perhaps Zosimus had to contend with the generally favorable impression that Zenobia left on classical writers. It is noteworthy that according to him (I.58) she died on her way to Rome after abstaining from food or being taken ill, while the general consensus is that she died in her villa at Tibur.

of *pronoia* is the good pagan emperor, Aurelian, who builds a temple to Sol in Rome and whose victory is foretold in an oracle; (3) the defeat of the Palmyrenes is foreordained by the gods, who tell the Palmyrenes the outcome beforehand.

(*b*) Striking in this account is its *detailed* nature, as it runs through so many sections of Book I. This raises a further question, namely, his reason for writing what seems at first sight an inordinately long account. But a close examination of the account in its entirety, both the factual and the interpretative features, suggests the following answer. Zosimus clearly realized that the revolt of Palmyra was the climax of the period of the imperial crisis in the third century as it represented the most serious and almost successful attempt at separatism, when the whole of the *pars orientalis* or most of it actually passed from the dominion of Rome to that of Palmyra. The dimensions of the Palmyrene crisis then provided him with material for illustrating in a large way the thesis he wanted to maintain on Roman decline.

(*c*) But the unusual interest of Zosimus in the Palmyrene crisis remains striking even after what has just been said on the function of the account as an illustration of the working of *pronoia* in the third century of the imperial crisis. In this account, Zosimus does not limit himself to reflecting on Roman history in the past of the third century; he goes out of his way to speak in strong terms of the later period when the empire was barbarized and shrunken and of his desire, in due course, to discuss causes and cite oracles. This justifies at least a suggestion that the Palmyrene episode had another function in the structure of his work.

(1) The *Historia Nova* in its extant form ends just before the sack of Rome in 410. In the period that had elapsed between the Palmyrene crisis and Alaric's sack of Rome in 410, much had happened to the empire. The barbarians had won the battle of Adrianople, had secured a favorable settlement with Theodosius in 382, and finally had succeeded in capturing Rome itself. The same period also witnessed the triumph of Christianity; but the simultaneous triumph of the two processes of barbarization and Christianization could not have been fortuitous. In the pre-Christian period of Roman history, the Palmyrene crisis had been weathered by Aurelian because that emperor had observed the rites of the old Roman religion, but in the fourth century these rites were

neglected, and as a consequence the empire of the Romans suffered these grievous losses.

(2) By 410 much had happened to the empire in the way of barbarization, including territorial losses, to justify some comparison with the temporary loss of territory to Palmyra. But towards the end of the fifth century, many more losses had been sustained, nothing less than the fall of the *pars occidentalis* to the barbarians and the establishment of the Germanic kingdoms. This was a much more convincing parallel to the Palmyrene crisis, since the fall of the *pars orientalis* to the Palmyrenes would truly balance the fall of the *pars occidentalis* to the Germans. If Zosimus's *floruit* was not the early but the late one, then the Palmyrene crisis would have functioned in his work as substantiation of his views on the loss of the *pars occidentalis* in the fifth century.[18]

III

After his account of the Arabs in the pre-Christian period in Roman history, the third century, Zosimus includes a last account of them in section 22 of Book IV, in the new world of the fourth century, barbarized and Christianized by Constantine. It pertains to the Arab contribution to the Gothic War of Valens's reign. It is both a valuable and a fair account, written from a strictly technical, military point of view.[19] The Arabs, however, are presented as Saracens, and the historian is completely silent on the queen whose mounted pikemen contributed to the deliverance of Constantinople

[18]Conversely and at the cost of some circularity, his account of the Palmyrene crisis, replete with views on Roman decline, could argue that Zosimus had in mind the fall of the Western Empire in the fifth century and consequently that he did indeed write his work in the late period. The date of the *HN* has been assigned to as early as the reign of Theodosius I and as late as that of Anastasius, for which see Goffart, "Zosimus," pp. 420–23. The generally held view is that he wrote in the second half of the fifth century, and some extend this late period to include the first decade of the sixth in the reign of Anastasius (491–518); see E. Stein, *Histoire du bas empire* (Paris, 1949), vol. 2, pp. 707–8; Moravcsik, *Byzantinoturcica*, vol. 1, p. 577; A. Cameron, "The Date of Zosimus' New History," *Philologus*, 113 (1969), pp. 106–10, with the comments of Goffart, "Zosimus," notes 49, 53.

[19]Unlike Ammianus, who was a contemporary and knew such personalities as Victor, Mavia's son-in-law, Zosimus was distant from these events and personalities, and for this reason wrote a more objective account than his fellow pagan, an illustration of how contemporary history is not necessarily better than noncontemporary. On Mavia and her contribution to the Gothic War, see chap. 4 on the reign of Valens in *BAFOC*.

from the Goths. Her Arabs are isolated from the various affiliations
to which they belonged and are presented anonymously.

It is possible that Zosimus was unaware of the relation of these
Saracens to Queen Mavia; but this is unlikely for the following
reasons: (*a*) He was writing in Constantinople itself, the scene of
the Arab exploit, which took place not in the distant past but in
the preceding century; recollection of the Arabs must have remained
alive in the city that owed its deliverance partly to them; furthermore, the Arabs are associated with one of the major battles of late
Roman history, the disaster of Adrianople, and consequently details
of the aftermath, including Arab participation, must have been
known to him. (*b*) He devoted many chapters to the fortunes
of another Arab queen, Zenobia, whose career affords an obvious
parallel to that of Mavia, even to the extent that the armies of both
queens reached the same waterway that divides Europe from Asia—
Zenobia's reached the Hellespont, while Mavia's even crossed the
Bosphorus into Byzantium itself. The parallel is too striking not
to have been noticed by Zosimus, and consequently the omission of
any reference to Mavia is likely to have been deliberate. (*c*) Zosimus
lived not long after the composition of the ecclesiastical histories
of Socrates and Sozomen and, what is more, in the very same city
in which these lived, worked, and wrote—in Constantinople itself.
The works of these historians must have been known to him, especially as his was a counterblast to those of the Christian apologists
on the decline of Rome.[20] If he read Socrates and Sozomen, he must
have known that the Saracen troops he wrote about were those sent
by Mavia, as clearly stated by these two historians.

It is not to be expected that Zosimus would write an extensive
account of Mavia in his work; the case of Zenobia, however, proves
that if he had wanted, he could have written something that identified these Saracens whose exploits he described. But the new
Zenobia was both Christian and barbarian and, what is more, loyal
to Rome for which she fought; this he understandably avoided
recounting. The case of Mavia would have illustrated for the reader
the new look of Arab queens, drawn to an empire by the new bond
of Christianity, and would thus have invalidated the thesis that
Zosimus was maintaining for the post-Constantinian period in

---

[20]On these ecclesiastical writers in this context, see Kaegi, *Byzantium and the
Decline of Rome,* and also his chapter on Zosimus, pp. 99–145.

Roman history, namely, the setting in of the decline through barbarization and Christianization. The sharp contrast between the careers of the two Arab queens—the first belonging to the world of the third century, pagan and disloyal to Rome, the second, belonging to the new world of the fourth century, Christian and loyal— would have been attributed only to the success of the Constantinian experiment. It invalidated his thesis, and he suppressed the relevant facts[21] as he had suppressed certain facts about Philip the Arab and for much the same reasons.

IV

For Zosimus, the reign of Constantine is the watershed in the periodization of Roman history, which thus may be divided into pre-Constantinian and post-Constantinian. Rome, pagan Rome, fared well before Constantine,[22] and *pronoia* enabled it to weather all the storms. After him, the process of decline set in as the old gods were abandoned, and whatever good fortune the Romans continued to enjoy, e.g., the prosperity of Constantinople, was due to some form of persisting *pronoia*.[23]

An examination of the sections in the *Historia Nova* in which the Arabs appear or are made to appear reveals that the choice of rejection of data pertaining to them was governed by the degree to which these data contribute towards validating or invalidating Zosimus's thesis on the process of Roman decline. Two major episodes in which the Arabs are involved, the principate of Philip and the revolt of Palmyra, belong to the pre-Constantinian period, while the third and last major one took place in the post-Constan-

[21]It is noteworthy that he does not call them Arabs but Saracens, whom his predecessor Ammianus had identified with the Scenitae, and this would have separated, in the mind of the reader, Mavia's Arabs from those of Zenobia, whom he always refers to as Palmyrenes.

[22]For Zosimus as the last representative of a line of thought hostile to Constantine and which began with Julian, see J. Vogt, "Kaiser Julian über seinen Oheim Konstantin den Grossen," *Historia,* 4 (1955), pp. 351–52.

[23]On the oracle that Zosimus dug out in order to explain the prosperity of Constantinople in pagan terms, see *HN*, II.36–37. His view that Constantinople is watched over by Athena and other guardian deities (V.24) may be a counterblast to a Christian view which might have arisen in the fourth century, and which Ammianus already may have expressed by the introduction of a pagan *numen* to explain the deliverance of Constantinople from the Goths, for which, see *Res Gestae*, XXXI.16.4, and the discussion in "Ammianus and the *Foederati*" in *BAFOC*, chap. 7, sec. II.

tinian period, and all of them illustrate the principle of choice or rejection.[24]

In his conception of Roman history, Zosimus brings to mind his fellow pagan Ammianus, and so does he, also, in the way he presented the Arabs in his work. The early books of the *Res Gestae*, including the pre-Constantinian ones, are lost and with them Ammianus's account of the Arabs during periods such as the principate of Philip and the revolt of Palmyra. What he said about them, if he said anything, could only be *inferred*, but the explicit statements of Zosimus could help in the process of reconstructing Ammianus's account of the reign of Constantine which has not survived. Also, he did not include an account of the reign of Theodosius in the *Res Gestae*, which stops just before the latter's accession. What he thought of both emperors is a matter of inference, but Zosimus's accounts of both Constantine and Theodosius have survived, and they are couched in strong denunciatory tones of the two emperors of the fourth century.[25]

It is possible to conclude that the two pagan writers held similar or almost similar views on Roman history and that their two works are mutually illuminating. But Zosimus was in a better position to write on Roman decline because he lived later than Ammianus and could support his thesis by appeal to the extraordinary events that took place in the fifth century in the western part of the empire. Ammianus, on the other hand, had lived in a period when the case against the two agents of decline, namely, Constantine and Theodosius, was not so clear: Theodosius had contained the thrust of the Goths by the Settlement of 382 and had put the house of the *ecclesia* in order at the Council of Constantinople the year before. Besides, Zosimus was temperamentally different from Ammianus, less inhibited and more outspoken. It is possible that had Ammianus lived later than he did and been temperamentally otherwise than he was, he would have expressed himself on the process of Roman decline in similar or identical terms.

[24]On the *HN* as *histoire raisonnée*, see J. F. Reitmeier, in Goffart, "Zosimus," p. 414.

[25]For Zosimus on these two emperors, see F. Paschoud, *Cinq études sur Zosime*, Collection d'études anciennes Budé (Paris, 1975), which also has more on the sources of Zosimus (*supra*, note 2).

IX

The Term *Saraceni*
and the Image of the Arabs

The Arabs were referred to in the Graeco-Roman sources by many terms—*Arabes, Saracenoi/Saraceni, Ismaelitae,* and *Hagarenoi/Hagareni*. The second of these terms, *Saraceni,* acquired in these sources a wide vogue in pre-Islamic and Islamic times both in the Greek East and the Latin West throughout the Middle Ages. Of these four terms, it is *Saraceni* that has presented a problem to the etymologist, as it still does, a problem complicated by the semantics of the term and its development from being the equivalent of *Scenitae,* "Tent-dwellers," to a much wider denotation coterminous with the most generic of all the four terms, namely, *Arabes*. Furthermore, the two problems, the etymological and the semantic, entangled with each other, are related to the more important problem of the image of the Arabs in ancient and medieval times. The etymology of the term *Saraceni* is therefore of more than purely linguistic interest and deserves a close and detailed examination.

I

Various etymologies have been suggested for the term *Saraceni* by Orientalists[1] in the nineteenth and twentieth centuries, but not

---

[1]The fruits of this Orientalist scholarship are succinctly and conveniently presented in two short articles by B. Moritz and J. H. Mordtmann. The first appeared in 1920, for which, see *RE*, Zweite Reihe, I.A, cols. 2387–90, *s.v.* Saraka; the second in 1934, for which see *EI*, 4, pp. 155–56, *s.v.* Saracens. The two articles have certainly not outlived their usefulness and are still important contributions to this problem both in respect to the relevant data assembled in them for the discussion of it and to the arguments that have been put forward for and against the various etymologies suggested; they will be cited hereafter as Moritz, "Saraka," and Mordtmann, "Saracens."

one of them has been universally accepted and only varying degrees of probability have attached to the various suggested etymons. Since the forties,[2] no new ones had been proposed until the appearance in 1977 of "The Origin of the Term Saracen and the Rawwāfa Inscriptions,"[3] a substantial article in which the two authors, after a detailed discussion of all the previous etymologies, not only suggest a new etymon but also present a new approach to the solution of the problem. Thus their contribution is methodological as well as substantive. In view of the importance of their article, the discussion of *Saraceni* in this section will, therefore, first review the previous etymologies and then devote a special section to the examination of the new one.

A. The Old Etymologies

These etymologies may be divided, following Graf and O'Connor, into linguistic, ethnic, and geographical ones;[4] as to the patristic etymology, it may be left out for the time being.[5] Since these old etymologies have often been discussed and have lately been reexamined by Graf and O'Connor, there is no need to restate the old arguments; only a few new observations by the present writer will be included to supplement the old ones[6] or to revive those that have been erroneously deemed invalid and relegated to obscurity.

[2]Which witnessed the appearance of C. C. Murphy's "Who Were the Saracens?" in *The Asiatic Review*, 41 (1945), 188–90.

[3]See David F. Graf and M. O'Connor, "The Origin of the Term Saracen and the Rawwāfa Inscriptions," *Byzantine Studies,* 4 (1977), pp. 52–66 (hereafter cited as *OTS*). The article has such a comprehensive bibliography on the term *Saracen* that it is superfluous to burden the pages of this book by duplicating it. Only a few important bibliographical items will be cited in these notes, while for the rest the reader is referred to the footnotes of *OTS*. In the following year, Graf published "The Saracens and the Defense of the Arabian Frontier," in *Bulletin of the American School of Oriental Research*, 229 (1978), pp. 1–26 (hereafter, *SDAF*). In addition to the reprise of the etymological theme of the term *Saracens* on pp. 14–15, Graf devotes pp. 9–10 to the Ruwwāfa inscriptions, the texts of which are given, and treats other topics, all of which are related to the etymology of *Saracens*.

[4]*OTS*, pp. 61–64.

[5]For a brief treatment, see *supra*, p. 105 note 63. The patristic etymology is treated more extensively in *BAFOC* as will the Arab biblical image be in *BAFIC*.

[6]For these, see Moritz, "Saraka," and Mordtmann, "Saracens."

1. The first etymon is *sharq/sharqī/sharqiyyīn*, meaning "east/easterner/easterners."

The derivation from *sharq/sharqiyyīn* does not sound so implausible when it is remembered that (*a*) *sharq* is a relational or directional term: it is so in relation not to Palestine but to the Nabataeans, who, as will be argued further on, are the ones who could have mediated the term to the Graeco-Roman world; (*b*) ethnographic maps charted according to the data supplied by Ptolemy show the Saracenoi settled to the south rather than to the east of the Nabataeans,[7] but that was in the second century, and the Saracenoi may have lived to the east of the Nabataeans when the term was first applied to them by the latter; and (*c*) the Nabataean empire extended deep in the south of Ḥijāz, and so the Saracenoi, even according to Ptolemy's conception of their location, could have lived due east of the southern Nabataeans.[8]

2. The second etymon is *sāriq/sariqīn*, meaning "thief/thieves—marauders—plunderers."

In support of a derivation from the root S-R-Q, "to steal, rob, plunder," it may be said that (*a*) this would have been a natural designation of the nomads by the sedentaries of the Nabataean kingdom, a designation that has parallels in the application by the Romans of the term *latrones*, "robbers," to practically all the barbarian peoples outside the *limes*;[9] (*b*) as self-designation, too, it does

---

[7]See the map drawn by O. Blau for his article "Die Wanderung der sabäischen Völkerstämme im 2. Jahrhundert n. Chr. nach arabischen Sagen und Ptolemäus," *ZDMG*, 22 (1968), between pp. 654 and 655; and that drawn by Carl Müller for his edition of *Claudii Ptolemaei Geographia, Tabulae* (Paris, 1901), p. 35. The Byzantine theme of the seventh century, Anatolikon, provides a parallel. It derived its name from the Orient when its troops were stationed in that diocese; after the Persian Conquest it moved, according to one view, to western Asia Minor but kept its name, Anatolikon.

[8]People do designate those that live to the east of them as easterners. The western inhabitants of the United States do this, as do those of Ḥijāz in present-day Arabia when they refer to the inhabitants of Najd, calling them al-Shurūq (according to a Saudi Arabian informant and friend); see also A. Musil, *Arabia Deserta* (New York, 1927), p. 494, on the term *East* (*Šerk*) as applied to the inner desert in central Arabia. Most relevant in this context is the attestation of the term *Sharqī* ("easterner") as a proper noun in the Sinaitic inscriptions of the 2nd–3rd centuries A.D., for which, see Moritz, "Saraka," col. 2389, and J. Cantineau, *Le nabatéen* (Paris, 1932), vol. 2, p. 154, where it appears as *šrqyw*.

[9]Even the Arabic Qur'ān refers to the Arab nomads in pejorative terms as *al-Aʿrāb*.

not seem improbable; Moritz refers to the Sauwārke, the tribe in Sinai that lived between Gaza and Pelusium, while names derived from that root, such as Masrūq and Surāqa, are not uncommon in Arabic.[10] The term may have been differently nuanced in this ancient period and consequently may not have had the strongly pejorative tone imparted to it in later times. It may have meant simply "marauder," as an attribute of a doughty warrior, hence the possibility of such self-designations as those listed above.[11]

3. The third etymon is $S^e r\bar{a}q$,[12] meaning "emptiness" or "barrenness," and thus Saraceni are those "who live in barren land."

The main objection to this etymon is that it seeks the solution not in Arabic but in a cognate language, Aramaic, whereas the probabilities are in favor of an Arabic derivation because the term *Saraceni* is likely to be either a self-designation or one given by another Arab group, such as the Nabataeans. Furthermore, the common word for "desert" in Aramaic is *madbrā*, and it is therefore more natural to expect a designation for the desert people to be related to this term.

4. The fourth etymon of the term *Saraceni* is derivable from the name of an Arab tribe which became prominent in the third century[13] and whose name became synonymous in Graeco-Roman usage with the Arab inhabitants of north Arabia and Sinai.

This derivation has not had the fair hearing that it deserves. It has the authority of Ptolemy for at least the first stage—that of a specific tribe by the name of *Saraceni*—while the second stage—

[10]See Moritz, "Saraka," col. 2388, both for "Sauwārke" and for the biblical place name Masreka in Idumaea.

[11]A variant reading of the term *Saracenus* is noteworthy; it is spelled with a double *r* and appears as *Sarracenus*. If this is not a transcriptional error, it could clinch the point that the derivation is Arabic and comes most probably from the root S-R-Q, since this variant reading would reflect the intensive form in Arabic. Although it could conceivably be expressive of Arabic *sharrāq*, it is more likely to be a reproduction of Arabic *sarrāq*. However, since the name Sarah is sometimes spelled with a double *r*, this variant reading of *Saraceni* may be related to this alternative orthography of Sarah, for which, see Richard Southern, *Western Views of Islam in the Middle Ages* (Cambridge, Mass., 1962), p. 18.

[12]Suggested as *Srāk* by Murphy, "Who Were the Saracens?" (p. 190). See the comments of Graf and O'Connor on his views in *OTS*, p. 63.

[13]Originally suggested by Moritz, "Saraka," col. 2388; Mordtmann added the detail on its prominence in the third century, for which, see his "Saracens," p. 156.

the development of the term from the specific to the generic—is paralleled by that of Ṭayy, which had been the name of an Arab tribe before it became the generic Ṭayāyē, "Arabs" in the idiom of the Syriac writers. Moritz's reference to the Sauwārke of Sinai[14] is precious, not because of the remote possibility of their being the descendants of the Saraceni of classical times,[15] but because of its being an evidence for the journey of the term from the appellative to the denominative stage, a development which thus could have happened in classical times. That the term does not appear in the genealogical works of medieval Arab writers is not a valid argument against this derivation; the knowledge of the Arab genealogists did not go back very far, and the Nabataeans themselves are unknown to the Arab genealogists.[16] All these old tribes were lumped together by the genealogists under the umbrella title of "al-ʿArab al-Bāʾida," "the extinct Arabs," some of whose names have survived while others have not.

5. The fifth etymon of the term *Saraceni* is a place name such as Sarakēnē or Saraka,[17] as suggested by Ptolemy and Stephanus respectively.

The authority of these writers cannot be lightly dismissed. That such a name or one related to it existed somewhere in northwestern Arabia is certainly a possibility.[18] It could have been Sharq, Sharqiyya, or Shāriqa.

---

[14]*Supra*, p. 126 and note 10.

[15]Mordtmann thought it possible that these were the particular group of Saracens mentioned by Eusebius exactly in that region—Sinai; see his "Saracens," p. 155.

[16]In the Arabic works, *Nabīṭ* does not denote the Nabataeans; see Nöldeke, "Die Namen der aramäischen Nation und Sprache," *ZDMG*, 25 (1871), pp. 113–31. Incidentally, the view that the Saracens had been a specific tribe before their name became generic and before they themselves disappeared as Saracens from the consciousness of the genealogists is Nöldeke's considered judgment, for which, see *Philologus*, 52 (1894), p. 736.

[17]For this, see Moritz, "Saraka," col. 2388.

[18]For the biblical toponym Masreka in Idumaea, see *ibid*. Sarha in South Arabia suggested by A. M. al-Kirmilī is out of the question; see *al-Machriq*, 7 (1904), p. 341. Closer than South Arabian Sarha and less improbable is the Sarāt mountain range in northwestern Arabia not far from which the Sarakēnoi are located by Ptolemy. According to this derivation, the Sarakēnoi would have been the inhabitants of the Sarāt range; but one has to account for the appearance of the *kappa* of *Sarakenoi* and the disappearance of the *t* of *Sarāt*.

B. The New Etymology

Graf and O'Connor have argued "that the term *Saraceni* was derived from a pre-Islamic Arabic cognate of classical Arabic 'šrkt' which meant 'association' in the politically restricted sense of 'federation'. This term was taken over into the Nabataean lingua diplomatica and thence passed into Latin and Greek usage. Although perhaps initially applied only to the Thamudic confederates of the Antonine period, the term was generalized, after the collapse of that peace, from the Thamud to include their congeners and neighbors."[19] The statement is amplified with pertinent observations on the following two pages.

This view is not implausible phonetically, geographically, and chronologically. And yet, this new,[20] even exciting, etymology is not convincing, and reservations about it may be expressed through the following observations.[21]

1. Thamūd, not *sharikat*, remains the proper name for the Arab people of the Ruwwāfa inscription, and it would seem strange that the Romans should have chosen to designate this people with a term that reflected their internal social and political organization, a matter of concern to the Thamūd or more the concern of the Thamūd than of the Romans.[22] If *sharikat* in the inscription reflected the federate status of the Thamūd with the Romans—that they were their allies, their *foederati*—then it would not seem utterly strange on the part of the Romans to refer to their allies, their *foederati*, their *sharīks*,[23] by the latter's own term for themselves, although even this would have been quite anomalous in the whole history of Rome's relations with its *foederati*, who are uni-

---

[19]*OTS*, p. 65; for the proposal of the new etymology in its entirety, see pp. 64–66. Epigraphic *šrkt* will be vocalized *sharikat* in this chapter as it is in classical Arabic.

[20]On a related etymology suggested by A. Sprenger in 1875, see *ibid.*, p. 53 note 4. Sprenger's *sharīk* in the sense of "ally of Rome" was rejected by Mordtmann in "Saracens," p. 156.

[21]For an examination of the term *sharikat* in the sense of "federation," on which the etymology is based, see *infra*, Appendix, pp. 138–41.

[22]The explanation of the "transference of the term *šrkt* to the Roman world" is not entirely convincing; see *OTS*, p. 65. Furthermore, and as will be argued in the Appendix (*infra*, pp. 138–41), it is not certain that the term *šrkt* in the Ruwwāfa inscriptions means "confederation."

[23]On Sprenger's *sharīk*, see *supra*, note 20.

formly referred to by their own proper names. *Sharikat* is not a proper but a common noun and, what is more, indicative of an internal tribal organization.

2. Ptolemy is the earliest serious source[24] on the Saraceni and is relatively informative. He makes it quite clear that this Arab people is quite distinct from the Thamūd and from the Ṭayāyē, too, and was not part of a federation of Thamūd that included other tribes. Furthermore, Ptolemy and later Stephanus of Byzantium speak of localities, Sarakēnē and Saraka respectively, and not only of a tribe or people by the name *Saraceni*.[25]

3. This very tribal group appears later in the *Notitia Dignitatum,* represented by two military units in the Roman army.[26] In Palestine, "Thamūd" appears as such without the qualification "Saraceni," and it would be difficult to understand why, if indeed the Thamūd were the people or the tribal group whose own term *sharikat* gave rise to the term *Saraceni*. In the *Limes Aegypti*, the term *Saraceni* is used to qualify *Thamūd* in the designation of the second military unit.[27] This qualification is not easy to explain,

[24]On the reference to *Saracen* in an earlier source, Dioscurides of Anazarbus, and the uncertainties that attend it, see Mordtmann, "Saracens," p. 155, and *OTS,* p. 57.

[25]According to Graf and O'Connor, the references to the Sarakēnoi in Ptolemy's *Geography* may be confused because he places the Sarakēnoi in two different places, in northern Ḥijāz and in Sinai; see *OTS,* p. 57. But even if his references are confused, he remains the most reliable early source for the existence of the Sarakēnoi in the second century, since it is a matter of detail whether they were represented in one or two regions. However, the "confusion" imputed to Ptolemy calls for two comments. (*a*) There may have been two different tribal Arab groups that carried the same name *Sarakēnoi,* but who lived in two different parts of the region, one in Ḥijāz, the other in Sinai. Many Arab tribes carried the same name although they were unrelated and lived in different parts of the Peninsula. (*b*) It may be that the references in Ptolemy involve two tribes with two different but similar names, the one deriving from *sharqiyyīn,* the other from *sāriqīn;* Greek could not reproduce the Arabic *sh,* and thus it expressed both the *sh* of *sharqiyyīn* and the *s* of *sāriqīn* through the single sound *sigma,* and in the process produced two homophones.

[26]On the Equites Saraceni Thamudeni in *Limes Aegypti* and the Equites Thamudeni Illyriciani in Palestine, see *supra,* p. 57 note 28; p. 60 note 37.

[27]*Saraceni* as applied to this unit presents further difficulties: the term in the fourth century was equivalent to *Scenitae,* but the unit is not likely to have been composed of Arab Scenitae since the Thamūd were a sedentary people in the second century; even if some of them went through the process of bedouinization, this particular group serving in the Roman army was not nomadic and, what is more, its members were most probably *cives.*

but it does not seem to make easier the descent of *Saraceni* from Thamudic *sharikat*.

4. Although phonetic plausibility can be predicated of this derivation, there are some reservations which might be expressed not only on phonetic but also on other grammatical grounds: (*a*) consonantally, one has to account for the disappearance of the final *t*, a problem that does not arise with the derivation of *Saraceni* from such terms as *Sharq* (east) or *Sarq* (theft); (*b*) the vocalic sequence in *Saraceni* does not quite suggest *shirkat* or *sharikat* and is more in harmony with the other two derivations from sh-r-q or s-r-q, especially the latter, from which may be derived the verbal nouns *saraq* and *saraqat*; (*c*) even the suffix (if Semitic and not just the Latin or Greek *enus*/ηνός) is easier to accept as the Arabic plural suffix in the objective case than the author's suggestion that it reflects a hypocoristicon, especially as the point of the hypocoristicon in such a term is not clear.[28]

5. Noteworthy is the reference to the Saracens in one of the earliest and most important *loci classici* on this term, namely, that precious passage in the Syriac author Bardaiṣan[29] (ca. A.D. 200). There the Syriac form of *Saraceni,* "Sarqāyē," is spelled not with a *kāf*, a kappa, but with a *qāf*. This orthography allies *Saraceni* not to a word that has a *kāf*, such as Thamudic *sharikat*, but to a word that has a *qāf* as one of its radicals, such as *sharqiyyīn* or *sāriqīn*.[30]

Thus in spite of the originality of the new proposal, it cannot be said to have solved the etymology of *Saraceni*. Many questions remain unanswered, perhaps too many, for the new proposal to carry conviction.[31] More important than the concrete etymon which the two authors have suggested is their insistence on a historical

---

[28]See *OTS*, p. 65. The hypocoristicon is functional, expressing such notions as endearment or contempt, but its function in a term that is supposed to mean "confederation" is not clear.

[29]See Bardaiṣan, *Laws*, p. 50, line 11.

[30]Much depends on whether Bardaiṣan was translating the term from Greek or from Arabic. If *Saraceni* reached him through Greek, the argument from his use of the *qāf* and not the *kāf* loses some of its force since a cognate Semitic language, Arabic, transliterates the kappa in Greek *Sarakenoi* sometimes with a *kāf* and sometimes with a *qāf*, as in the well-known passages in Ibn-Baṭṭūṭa and Ibn-al-Athīr, for which, see al-Kirmilī in *al-Machriq*, 7 (1904), p. 341.

[31]See also Appendix, *infra*, pp. 138–41.

context within which can be understood the rise and development of the term *Saraceni*.[32] The present author shares with them this insistence. The key to the solution of this problem is not in the hands of the traditional etymologist but in that of the historian, and what remains is to discover the right historical context within which the term arose and developed. An alternative to the one offered by the two authors will be suggested in the following section.

II

The arguments that can be propounded with plausibility for each of the many etyma suggested for the term *Saraceni* indicate that for the time being the term is not definitively etymologizable and that more data are necessary, especially epigraphic, from the northwestern Arabian region before the question can be settled decisively. However, a wide range of possible etyma has been suggested, and the correct one almost certainly is bound to be found within this range.[33] But the problem of *Saraceni* has other dimensions, the semantic and the historical, and it is these non-etymological dimensions that are more important[34] to explore for the history of Arab-Roman and Arab-Byzantine relations, especially as some confusion exists about the signification of the term which, moreover, has been indiscriminately applied to various Arab groups.

A

1. Ptolemy is surely the safest guide[35] as a starting point for the investigation of the problem of the term *Saraceni*. The specificity that informs his account, short as it is, must command respect for its authenticity, especially as he is confirmed by other important sources.[36] According to his account, the Saraceni were a

[32]See *OTS*, pp. 52, 65–66.

[33]For this, see *supra*, section I.A, pp. 124–27.

[34]And yet the etymological dimension of the problem is not of purely philological interest but is of some relevance to the historical dimension of the term *Saraceni*. Curiously enough, it is the clearly erroneous etymology, the patristic, that is most relevant to a discussion of this historical dimension, in what might be termed the genealogy of error concerning the image of the Arabs in medieval Christendom; see the discussion of this in *BAFOC*.

[35]On certain negotiable difficulties in Ptolemy, see *supra*, note 25.

[36]Such as Stephanus of Byzantium; in spite of his later *floruit*, possibly in the sixth century, and the variant reading he gives for the toponym involving the Saracens (*Saraka* instead of the *Sarakēnē* of Ptolemy), he remains an important

differentiated tribe in the first half of the second century, quite distinct from the Nabataeans and the Thamūd; and they inhabited the region which lay to the south of the Tayēnī, another important tribe for the discussion of the fortunes of the term *Saraceni* in non-Arabic sources.

The Graeco-Roman world must have known about this tribe of Saraceni[37] before Ptolemy, but it was in the second century that this awareness or knowledge apparently assumed some significance. The evidence from Josephus, negative as it is, is valuable. This Arab tribal group is unknown to him, and if it had been an important group in the first century A.D., the Jewish historian, who had occasion to mention the Arabs repeatedly, would have included mention of it in his work.

Thus it may be assumed with a reasonable degree of certainty that the northwestern Arabian tribe of Saraceni began to assume some significance in the second century of the Christian Era.

2. The second safe guide after Ptolemy is Ammianus Marcellinus of the fourth century. When writing of the Arab Scenitae, the "Tent-dwellers," he informs his readers that they are now (*nunc*) called Saraceni, and in another passage he speaks of how the Scenitae were called Saraceni by *posteritas*.[38]

It is clear from Ammianus that in the fourth century the term *Saraceni* was certainly used to denote the Arab Scenitae, but he leaves the question open as to when this process or development in the semantic journey of the term *Saraceni* from the specific to the generic took place. His reference to the Arabs as Saraceni during the reign of Marcus Aurelius[39] in the second half of the second

---

source corroborative of Ptolemy, both deriving their information on the Saraceni from the same type of ancient and reliable sources (Mordtmann, "Saracens," p. 155). Bardaiṣan, too, ca. A.D. 200, is supportive of Ptolemy in spite of the fact that by his time the term *Saraceni* had become generic if not for all the Arab Scenitae at least for those of the western half of the Fertile Crescent; see *infra*, p. 133.

[37]On the possibility that Uranius, one of the two authorities of Stephanus of Byzantium on the Saracens, belongs to the period of the last Diadochi, see Mordtmann, "Saracens," p. 155.

[38]On the two quotations from Ammianus, see *Res Gestae*, XXII.15.2; XXIII.6.13. On the image of the Arabs in Ammianus, see "Ammianus and the Arabs" in *BAFOC*, chap. 7, sec. I.

[39]*Ibid.*, XIV.4.2 The use of *Saraceni* by Rufus Festus in his account of the campaign of Lucullus in Armenia is an anachronism; see *The Breviarium of Festus*, ed. J. W. Eadie (London, 1967), sec. XIV.

century may be anachronistic, but on closer inspection it may be maintained that by the end or second half of the second century the term *Saraceni* had become generic. Confirmation of this comes from that precious passage in the Syriac writer Bardaiṣan who in speaking of the Arabs uses the two terms *Sarqāyē and Ṭayāyē*;[40] and it is amply clear from the context and the cultural matters which he was discussing that the two terms could have been used by him only in the generic sense of Arab nomads. Those of the western half of the Fertile Crescent in the Syro-Arabian desert and neighbors of the Romans were called the *Sarqāyē*, while those of the eastern half of the Fertile Crescent and neighbors of the Persians were called the *Ṭayāyē*.[41]

B

The question arises as to why the Romans found it necessary or convenient to apply a term such as *Saraceni* as a generic term to denote the Arab Scenitae, the "Tent-dwellers." To this historical question are allied or related a number of others.

1. The chronological and geographical data extracted from Ptolemy and fortified by other data from Bardaiṣan and Ammianus point to the second century and to Nabataea in the larger sense as the period and the area respectively within which the development of the term *Saraceni* from the specific to the generic took place.[42] But in the second century and in this very sector in the Orient took place the most important of all Arab-Roman confrontations before the fall of Palmyra, namely, the annexation of Nabataea and its conversion into the Provincia Arabia in A.D. 106. This then is the large and significant fact in the history of Arab-Roman relations within which can be fruitfully sought the answers to the historical questions posed earlier in this section.

2. The fall of the Nabataean kingdom, the Arab shield of Rome against the Peninsula, brought the Romans in direct contact with the Arabs of the Peninsula. All contacts with the vast area that now opened to the Roman soldier and administrator had before been conducted for them by the Nabataean Arabs, familiar

[40]Bardaiṣan, *Laws*, p. 50, line 11.
[41]On this, see Nöldeke, *Philologus*, 52 (1894), p. 736.
[42]The two works of Ptolemy and Bardaiṣan, the *Geography* and the *Laws*, thus represent the two termini of this crucial period in the development of *Saraceni* from a specific to a generic term; see *supra*, notes 7, 29.

with the world of their nomadic or semi-nomadic congeners. But after A.D. 106, Roman arms and diplomacy had to deal directly with this world of the Arabian Peninsula, teeming with Scenitae, divided into many tribes. It was necessary to employ a term to describe these new neighbors homogeneous in their nomadism and thus calling for one term to designate them. The generic term *Arab* was clearly inadequate. It was too inclusive, comprehending all varieties of Arab groups who were of different levels of cultural development—nomads, semi-nomads, and sedentaries—and so it was not precise enough. But the more important reason that impelled the Romans to adopt the term *Saraceni* must have been the new situation that arose with the annexation of Nabataea in A.D. 106. The Graeco-Roman world knew the inhabitants of Nabataea as *Arabes*, civilized sedentaries, who in A.D. 106 had acquired a new status, that of Roman provincials, and since then had crossed another milestone in their Roman journey in A.D. 212 when they became Roman *cives*. It was therefore necessary to find for the Arabs outside the *imperium romanum* a term that was distinct and did not confuse the nomads of the Peninsula with the Roman *cives* of the Provincia.[43] Thus the term *Saraceni* was convenient as it denoted the Arabs who were Peninsular,[44] nomadic, and non-citizens, and distinguished them from the inhabitants of the Provincia who were provincial, sedentary, and, after A.D. 212, Roman citizens. Furthermore, the term *Scenitae* was not peculiarly Arab since it could be applied to non-Arab tent-dwellers, hence the term *Saraceni* served the two purposes of reflecting the Arabism as well as the nomadism of the Arab Scenitae.[45]

3. A return to the etymological dimension of this question, from which this investigation has been temporarily disentangled, is now necessary in order to answer the question why the Romans

[43]Even as late as the reign of Justinian in the sixth century, the Provincia Arabia was to the emperor himself "the country of the Arabs," τὴν 'Αράβων χώραν; see *supra*, p. 15 note 41.

[44]And sometimes some Arab nomadic groups who were living in the Orient.

[45]The new Roman designation for the Arabs and their territory may have been influenced by the idiom and conceptions of the classical geographers who divided Arabia into Petraea, Deserta, and Felix. In A.D. 106, the first of these three Arabias, Petraea, disappeared as such, and emerged as the Provincia Arabia, while the Arabs of Deserta became *Saraceni*, not an inappropriate term for the desert-dwellers.

chose this particular term *Saraceni* for designating the Arab Scenitae and thus gave it vogue as a generic term. Two answers may be given to this question and they are not exclusive of each other.

(*a*) It could be maintained that it was the Roman response to the fact that the tribe Saraceni, one specific tribe in north Arabia according to Ptolemy, had become so powerful as to impose itself and its name on the attention of the Romans.[46] As it was possibly the closest to the new Roman *limes*, extended after the annexation of Nabataea in A.D. 106, the Romans may not have found it too difficult to call all the neighboring Arab tribes, nomadic and semi-nomadic, by that term.[47] This would have been just another instance of the application of the particular to the general and could derive much support from the parallel cases of such terms as *Persians*, *Greeks*, and *Allemands*, but most importantly from the development in Syriac of the name of the sister tribe in Ptolemy, that of the powerful and numerous Ṭayāyē, to designate the Arab Scenitae of Mesopotamia.

(*b*) Alternatively, the name *Saraceni* may not have been that of a specific tribe, but a descriptive term, either "easterners" or "marauders, plunderers," *sharqiyyīn* or *sāriqīn*, which the Nabataeans could have applied to their less-fortunate congeners in Arabia Deserta to their east and which the Romans thus inherited to describe this new world of the Arab nomads or Scenitae which after A.D. 106 had become very much their concern.[48] The importance of the provincial Nabataean Arabs in the affairs of the Provincia, its administration and its defense,[49] especially after A.D. 212, cannot be underestimated, and it is perfectly possible that the term

[46]Suggested by Moritz, "Saraka," col. 2388, and developed by Mordtmann, "Saracens," p. 156; it is also Nöldeke's view, but without reference to the tribe's becoming powerful or aggressive to the Romans; see Nöldeke, *Philologus*, 52 (1894), p. 736. See also the paragraph on "the extinct Arab tribes," *supra*, pp. 126–27.

[47]Proximity as well as power may have been an important factor in the process. Ptolemy's conception of the level of social development reached by his Sarakēnoi is not entirely clear, but the presumption is that he considered it a semi-nomadic tribe of north Arabia, one among many Arab tribes that lived outside the limits of the *imperium*.

[48]See the argument for *sāriqīn* ("plunderers, marauders") as the etymon of *Saraceni*, *supra*, p. 125.

[49]For native troops serving in the Roman army in former Nabataean territory, see the list of units in the two provinces of Palestine and Arabia in the *Notitia Dignitatum*, *supra*, pp. 60–61, 62–63.

was thus mediated to the Romans through the "Nabataean lingua diplomatica"[50] of the period.

4. The vogue that the term *Saraceni* experienced as a generic term for the Arab Scenitae probably passed through many stages. Ammianus, the main source on this point, is very laconic, but certain landmarks in Arab-Roman relations in the course of the first three centuries of the Christian Era could be helpful in charting the possible phased journey for the vogue of the term.

(*a*) The first phase must have been opened by the annexation of Nabataea and its conversion into the Provincia Arabia in A.D. 106. Within this phase involving the Provincia Arabia, the year 212, that of the Edict of Caracalla, may have been another significant date, as suggested above.

(*b*) The second phase in the vogue of the term may have opened ca. A.D. 240, when Gordian put an end to the independence of the Arab kingdom of Edessa in Osroene, which became a Roman colony. This again brought the Romans into direct confrontation with the Arab Scenitae of the Trans-Euphratesian region, partially screened from them before by the Abgarids, the Arab kings of Edessa.[51]

(*c*) The third phase in its vogue could have been opened by the Roman encounter with Arab Palmyra and the subsequent destruction of that city in A.D. 272, which brought about another major confrontation between the Romans and the Scenitae of the middle sector of the Orient, in much the same way that the annexation of Osroene in the north and Nabataea in the south had done before.

---

[50]See *OTS*, p. 65. The gradual disappearance of the name of specific Arab tribes, the many Arab tribes, which appear in the works of the Greek and Roman geographers and the subsequent vogue of such generic names as *Arabes* and *Saraceni* is a striking phenomenon. In addition to what has been said in the text of this chapter, the following observation may be made to explain this phenomenon. Perhaps many of these tribes lost their identity after being ruled or controlled by, or even absorbed in, the larger political structures erected by the three groups of Arabs who moved in the Roman orbit, the Nabataeans, the Palmyrenes, and the Edessans.

[51]The fall of Arab Ḥatra, to Shāpūr I, also ca. A.D. 240, must also have contributed to a certain degree of nomadization in the Persian section of the region the effects of which must have been at least partially felt in Roman Mesopotamia. On the fall of Edessa and Ḥatra, see *CAH*, 12, pp. 87, 130–31; on "nomadization," see the following note.

Thus by the end of the third century the Arab urban establishment in the Fertile Crescent had been dismantled, and a state
of direct confrontation of Rome with the Arab Scenitae from the
Euphrates to Sinai and the Red Sea took place. No doubt, a certain
degree of nomadization[52] ensued with the fall of the strong Arab
urban centers that had controlled the Arab Scenitae and their transhumance, but the more significant historical consequence of the fall
of these Arab urban centers was the direct confrontation of the
Romans with the vast world of the Arab Scenitae.[53] It was only
natural, in view of the importance of this homogeneous world of
nomads, that a term which had been adopted in the second century
should have been extended to designate this world in its entirety
in the third.

Postscript: The pre-publication comments of one reader have made it
necessary to clarify my views on Roman usage of the term *Saraceni, supra,*
pp. 133–37.

1. There is no positive evidence for the circumstances that brought
about Roman usage of the term *Saraceni*. These can only be reconstructed,
and I suggested as the most significant date A.D. 106, the year of the
annexation of Nabataea, and explained my reason for the choice of that
date, since "Saraceni" were now contrasted with the Arabs of the Provincia
Arabia, now Roman provincials. But they could also have been contrasted
with the Roman Arabs, not as provincials but as *cives*, after the promulga-
tion of the *Constitutio Antoniniana* in A.D. 212. Hence the reference to
the latter and the year 212 as a significant date. However, I am much
more inclined to think that the truly significant date in the story of
Roman usage of *Saraceni* is A.D. 106.

2. On pp. 136–37, I discuss *another* dimension of the Roman usage
of *Saraceni*, after its adoption with the annexation of Nabataea, namely,
its *vogue* and the *extension* of its usage after A.D. 106. I refer to two similar
annexations in the third century, that of Arab Osroene around A.D. 240

---

[52]On the concept of nomadization in this period, see W. Caskel, "The
Bedouinization of Arabia," *Studies in Islamic Cultural History*, ed. G. E. von
Grünebaum (Chicago, 1954), pp. 36–46, esp. pp. 40–41.

[53]Graf and O'Connor (*OTS*, p. 66) availed themselves of Caskel's "bedouinization" in the presentation of their proposal of the new etymology, but the place of
"bedouinization" in their proposal is different from its place in the argument of
this chapter in which it has experienced a shift of emphasis. For the two authors,
it accounts for "the later obscurity and confusion about the meaning of *Saraceni*";
for the present writer, it partially accounts for the rise and vogue of the term.

and of Palmyrena in A.D. 272, and suggest that it was these two annexations that finally were responsible for the widest vogue and extension of
the term to denote the nomads of the Arabian Peninsula.

Appendix

The etymology of the term *Saraceni* proposed by Graf and O'Connor
is based on J. T. Milik's interpretation of the term *šrkt* of the Ruwwāfa
Bilinguis, which he argued is a technical term meaning "federation."[1]
Section I.B in this chapter has examined the validity of this etymology
and this Appendix will address itself to examining its very foundation,
namely, whether the term *šrkt* does in fact mean "federation" or "confederation." The problem is important to the internal history of this
important Arab tribe, to the history of Ḥijāz in this period, and to the
history of Arab-Roman relations.[2] The etymology proposed for *Saraceni*
depending on it makes it important to Arab-Byzantine relations too.

In spite of the attractiveness of Milik's suggestion and the competence with which the arguments in support of it have been advanced by
Graf and O'Connor,[3] the present writer is not convinced of the validity
of Milik's interpretation of the term *šrkt*. Various types of arguments may
be put forward against the view that *šrkt* in the Ruwwāfa Bilinguis means
"federation."

A

1. The term *šrkt* is unknown as a term in the political terminology
of the Arabs, both before and after the rise of Islam, in the technical
sense of a federation or a confederation. The chances are slim that it

---

[1]For the Ruwwāfa inscriptions, see Graf, *SDAF*, pp. 9–10, where the texts
of the relevant inscriptions are given with a commentary; for Milik's interpretation of *šrkt* as "federation," see also *OTS*, pp. 64–65, which also have much
relevant material in their footnotes. J. T. Milik's article, entitled "Inscriptions
grecques et Nabatéennes de Rawwafah," had appeared in *Bulletin of the Institute of
Archaeology* (University of London), 10 (1971), pp. 54–58.

[2]For the views of Graf and O'Connor on the historical importance of what
they consider the rise of a Thamudic confederation in northern Ḥijāz in the second
century, see *OTS*, pp. 65–66, and also *SDAF*, pp. 10–12, 15–20.

[3]*OTS*, pp. 64–65; also, Graf in *SDAF*, pp. 14–15.

became obsolete and that its obsoleteness explains its non-attestation in classical Arabic in this sense. Arabic and the other Semitic languages are full of homophonous but non-synonymous roots and lexemes, and *šrkt* in the Thamudic inscriptions could be an instance of this non-synonymity.[4]

2. The common term in Arabic for federation or confederation is *ḥilf*.[5] It is an old and well-attested term in pre-Islamic Arabic and was widely used in various parts of the Peninsula. One would expect this term to have been used if it had been the concept of federation that was wanted to describe the political organization of Thamūd.

3. That *šrkt* is not "confederation" is further confirmed by the second part of the grammatical construct in which it appears, namely, Thamūd. When a confederation or a federation in pre-Islamic Arabia came into being, it was usually given a new name exclusive of that of each of its constituent member tribes, such as Tanūkh, or sometimes a *pater eponymus*, such as Ma'add.[6] The employment of the term Thamūd, the name of the well-known tribe,[7] rather than a new name for the presumed Thamudic confederation indicates that *šrkt* is not expressive of that concept.

B

Even more important than the employment of Thamūd in the construct phrase of the Aramaic inscription is the rendition of that phrase in the Greek version. Without the Greek, it would not be inconceivable to argue for "confederation" as a signification for *šrkt*. But the Greek clinches the point, and it does throw a bright light both on what *šrkt* is and what it is not.

1. It proves almost conclusively that *šrkt* is not "confederation." If it had been, the translator[8] would have used the right Greek term for confederation or alliance, a term such as συμμαχία. The fact that he does not use such a term but instead another one, ἔθνος, which does not signify it, indicates that the term *šrkt* simply meant "tribe" or "people" and

---

[4]That is, in classical Arabic it means "association" but in the Thamudic inscription it means something else, just as in classical Arabic *sharak*, derived from the same three radicals as *šrkt*, means "snare," something completely unrelated to "association," or so it seems.

[5]See *EI*, 3, pp. 388–89, *s.v.*

[6]Even though some of these eponyms were fictitious. When the name was not exclusive, it included *all* the constituent members of the *ḥilf*, the federation, such as *ḥilf* Qaḥṭān and Rabī'a or *ḥilf* Kalb and Tamīm.

[7]Whose longevity as well as distinctness as a tribe was remarkable, going back to Assyrian times.

[8]Whether they were the bilingual Thamudites or, in Graf's phrase, the "linguistic specialists who were familiar with the native language of the desert Arabs," *SDAF*, p. 15.

was not a politically significant new term, for the rendering of which
ἔθνος would have been inadequate.

2. On the other hand, the Greek version of the inscription with its
ἔθνος gives a clue as to how to translate this rare term, *šrkt*, which in
this context should mean "tribe" or "people." This should not be surprising since Arabic has a wide variety of terms to signify tribes and
tribal subdivisions, such as *qabīla*, *ḥayy*, *shaʿb*, *ʿimāra*, *baṭn*, *fakhḏ*; and
šrkt may well have been one of these terms[9] in the Arabic of Ḥijāz in the
second century A.D.

C

Thus the employment of *Thamūd* immediately after *šrkt* in the construct phrase of the Aramaic inscription and the translation of *šrkt* by
ethnos in the Greek version of the inscription fortify each other and indicate
that *šrkt* does not mean a confederation of tribes that included Thamūd
and other non-Thamudic tribes. Although it has been suggested that all
the evidence leads to the conclusion that it simply means "tribe," it is
not impossible to argue for a signification of the term *šrkt* which partakes
of both, "tribe" and "confederation."

1. The confederation, *ḥilf*,[10] was of more than one variety. The *ḥilf*
proper was composed of separate and different tribes, often amalgamated,
to which a common eponym was given, which *šrkt*, it has has been argued,
is not. Another type is the *ḥilf* that obtained among the various clans
of one and the same tribe "through which they settle on a line of conduct
in the general interest."[11] *Šrkt* could have been used in this sense of *ḥilf*,
"confederation."

2. This interpretation could receive considerable fortification from
the employment of the term *qdmy*, in the plural, to indicate the elders
or leaders of the *šrkt* in the phrase *qdmy šrkt*.[12] The various elders then
could be the heads of the various clans within the tribe of Thamūd, and

---

[9]The closest signification that might be suggested for this epigraphic term
šrkt and one which would ally it semantically to the cluster of Arabic terms
enumerated above would be "community." This signification can be supported by
appeal to the meaning of the root š-r-k, from which such a term as *mushtarak*
("common") is derived. Parallels to this would be Latin *commune* as substantive,
meaning "state," "community," and Greek τὸ κοινόν in the same sense, not
in that of "league," which it can also have.

[10]Strictly speaking, *ḥilf* is the covenant or compact that brings about the
confederation or alliance.

[11]For this, see *ḥilf*, *EI*, 3, p. 388.

[12]For the phrase, see Inscription B in *SDAF*, p. 9, and its French translation
on p. 10.

in this restricted sense *šrkt* may be a confederation,[13] but quite different from the one that has been conceived for *šrkt* and without the historical significance that has been attributed to it.

[13]One might add a final signification for *šrkt*, that of a "partnership" as a commercial term, which would be the natural translation of classical Arabic *šrkt*. In view of the importance of trade for a community such as that of Ruwwāfa, settled on the caravan route, "partnership" may turn out to be the most suitable signification. Lammens's term for Mecca, the much greater caravan city of pre-Islamic Arabia, namely, "the commercial republic," naturally comes to mind. The frequent attestation in this area of proper names derived from the root *šrkt* (*OTS*, pp. 64–65, and note 62) could confirm this signification of "partnership" suggested for *šrkt*. A proper name derived from *šrk*, such as *Sharīk*, clearly means "partner," "commercial partner"—a natural appellation in an area that was a commercial bridge for the caravan trade between Arabia and the Mediterranean region. On the use of ἔθνος in the papyri for a trade association or guild, see Liddell and Scott, *Greek-English Lexicon*, *s.v.* Thus, the "commercial community" of Thamūd may be a good translation of the term *šrkt Thamūd*, combining the notion of "partnership" suggested in this note with that of "community" suggested *supra*, note 9.

A final paleographic observation may be made: in the Nabataean script the two letters *k* and *b* bear a striking resemblance to each other. Consequently, *šrkt* could really be *šrbt*, which thus rules out "federation" and accurately renders ἔθνος as "tribe" or "people."

PART THREE
SYNTHESIS AND EXPOSITION

I

When Pompey appeared on the stage of Near Eastern history, a substantial portion of the Orient was possessed by various Arab groups some of whom had taken advantage of the decay of the Seleucid and Ptolemaic Empires, effected deep penetrations into the Fertile Crescent, and carved for themselves principalities and small city-states from the Euphrates to the Nile. Such were the Osroeni of Edessa, those of the chief ʿAzīz in the region of Antioch, those of Alchaedamnus, Gambarus, and Themella in Chalcidice; the Arabs of Palmyra, those of Sempsigeramus in Emesa and Arethusa; the Ituraeans of Lebanon, Anti-Lebanon, Batanaea, Trachonitis, and Auranitis; the Idumaeans of Palestine; the Nabataeans of Petra; and the Arabs of Egypt between the Nile and the Red Sea.

The extent of this Arab presence in the Orient has been obscured onomastically by the specific designations, both gentilic and geographic, given to these Arab groups, which have concealed their common Arab origin throughout the four centuries or so of this Roman period. Only the application of the term *Arabia* in the terminology of the Roman administration to three regions, "the three Arabias" of Mesopotamia, Trans-Jordan, and Egypt, could have suggested that the inhabitants of these regions were ethnically Arab. This obscuration of their identity was further accentuated by their assumption of Graeco-Roman names.

This extensive and intensive Arab presence has passed almost unnoticed. Analysts of the ethnic and cultural map of the Orient speak of two constituents—the Greek and the Aramaic. But the reading of the cultural map in bipartite terms is misleading. By subsuming the Arab element under the Aramaic, it obscures both the extent and reality of the Arab presence, which was an enduring factor in Roman history in the Orient in both Roman and Byzantine times. The ethnic and cultural cartography of the region must be understood in tripartite terms—Greek, Aramaic, and Arab—dissociating the third from the second, and presenting the third as related to the second but distinct from it in the larger context of Semitic. This is all the more necessary to do not only because it is

correct ethnic and cultural cartography, but also because it was
the Arabs, not the Aramaeans, that were the Semitic force in the
dynamics of Roman history in the Orient during these centuries.

In spite of acculturation and sometimes assimilation to the
Graeco-Roman and Semitic cultures of the Orient, the Arabs retained their identity in varying degrees, reflected in the retention
of their Arab ethos and mores, of their language, religious rites,
and ancestral customs. They were able to do so because of the
antiquity of their settlement in this area long before the Romans
appeared in the first century B.C.; because for a long time the
latter left their political and social structures intact through the
device of the clientship; and because of their proximity and sometimes contiguity to that large ethnic and linguistic reservoir, the
Arabian Peninsula, their homeland. And it was this that determined the degree of that identity: (a) those of the Mediterranean
littoral, such as the Idumaeans and the Ituraeans, were Judaized,
Hellenized, and Romanized, and thus lost much of their Arab
cultural identity; (b) less so than these were the Arabs of the Valley
of the Orontes, those of Emesa and Arethusa; (c) but it was in the
Roman limitrophe in those provinces or areas that were closest to
the Arabian Peninsula that Arab identity remained strong, namely,
in Palmyrena and Nabataea, even more pronounced in the latter
than in the former. And it is in this limitrophe that one can
identify most distinctly an Arab zone in the ethnic and cultural
map of the Orient.

If an Arab presence, pervasive and deep, can thus be predicated in the Orient in the first century B.C., and if the Arabs did
not lose their identity after the Settlement of Pompey, then it is
possible, even necessary, to speak of the Arab factor in the structure
of Roman history in the Orient, especially as the Arabs remained a
force in the dynamics of that history until the latter part of the
third century, the century of the imperial crisis, which witnessed
the climax of Arab-Roman relations.

Just as the Settlement of Pompey was a landmark in the history of Roman expansion in the eastern part of the Mediterranean,
so it was in the history of the Arabs in ancient times. These had
replaced the Seleucids as the new masters of certain portions of the
Orient, and had it not been for the sudden and unexpected appearance of Pompey, the Arabs would or might have developed the

Orient, especially the western half of the Fertile Crescent, along lines different from those of the Seleucids and the Ptolemies, new lines that would have returned the western part of the Fertile Crescent to Semitic rule just as it had been before its fall to the Achaemenids in the sixth century B.C. Pompey's Settlement ensured that Rome, not the Arabs, was to be the heir and successor of the Hellenistic kingdoms and the continuator of their cultural policies, and thus a new lease on life was given to Hellenism and to the prolongation of what might be termed the Indo-European era in the history of the Semitic Orient.

Pompey's Settlement frustrated the unfolding of Arab history in the Fertile Crescent in the first century B.C., forced it into a new groove in which it was to run for many centuries during which the Arabs moved in a new historical orbit, that of Mediterranean Rome, and delayed the Arab successful self-expression for seven centuries. It was not until the Arabs of the Peninsula were united under the banner of Islam in the seventh century A.D. that they were able to recover the western half of the Fertile Crescent, the Orient, from Roman hands, to terminate what might be described as the Graeco-Roman millennium which began with the conquests of Alexander in the fourth century B.C., and reassert the Arab political and military presence, which had been frustrated by Pompey in the first century B.C.

Pompey's Settlement turned out to be the beginning of a long involvement of the Arabs with Rome, lasting for seven centuries, at the end of which the Arabs succeeded in severing their Roman connection. The most important problem, and the most complex in the history of Arab-Roman relations, is, of course, the Arab Conquests in the seventh century and the blow which the Arabs administered to East Rome, thus changing the course of Roman and Mediterranean history. How they succeeded is a big question, but the close examination of the first major Arab-Roman encounter in the first century B.C. is relevant to answering that question, at least insofar as it illuminates it with comparisons and contrasts. Unlike the Arabs of the seventh century A.D., those of the first century B.C. who crossed the path of Pompey were disunited— many dynasts who did not concert action—and thus Pompey could deal with them separately, one after the other. They were also set- tled not in remote, inaccessible regions of the Arabian Peninsula but in cities within the confines of the Orient, and thus they could not elude the grasp of the Roman commander who could easily disperse them. Finally, Pompey was the commander of an army which, unlike that of Heraclius in the seventh century, had not sustained crushing defeats and then won Pyrrhic victories which had exhausted it for some twenty years. Thus he was able to settle in favor of Rome the first major Arab-Roman confrontation.

II

The Settlement of Pompey ushered in a period of four centuries of Arab-Roman relations, a genuine historical era, within the longer period of these relations which lasted throughout the Byzantine period. Its terminus is the revolt of Palmyra in the third century, the most serious Arab-Roman military confrontation before that with Islam in the seventh century. The internal history of the Orient in these four centuries turns largely round the question of how Rome dealt with its Arabs throughout these centuries from the Settlement of Pompey to the reign of Diocletian.

The course of these relations between their submission in the first century B.C. and their revolt in the third century A.D. is divisible into two parts: (1) in the first period, which is roughly the first two centuries, Rome rested its rule on the *status quo*, confirming the various dynasts, and making of them clients; these in turn served Rome well and became acculturated, appearing as philhellenes, *philorhomaioi*; (2) the second period is that of absorption and direct rule through annexation, which had already begun in the first century A.D. with the incorporation under the Flavians of Ituraea, but which in the second and the third centuries is applied to much more important Arab groups—the Nabataeans in A.D. 106, the Osroenians in A.D. 244, and the Palmyrenes in A.D. 272. These three annexations, especially the first and the last, completed the absorption of the Arabs of the Orient within the Roman system, effected important changes in Roman frontier policy, and brought the Romans face to face with the Arabs of the Peninsula, thus giving the Romans a long frontier with Arabia.

Perhaps nothing reflects better the extent to which Rome had succeeded in solving the Arab problem throughout these centuries than that document dated to the early part of the fifth century, namely, the *Notitia Dignitatum*. Although it is an early fifth-century document, yet the Roman substrate in it is recognizable, and this substrate reflects conditions that obtained in the Roman, pre-Byzantine period. The large number of Arab units that have been included in the document reveal both the nature and extent of the Arab contribution to Rome's war effort and also the fact that after fighting them Rome enlisted the Arabs in its service.

The presumption, the strong presumption, is that these were Roman citizens, either through regular service in the Roman army or that they had been already citizens after *civitas* had been extended to them in A.D. 212 by the Edict of Caracalla. Thus the large number of units described as *indigenae* in the provinces of the Orient with strong Arab ethnic complexion were Roman provincials of Arab origin who served in the army of the empire of which they were now citizens.

III

Although the Arabs had been a permanent element in the history of the Orient from the time of Pompey's Settlement, it was in the third century A.D. that the element became a factor in the making of Roman history throughout that century—in its first half, towards its middle, and in its second half. This factor is represented by the Arab component in the making of the Severan dynasty, by the principate of Philip the Arab, and by the reigns of Odenathus and Zenobia of Palmyra.

The Arab character of this extraordinary self-assertion in the third century has not been fully grasped. Even when the Arab character of each of the three components of the factor has been recognized, the three were treated as separate and unrelated chapters in the history of the third century. It is difficult, however, to believe that there was no filiation or genetic relationship among the three of them. The wife and the successors of Septimius Severus, Philip the Arab, and Odenathus and Zenobia all hailed from the three Arab cities of Emesa, Philippopolis, and Palmyra respectively. These were cities quite close to one another and their Arabs were neighbors. Surely the spectacle of Arabs from Emesa attaining to the purple could have whetted the appetite of the Arab from Philippopolis, just as the spectacle of the Arab from Philippopolis attaining to the principate and celebrating the Millennium could have whetted the appetite of the lord of Palmyra, Odenathus, and more clearly his widow, Zenobia.

In addition to filiation, it is possible to detect some relevant features of background in certain spheres of their activities. (1) The *Constitutio Antoniniana* could have been partly inspired by the fact that the promulgator did not belong to the Graeco-Roman establishment but was a provincial himself. If so, it was the half-Arab Caracalla and his Arab mother, Julia Domna, that completed the work begun by Julius Caesar. (2) The Arab background is clearer in the religious policy of the Severi. Julia Domna's aggressive championship of paganism against Christianity could be explained only by the fact that she was the daughter of the priest of the Arab sun-god of Emesa himself, while the installation of the sun-god in Rome by Elagabalus, its quondam priest in Emesa, speaks for itself.

Some facets of the Arab factor are noteworthy:

1. Arab participation in the making of Roman history is no longer on the low, provincial level, but on the highest—in the court itself, the principate, to which the half-Arab emperors of the Severan dynasty attained, as did Philip. Through the highest office, the principate, these Arab figures, especially the Severi, were able to make fundamental changes in the structure of Roman history and in the principate itself.

2. After three centuries or so of acculturation or even assimilation, these Arab figures are part of the Roman system. They now belong to an empire of which they are proud to be citizens. Thus they all, from Julia Domna to Odenathus, work for the imperial idea and their loyalty is not in question.

3. Remarkable is the number of Arab women who figure prominently in this century: Julia Domna, Julia Maesa, Julia Soaemias, and Julia Mammaea, the empresses of the Severan dynasty; Marcia Otacilia Severa, Philip's wife; and Zenobia, Odenathus's wife. Two of them, the most celebrated, were most active when widowed. It was as widows that Julia Domna attained the acme of her ambition and Zenobia threw a challenge to the might of Rome.

The operation of this Arab factor in the third century is evident but not striking for the period of the Severi and Philip, *cives* of Arab origin, who were fighting the wars of an empire of which they were rulers. It was different in the case of the more recognizably Arab Odenathus and Zenobia. Their military operations were not conducted from Rome as their capital but from the Arab city of Palmyra, the caravan city of the Syrian desert, with Arab troops, and sometimes following the principles of desert warfare.

The scale of operations was gigantic and is measurable by the fact that the Palmyrene Arab took on no less than the empire of the Sasanids, avenged the capture of Valerian, and richly merited such titles as *dux Romanorum* and *corrector totius Orientis*. As he changed the course of events in the East in his lifetime, so did he change it by his death, since he was succeeded by his ambitious wife, Zenobia, who *inter alia* endowed Roman history with its most romantic episode since the days of Cleopatra. Her war was on an even more gigantic scale than that of her deceased husband. She succeeded in occupying the whole of Syria from Taurus to Sinai, Egypt, and Asia Minor. In Zenobia's revolt even more than in the career of her husband one can detect some filiation, the spectacle of one Arab imitating another, Zenobia imitating Julia Domna. It was Zenobia's ambitions that brought Palmyra and Rome on a collision course, and it was the elimination of Palmyra and its destruction by Aurelian, caused by her revolt, that brought about those far-reaching changes in the history of the Orient that were to obtain throughout the three centuries of the Byzantine period.

The Romans both made and unmade Palmyra. They had given her a spacious opportunity to prosper after the annexation of Nabataea in A.D. 106 and the two swift campaigns of Aurelian brought about first her submission and then her destruction. The revolt was atypical of the course of Arab-Roman relations; Palmyra's prosperity as a commercial empire and a liaison station between the East and the West depended on cooperation with Rome. Hence the revolt of Zenobia has to be sought in the psychology of the Arab queen—her desire to emulate the example of her illustrious neighbor from Emesa. The destruction of the city by Aurelian brought to a close that period in Arab-Roman relations during which the Arabs were represented by well-defined groups and major urban centers: such were the Arabs of Emesa, those of Petra, and those of Edessa. Palmyra was the last city of this arc of Arab urban centers to fall and, what is more, unlike the others it sank into complete, or almost complete, oblivion.

The revolt of Palmyra convulsed the *pars orientalis* and proved to be a major episode in the history of the Roman Orient, especially in the century of the imperial crisis of which it was the climax. For the first time in Roman history, the separable, that is, the *pars orientalis* in its entirety, became in actual fact separated. And had the *princeps* who was responsible for crushing the Palmyrene revolt been less distinguished than Aurelian, the course of Roman history might have been changed. Aurelian's generalship possibly averted a great historical might-have-been.

More important and relevant is the exploration of the Arab-Roman dimensions of the revolt of Palmyra and its fall for a better understanding of these relations in the Roman and Byzantine periods and in the seventh century, that of the Arab Conquests. The occupation of the *pars orientalis* and especially the Semitic Orient from the Taurus to Sinai inevitably evokes the historical situation that had obtained in the first century B.C. when a substantial portion of the same area was virtually in the hands of the Arabs and of Arab dynasts who had relieved the last Seleucids and Ptolemies of their Asiatic possessions. The Palmyrene occupation signaled the return of the area to Arab rule, however temporarily, four centuries after the Settlement of Pompey, and brought about the second major Arab-Roman confrontation of the period. It was also the much more serious one for Rome. The Arabs of the first century presented a disunited front, and this has been presented as a partial explanation for their failure to cope with the Roman adversary. But in the third century, Zenobia succeeded in presenting a united front, and yet Aurelian was able to defeat her notwithstanding. In addition to the superiority of Roman generalship over the mediocre Palmyrene commander Zabdas, the Arab defeat is explicable by the fact that the power of the Palmyrene Arabs was entirely dependent on a city, one single city, which, moreover, was within striking distance of the legions in Antioch or Emesa. Once that city fell, the Palmyrene resistance disintegrated and collapsed.

The two Arab-Roman confrontations of this period, the one in the first century B.C. and the other in the third century A.D., are relevant to solving the problem of the Arab Conquests in the seventh century, the investigation of which must both take into account the two previous Arab military efforts that failed and study the causes of that failure. The Arab success in the seventh century thus receives considerable illumination by comparison and contrast with the Arab failure in the first century B.C. and the third A.D. An entirely new and complex situation arose in the seventh century, with which the emperor Heraclius was unable to cope, but its complexity becomes easier to probe when set against the background of the two previous confrontations with which Pompey and Aurelian had had to deal.

IV

The subjection of the Arabs to the processes of Romanization and Hellenization for four centuries or so naturally resulted in a considerable degree of acculturation and assimilation to Graeco-Roman civilization. The extension of *civitas* to them in A.D. 212 must have enhanced the degree of this acculturation and assimilation as it gave them a sense of belonging to the empire of which they were now citizens. The Arab involvement in this Graeco-Roman culture and in that of the Semitic Orient may be presented as follows.

The vogue of the term *Saracens* for the Arabs and the equation of this term with the Scenitae, the "Tent-dwellers," has *inter alia* obscured the fact that the Arabs had made a substantial contribution to the cultural life of the Orient by their foundation of important urban centers or their development of centers already founded by others. Of the various groups of Arabs who made important contributions towards the urbanization of the region, the Idumaean Herodians of Palestine and the Nabataeans of what later came to be the Provincia Arabia are the most important. The contribution of the Nabataeans was the more remarkable since it was made in the arid areas of Trans-Jordan, Trans-'Araba, the Negev, and northern Ḥijāz. The Arabian limitrophe witnessed the rise of two of their major foundations, Petra and Bostra, both built and developed by the Nabataeans. To the north of the Nabataean city of Bostra, the Palmyrenes made of an old Semitic foundation, Tadmur, the greatest Arab caravan city of the Roman period— Palmyra. To the west of Palmyra, there was Emesa, the famous seat of the cult of the sun-god, of the dynasty of Sempsigeramus, and the home of the empresses of the Severan dynasty. Across the

Euphrates, the Arab Abgarids possessed themselves ca. 130 B.C. of Seleucid Edessa and continued to be its rulers until the middle of the third century A.D.

A high form of material culture developed in these Arab cities. What is more important in this context is the unfolding of a vigorous literary and intellectual life. The Arab dynasts, who enjoyed a certain degree of autonomy or independence as client kings before Rome annexed their kingdoms, contributed to the cultural life of the Orient by making their cities the centers of important cultural circles. Three of these Arab dynasties may be mentioned: the Sempsigerami of Emesa, the Abgarids of Edessa, and the house of Odenathus in Palmyra. Julia Domna patronized Papinian, Ulpian, Diogenes Laertius, Dio Cassius, Philostratus, and Galen; Abgar VIII, Bardaiṣan; and Zenobia, Longinus.

The involvement of the Arabs of this period in Neo-Platonism is noteworthy. Under the patronage of Zenobia, Amelius founded a Neo-Platonic school at Apamea. But the involvement went beyond patronage; the Neo-Platonist Iamblichus was certainly an Arab and so was possibly one whose original Semitic name had been Malik— Porphyry.

The rise of a new monotheistic religion in Arabia in the seventh century has so associated the Arabs with Islam that it is not often realized how deeply involved in Christianity and indeed in all the religious currents of the Orient the Arabs of the Roman period had been—in paganism, Manichaeism, Judaism, and Christianity. Specifically Arab were the panthea of such cities as Petra, Emesa, Palmyra, and Edessa, important in the religious life of the Arabs and of these cities. The most important in this context is that of Emesa, since it contributed the sun-god that was installed in Rome itself by Elagabalus, the Severan emperor.

It was, however, their involvement in Christianity that was the most significant.

1. The Arabs were one of the first groups in the Orient, and indeed in the world, to adopt Christianity. That religion spread quite early and extensively in the Provincia Arabia. The Arabs of that province exhibited much intellectual vigor when they wrestled with the theological problems of early Christianity, but at the same time they brought upon themselves the denunciations of orthodox Christian theologians who branded them as heretics and heresiarchs.

2. Besides being one of the earliest ethnic groups to be converted to Christianity and to participate in the growth and development of early Christian theology, the Arabs contributed some of the martyrs and saints of the Christian Church in this Roman period. The most celebrated of their saints were Cosmas and Damian, the *anargyroi*, "the silverless saints," the patrons of physicians. Both were appropriately buried in Edessa, the city of the Arab Abgarids.

3. Striking is the contribution of the Arabs to the progress made by Christianity in reaching the imperial court. It was an Arab, Abgar the Great, the ruler of Edessa, who around A.D. 200 was converted to Christianity and in so doing became the first ruler in history to adopt Christianity and make it the official religion of a Near Eastern state. And it was another Arab, Philip, who became the first Christian Roman emperor. When Philip died in A.D. 249 after a rule of only five years, he was a relatively young man of forty-five years. Had he ruled as long as Constantine, he might have made significant contributions to the fortunes of Christianity and might have effected important changes in the course of Roman history as the half-Arab emperors of the Severan dynasty had done.

The conversion of the two Arab rulers provided Christianity— then a persecuted sect—with what it needed most, protection, and, what is more, royal protection and patronage.

Of all these Arabs who cut a large figure in the cultural history of the Orient, such as Herod, Julia Domna, Philip, Abgar, and Zenobia, it was Abgar and his house, the Abgarids of Edessa, whose contribution turned out to be the most enduring—the city of Edessa itself.

Even before their conversion ca. A.D. 200, the tolerant rule of the Abgarids had made possible the development of Edessa as a Christian center. It was possibly there that the Diatessaron was composed and the Peshitta was translated, thus marking the inception of the rise of Edessa as a center in which nascent and persecuted Christianity found refuge. The conversion of Abgar the Great was one of its earliest triumphs; it immediately became the state religion of Edessa, and it was there and at the court of Abgar that Bardaiṣan lived and worked.

The fall of the dynasty half a century after its conversion did not affect the status of Edessa as a Christian center. It remained such, and in the following century it welcomed St. Ephrem, who transferred thither his school from Nisibis, and so Edessa became the mother of the Syrian Christian Church of the Semitic Orient— the rival of Greek Antioch. Not only did it develop as a great center of Christian learning but it became, with the translation of the relics of St. Thomas and those of the Arab saints, Cosmas and Damian, a Holy City, "The Blessed City."

The Arab character of Edessa started to fade with the fall of the Abgarids. Unlike Palmyra and Petra, the two other cities of the Arabian limitrophe, Edessa had been a Seleucid city before the Arabs possessed themselves of it ca. 130 B.C., and, more importantly, it was located in Mesopotamia, where the language of cultural dominance was not Arabic but Aramaic. Indeed it was in Edessa that one of the Aramaic dialects, Syriac, developed and became the lingua franca of *Oriens Christianus*. Although the memory of the Abgarids was green when Egeria visited Edessa towards the end of the fourth century, and remained so even in Crusader times, few who visited or wrote about Edessa in that period realized that it was an Arab dynasty that made Edessa the Holy City of the Christian Orient.

V

The image of the Arabs, who played this extensive and varied role in Roman history, does not emerge from the pages of classical literature with perfect clarity. This is partly due to the fact that the Arabs appear in that literature not as one people but as many groups and, what is more, on various levels of cultural development. Besides, various specific names were applied to them, and this tended to obscure the ethnic affinity that obtained among these various group, so differently designated. The nomads among them, referred to as *Scenitae* in the Roman period, were a homogeneous and well-defined group and consequently their image is projected with tolerable clarity. In spite of the difficulties that attend the attempt to perceive the image of the Arabs on the basis of the data available in Graeco-Roman literature, it is possible to draw the following conclusions concerning that image.

The attitude of the historians and geographers to the Arabs was the classical attitude of these writers to all the non-Greek and non-Roman peoples of the empire, whom they considered *barbaroi*. In the case of the Arabs, the classical conception of them as *barbaroi* was fortified by another pejorative one, that of *latrones*, a conception perhaps partially justified by the fact that not all the Arabs in the Orient were sedentaries and that some were nomads and raiders. Thus from Strabo in the first century B.C. to Dexippus in the second half of the third century A.D., the picture on the whole is a reflection of the imperial and imperious Graeco-Roman attitude, which could not view the Arabs except as representing the second of the two terms of the conjugates *Greek* and *barbarian*. Perhaps the classical Roman attitude towards the Arabs was summed up best by two authors of the Byzantine period, Ammianus Marcellinus and Zosimus, who wrote ca. 500. The first almost equated the Arabs with the Scenitae/Saraceni and thus drew his well-known uncomplimentary picture of the Arabs; the second dealt mainly with the sedentary Arabs—the emperor Philip and the Palmyrenes—and drew of them a picture in dark colors, describing them as *ethnos cheiriston*. Between the two historians, the image of the Arabs in the Orient, both sedentary and nomadic, becomes fairly clear, and this seems to have been the judgment of the pagan classical world. Only one Arab group, the Nabataeans, elicited the admiration of two authors—Strabo and Diodorus Siculus—who conceived of the Nabataean Arabs as a civilized people to be admired for their lifestyle.

The image of the Arabs in the works of Eusebius is not much better than in the mirror of secular Roman historiography, and that image presented by the father of ecclesiastical history naturally influenced, sometimes dominated, the projection of that image in later ecclesiastical works. This view of the Arabs in ecclesiastical history, deriving from Eusebius, may be presented as follows.

1. The Arabs are descended from the first patriarch and are descendants of Abraham's firstborn, but they are Ishmaelites, outside the Promises. Thus their descent from Abraham does not assign them to a privileged place in the family of nations nor in the Divine Dispensation. Moreover, throughout the centuries which elapsed since Abrahamic times, they appear not at all as monotheists outside the Promises but downright pagans and polytheists who acquired repulsive practices such as human sacrifice to mollify

the wicked demons which they worshiped and also as barbarians with unwholesome habits and customs, to whom the higher forms of civilized life were denied.

2. In Christian times, their role was far from enviable. In addition to contributing Herod the Great, the would-be *theoktonos*, whose name is associated with the Massacre of the Innocents, they contributed Herod Antipas, who beheaded John the Baptist, and Agrippa I, who put to death St. James the Apostle. Thus through the three Herodians the Arabs appear as cruel tyrants in the annals of nascent Christianity. Furthermore, in the centuries that followed and that witnessed the rise and development of Christian theology, they appear as heretics and heresiarchs who had to be brought to the folds of orthodoxy by Origen—a view of the Arabs succinctly and trenchantly transmitted by the phrase *Arabia haeresium ferax.*

The only redeeming feature of the place of the Arabs in ecclesiastical history is the fact that they contributed the first Christian rulers, the Abgarids of Edessa and the emperor Philip. But even this redeeming feature is attenuated or obscured by the fact that the ethnic origin of the Abgarids is not explicitly stated.

The image of the Arabs in both currents of the historiographical stream experiences further deterioration towards the end of this Roman period with the vogue of the term *Saracen* to describe the Arab Scenitae and then the Arabs in general. The Romans most probably contributed to the vogue of the term *Saraceni*. In the second and in the third centuries, Arab-Roman relations were confrontational, and this resulted in the direct annexation of the three Arab kingdoms, Nabataea, Palmyra, and Osroene. These annexations brought the Romans face to face with the world of the Arabian Peninsula teeming with Scenitae/Saraceni, while the fall of the Arab urban centers entailed such a considerable degree of nomadization or bedouinization that the equation of Saracens and Scenitae or Arabs became natural. Whatever the route that this equation may have been, the term *Saracen* became the equivalent of *Scenites* and *Arab* in general, the term that for the secular historian had meant *scenites* culturally and *latro* politically and militarily. The ecclesiastical historian equated Saracen with Ishmaelite, and thus the term acquired a new semantic dimension from the Bible, namely, that the Saracens were not only *scenitae* and *latrones* but also Ishmaelites, i.e., outcasts, outside the Promises. The identification was clinched by the patristic etymology given to the term *Saracen* to be found in St. Jerome and possibly going back to Eusebius, involving Sarah and reiterating their being uncovenanted *scenitae* and *latrones*.

It was this image carried by the term *Saracen* that found a new field for its vogue, probably through the prestige of St. Jerome in Latin Christendom, even before the Arab appeared in North Africa and the Iberian Peninsula in the seventh and eighth centuries. Thus both the term and the image acquired their widest vogue in the Middle Ages not only in the Greek East but also in the Latin West.

VI

The conqueror of Arab Palmyra did not stay or live long enough in the Orient to reorganize its defense system, which needed a drastic reorganization after his destruction of that desert fortress. It was, therefore, left to another emperor to reap the harvest of Aurelian's victory over the Arabs and to complete and complement the work of its conqueror.

After pacifying the Arabs who were in revolt again, ca. 290, Diocletian attended to the task of dealing with Aurelian's unfinished work on the eastern front. Instead of reviving an Arab client-kingdom in Palmyrena, he constructed not only the *Strata Diocletiana* but also what might be termed the *Limes Diocletianus* in the Orient. The *limes* concept was now applied to the Arabian frontier in its entirety from the Euphrates to the Red Sea. It formalized militarily the Roman annexation of the Arab client-kingdoms and signaled Rome's direct shouldering of defense duties, entailing a total and direct confrontation with the world of the Arabian Peninsula. In so doing, Diocletian completed not only the work of Aurelian and the Flavians but also that of Trajan who after the annexation of Nabataea constructed the *Via Nova Traiana*. Diocletian constructed the *Strata* that carried his name, the *Strata Diocletiana*, which ran from Damascus to Sura on the Euphrates, passing through Palmyra, and carried out the extension of the fortification system, the military zone that ran from Petra on the Gulf of Aqaba to Sura on the Euphrates. The Arabian segment of the *Limes Diocletianus* in the Orient became for three centuries the frontier of Arab-Roman coexistence.

The construction of the *Limes Diocletianus* raises the question of Diocletian's employment of the Arab provincials of the Orient to defend it against the Arabs of the Peninsula. The military posts of his *limes* were manned by *limitanei*, and it has been argued that the many units called *indigenae* in the *Notitia Dignitatum*, which guarded these posts in the limitrophe provinces of the Orient, were Arabs and that these units as well as their distribution go back to the time of Diocletian, who thus not only built the static defenses of the *limes* but also manned its posts with Arab *indigenae*.

In addition to what has been said about them in a previous section, the nature and extent of their contribution to the defense of the Orient may be described as follows.

1. Although some of these units are described as *alae, cohortes* of infantry, and *dromedarii*, the overwhelming majority of these units are *equites, vexillationes,* the higher-grade cavalry; often they are *sagittarii*, and both reflect the importance of the Arab horse and bow and of the adaptations which Rome had to make in its strategy in view of the importance of these in the armor of their chief adversary in the East—first the Parthians, then the Sasanids.

2. The extent of this contribution may be measured fairly accurately by an enumeration of these units in each province in the Orient, and the units are mostly *equites* or *equites sagittarii*: (*a*) those that are certainly Arab are: three in *Limes Aegypti*, one in the Thebaid, one in Palestine, one in Arabia, two in Phoenicia, and one in Mesopotamia; (*b*) those that are likely to have been Arab are: nine units in the Thebaid, eight in Palestine, four in Arabia, seven in Phoenicia, five in Syria, one in Euphratensis, five in Osroene, and four in Mesopotamia.

These units in the *Notitia Dignitatum* may be described as Arab manpower in the service of Rome. Their presence implies that after four centuries Rome had solved the Arab problem, not only through direct annexation but, what is more important, by harnessing Arab manpower in the Orient and absorbing it into the Roman army to fight her own wars both against the Arabs of the Peninsula and other foes in the West as well as in the East. The former adversaries are tamed and appear as good Romans fighting the wars of their empire.

Thus the Roman period that opened with Pompey truly ended with Diocletian. His reorganization of the Orient was a milestone in the history of that region and in that of Arab-Roman relations. His enduring legacy is that impressive symbol of static defense and of the permanent presence of Roman arms in the Orient—the *Limes Diocletianus*.

Just as Diocletian closes the Roman period, he also opens a new one in the history of Arab-Roman relations. He ushers in a new phase in those relations lasting for some three centuries until it was brought to a close by the Arab Conquests in the seventh. The *Limes Diocletianus* is the key to understanding much about Arab-Byzantine relations in this long period, and the history of these relations, indeed, turns largely round this *limes*.

Diocletian bequeathed to his successors in the fourth century a stable front by the construction of his *limes* and the harnessing of the Arab provincials of the Orient in the service of Rome. After him, the Arab problem changes in character; it is no longer that of the Arabs of the Orient but of those of the Peninsula, who lived outside the *limes*, a problem which was adequately solved by the adoption and perfection of the system of *foederati* and *phylarchi* in the three centuries of the Byzantine period.

Epilogue

In collecting the data for the first three chapters of Part I, I have had to depend on standard works that embodied the agreed results of scholarship on these four centuries of Roman history. But the panorama of this history throughout these four centuries is vast, and it was inevitable that in the presentation some inaccuracies should have crept in and some overstatements should have been made in the formulation of generalizations. I am, therefore, especially grateful to Mr. Sherwin-White, a leading Roman historian within whose expertise this period falls, for reading the manuscript of this book in its entirety and for his detailed comments on these three chapters. Some of these I have incorporated in the text but others are such that they deserve to be treated separately. Often they deal with the possible implications of certain statements and the tenor of certain passages which sometimes could lead the reader into drawing conclusions that have not been intended by the author. As he said, "it is largely a matter of emphasis and focus," but these are important concepts in a historical presentation of this kind.

Chapter I

My goal in this chapter has been to indicate the reality of the Arab presence in the Orient and to disentangle the Arab zone from the general Semitic zone with which it has been confused. I did not wish to engage in detailed researches on the history of the Arab principalities of the first century B.C. I only wanted to make sense of the scattered references to them in the sources and to relate these references to an important theme instead of leaving them as data without a significant historical context.

1. Mr. Sherwin-White pointed out that there was room for clarification in the discussion of the political geography of the region "by bringing out the fact that the hard core of Hellenistic cities in the north, Laodicea, Seleucia, Apamea and its depen-

dencies, Antioch, etc. remained under Seleucid rule till the end. Likewise the Phoenician towns of the littoral, while Judaea, recently aggrandized by Alexander formed a solid block of the most prosperous zone of southern Syria."

This is important to remember; otherwise the extent and reality of the Arab presence in the Orient may be unduly exaggerated by forgetting that it did not extend to the Hellenistic and the Phoenician cities and to Judaea.

2. He also pointed out that the various Arab dynasts who appear in the Orient and who were a threat to its Greek urban centers could operate for only a short period, since from 84 B.C. to 69 B.C. these urban centers were protected by the large Armenian army of Tigranes which was in occupation of all Syria and Cilicia north of Judaea.

Even so, for the short period between 69 B.C. and the arrival of Pompey in 64/63 these dynasts appear in strength, and had Pompey not arrived they would have consolidated their hold on the region and fortified it. In speaking of the Arab presence in the Orient, a distinction should be drawn between the ethnic/demographic and the military presence. The first was old and extensive in all the eastern provinces of the limitrophe, the second was recent in the case of the dynasts of the eastern steppes. In the case of the Nabataeans, the two were combined; Nabataea in the south was an Arab kingdom whose dynasts had existed for centuries and whose Arabs were settled in a vast area in the Orient, long before Pompey appeared in the region. This was also true, although to a lesser extent, of Edessa and the Arabs of Osroene in the north. Thus the Arabs were demographically and politically in control of a substantial portion of the Orient.

3. He also raised the question of the Idumaeans—who, according to Strabo, were thoroughly Judaized—and whether they could be considered Arabs.

My views on the Idumaeans are not unlike those of Strabo, but after examining the problem of acculturation and assimilation in a large way for the fourth century A.D. in *BAFOC*, I am inclined to believe that Strabo was exaggerating (see *supra*, Chapter I, notes 26, 37). If the Idumaeans turn out to be the Arab tribe of Juḏām of Byzantine times, this might give the *coup de grâce* to Strabo's view that the Idumaeans were thoroughly Judaized.

4. It should not be concluded from my account of the Settlement of Pompey in the Synthesis that the confrontation between Pompey and the Arab dynasts was a bloody one. The two sides faced each other in a military context, but Pompey dispersed them and they submitted to him. Thus the word "confrontation" as used in the Synthesis and elsewhere to describe relations between Pompey and the Arab dynasts should not imply military action. As Mr. Sherwin-White says: "There was no fighting in Syria except at Jerusalem. . . . The essence of Pompey's Settlement from your point of view was the restoration of the Greek and Aramaic communities to autonomy under the Roman government and the cutting back of the Arab-Judaean infiltration."

5. The date of the Settlement of Pompey: according to *CAH*, 9, pp. 381–82, Pompey made "a provisional settlement of Asia Minor" in the spring of 64 while "the rest of 64 and part of 63 B.C. were spent in restoring order in Syria." Mr. Sherwin-White points out that as far as Syria was concerned the date of the Settlement is the spring of 63 B.C.

The year 64 B.C. makes the period from the Settlement of Pompey to the battle of the Yarmūk in A.D. 636 exactly seven hundred years! I have therefore adopted 63 as the year of the Settlement for Syria and kept 64 only as a terminus a quo when speaking of the seven centuries of Arab-Roman relations which ended with the battle of the Yarmūk in A.D. 636.

6. To my query about the number of legions and men that Pompey had with him in Syria, Mr. Sherwin-White made the following observations: the number of legions and men whom Pompey commanded in the East can only be surmised by indirect inference from the sums he distributed *per caput* as booty, altogether about forty-five thousand; i.e., some nine legions if at full strength, all of which he probably had in his Pontic campaign against Mithridates. There is no indication of how many he took into Syria, where he certainly concentrated a large part of them since most of his legates were with him. But prudence might require that he left three in Pontus, since Mithridates was still at large in the Crimea.

According to this reasoning, Pompey had with him in Syria five legions consisting of about thirty thousand men.

Chapter II

1. On Palmyra he writes, "There is no doubt that Palmyra was regularly within the Roman province in the first two centuries A.D."

I share this view; and I did not intend the section on Palmyra in this chapter to be understood otherwise. In addition to what Mr. Sherwin-White says about the Roman customs post in Palmyra and the regular military garrison stationed there, I have already expressed an identical view in the manuscript of *BAFOC*, in note 65 of the chapter that deals with the Arabic Namāra inscription, where I wrote of the Palmyra of the Roman period that "the elder Pliny's phrase that it was an independent buffer state between the two world powers, *inter duo imperia summa* (*NH*, V.88), cannot but be an anachronism." Pages 22–24, *supra*, emphasize Palmyra's role as a peacekeeper vis-à-vis the Arabs adjacent to Palmyrena in the Peninsula. Only in the time of Odenathus did it take on Persia and in so doing extend its role to more than dealing with the adjacent Peninsular Arabs.

2. Mr. Sherwin-White also made a useful addition to my account of the Arab auxiliary regiments in the imperial army which links up with the evidence of the *Notitia Dignitatum* of later times. He drew my attention to the list of regular auxiliary *cohortes* and *alae* during the early principate in G. L. Cheesman, *The Auxilia of the Roman Imperial Army* (Oxford, 1914), pp. 181–82, an old book which has not outlived its usefulness. The list is a welcome addition to the article on the archers in the Roman period noted in note 27 of this chapter.

3. Concerning Diocletian's reorganization of the oriental *limes* (section II of this chapter), he pointed out that the Mesopotamian *limes* goes back to Severus who may have followed the plan initiated by Trajan.

My account apparently could imply that the Tigris had not been reached before Diocletian or that Mesopotamia had not been acquired before him or that previous emperors had not established their *limites* in the region. My account should not be understood to imply this. In using the term *oriental limes* when speaking of Diocletian, I was thinking not only of the Mesopotamian sector

but of the *Limes Orientalis* in its entirety from the Tigris to the Red
Sea. I devote a special section to the *Limes Orientalis* in this sense
in *BAFOC*; see "The Arabs along the *Limes Orientalis*." On the
analogy of the *Strata Diocletiana*, I call this oriental *limes* from the
Tigris to the Red Sea the *Limes Diocletianus*; see p. 159 of the
Synthesis. Such a term is needed to denote the long *limes*, the Syro-
Mesopotamian one, conceived by Diocletian, who thus completed
the work of previous emperors as explained in the Synthesis, *ibid*.

Chapter III

1. Mr. Sherwin-White suggested that Septimius Severus was
not a Phoenician any more than Trajan or Hadrian were Iberians or
Celts because they hailed from Spain.

I am inclined to think that Septimius may have been more
aware of his African and ethnic background than Trajan or Hadrian
were of their Iberian one. I have enclosed Phoenician between quotation marks to reflect the attenuated sense in which the term
should be understood. He also thinks that his children "cannot
really be called half-Arab." It is true that they were educated in
Roman schools, but their mother, Julia Domna, was an Arab lady
from Emesa, and in this sense they can be described as half-Arab.
Perhaps part-Arab might be a better description as he suggests.

2. My account of the Arab factor represented by Palmyra in
the third century under Odenathus and Zenobia tends to ignore
the background of the continuous civil war in the central fifty
years and of the Sasanids.

When I wrote this chapter on the Arab factor I assumed that
the imperial crisis of the third century, well known to the Roman
historian, would be constantly in the background and in the mind
of the reader, and thus I concentrated on the Arab factor. But the
imperial crisis and the Sasanids should be kept in mind since it is
only against this background that the Arab factor can be fully
understood.

3. He reminded me that a powerful Roman army, not Palmyra, kept the peace in Syria in normal times and that its with-
drawal made the Palmyrene phase possible.

This is certainly true, but when I wrote of the role of Palmyra
in the defense of the Orient I was thinking only of the period

of Odenathus. When I implied other periods I was thinking of Palmyra's defense of the Roman frontier, coterminous with the Arabian Peninsula, not with Iran, either Parthian or Sasanid.

4. My account of Odenathus's military movements on p. 39 could give the impression that "the desert route by Palmyra was an army route."

I did not wish to imply this. I was speaking only in general terms of the area of his operations; Palmyrena where he moved his armies, the Euphrates region, and the road to Ctesiphon itself, are all arid zones, and it was these that I had in mind when I said that Odenathus was operating in arid and desert terrain with which he was familiar or when I said that "the desert was his field of operations against Shāpūr" (p. 39).

MAPS

Map I illustrates the Arab presence in Syria, from the Taurus to Sinai, in the first century B.C. This presence is represented by the Arabs of ʿAzīz in the region of Antioch; those of Alchaedamnus, Gambarus, and Themella in Chalcidice; those of Sempsigeramus in Emesa and Arethusa; the Palmyrenes; the Ituraeans of Lebanon and Anti-Lebanon; the Nabataeans of Petra; and the Idumaeans of southern Palestine. Arab cities or cities associated with the Arabs are printed in capital letters.

Hierapolis

Seleucia Antioch

CHALCIS AD BELUM

Chalcidicê

Laodicea

ARETHUSA

ARKA EMESA

Tripoli

PALMYRA

Byblus

Berytus

HELIOPOLIS
CHALCIS SUB LIBANO

Sidon

Damascus

Tyre

Ptolemais

Caesarea

BOSTRA

Neapolis

N

Joppa

Gerasa

Jerusalem

Philadelphia

Ascalon

Gaza

PETRA

MAP I

Map II illustrates the Arab presence in the Land of the Two Rivers both in its Roman-controlled and Persian-controlled parts. In the former, this presence is represented by Edessa (al-Ruhā), the city of the Abgarids, and the region around it in which lived the Osroeni Arabs, and in the latter by Ḥīra on the Lower Euphrates. Between the two and in the zone of Roman-Persian confrontation lay the city of Ḥatra and to its northwest Singara, in the vicinity of which lived the Praetavi Arabs. Bēth-ʿArabāyē between the Khābūr and the Tigris is "Arabia in Mesopotamia," the Arabia of Greek and Latin authors when they speak of the Mesopotamian region.

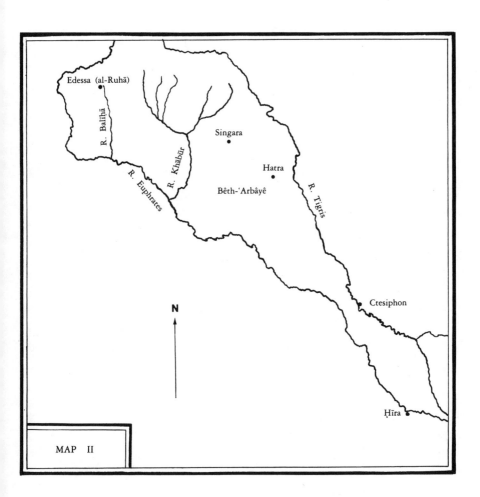

Edessa (al-Ruhā)

R. Balīḫā

R. Khābūr

R. Euphrates

Singara

Hatra

Bêth-'Arbâyê

R. Tigris

Ctesiphon

N

Ḥīra

MAP II

Map III illustrates the Arab presence in Egypt, where they lived in the area between the Nile and the Red Sea and in the Thebaid. The map shows two important areas of their presence in the north, not far from the Delta, namely, the oasis of Arsinoites (Fayyūm) and "Arabia in Egypt," the old Ptolemaic nome, called Arabia, the capital of which was Phacusa. Tendunias (*supra*, p. 57 note 28), in the *Chronicles* of John of Nikiou, identified by some with Thamudenas and thus considered an Arab center, was located to the north of Memphis on the road to Phacusa.

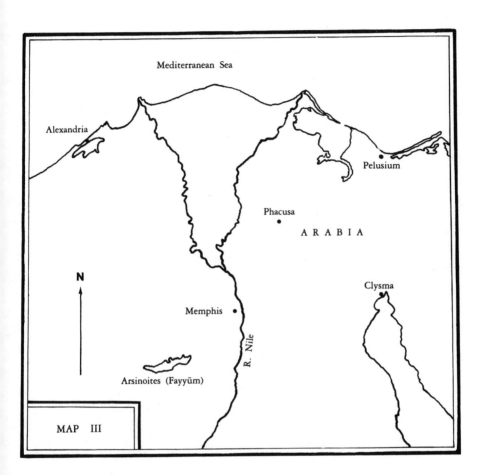

Mediterranean Sea

Alexandria

Pelusium

Phacusa

ARABIA

N

Memphis

Clysma

R. Nile

Arsinoites (Fayyūm)

MAP III

Map IV illustrates the Arab urban centers in the Orient in the Roman period. These were either Arab foundations, or the seats of Arab dynasts, or centers associated with the Arabs. Especially important is the triad of cities—Emesa, Philippopolis, and Palmyra—the native cities respectively of the empresses of the Severan dynasty, of the emperor, Philip the Arab, and of Odenathus and Zenobia, all historical personages of the third century, when the Arabs become an important factor in Roman history. The arc of Arab cities extends to the eastern half of the Fertile Crescent, controlled by Iran whether Parthian or Sasanid. The map shows Singara and Ḥatra since they belonged to the confrontation zone between Rome and Iran, and it also shows Ḥīra, on the Lower Euphrates, in view of its importance in the history of the Roman-controlled Orient. The better-known Arab foundations such as the Herodian Caesarea and Tiberias have been left out. For Arab centers in Arabia such as Dūma and al-Ḥijr, important for Arab-Roman relations, see Map III in *BAFOC*.

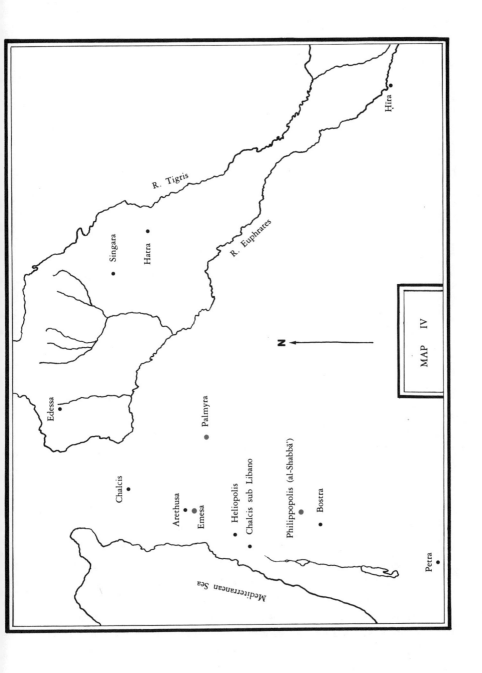

MAP IV

Hira

R. Tigris

Singara

Hatra

R. Euphrates

Edessa

Palmyra

Chalcis

Arethusa

Emesa

Heliopolis

Chalcis sub Libano

Philippopolis (al-Shabbāʾ)

Bostra

Petra

Mediterranean Sea

N

Map V illustrates the extent of the Palmyrene presence in the Pars Orientalis during the reign of Zenobia, when Arab arms reached Alexandria in Africa and the waterway that divides Europe from Asia, the Hellespont. This military expansion in the third century A.D. represents an advance on that of the first century B.C. when Arab military penetration of the Mediterranean region was virtually limited to Syria, from the Taurus to Sinai. Under Zenobia it included Asia Minor and Egypt and this penetration was the farthest that the Arabs effected before the rise of Islam. On the limits reached by Palmyrene arms under Zenobia, see H. Mattingly, *CAH*, 12, pp. 301–2.

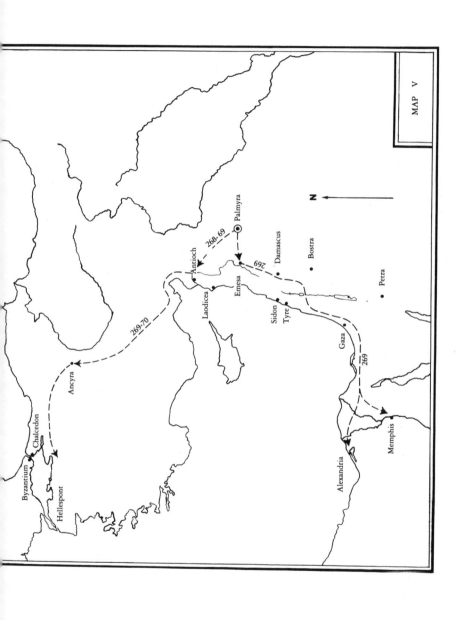

MAP V

Byzantium
Chalcedon
Hellespont

Ancyra

269-70

Laodicea
Antioch
268-69
Emesa
769
Palmyra

Sidon
Tyre
Damascus
Bostra

Petra

Gaza
269

Alexandria

Memphis

N

Index

Head of Julia Domna

Staatliche Antikensammlungen, Munich